CW01284364

Frontispiece An impression of a scene at Halton Lea Gate depot about 1840. The locomotives are *Rocket* 0-2-2oc (RS 19/29) ex-Liverpool & Manchester Railway, and *Belted Will* 0-4-0vc built at Kirkhouse in 1838/9.

(*Sid Barnes*)

LORD CARLISLE'S RAILWAYS

by
BRIAN WEBB
and
DAVID A. GORDON

Published by
THE RAILWAY CORRESPONDENCE AND TRAVEL SOCIETY
March 1978

This book is dedicated to the memory of the late David A. Gordon

Cover design by Brian Webb, ABID

Cover Drawing by Sid Barnes

Published by the Railway Correspondence & Travel Society

Copyright © Brian Webb

All rights reserved. No part of this publication may be reproduced, stored in a retrieval system or transmitted in any form or by any means electronic, mechanical, photocopying, recording, or otherwise, without the prior permission of the Copyright owner.

ISBN 0 901115 43 6

Printed by Ratnett & Co. Ltd.,
Knighton Junction Lane, Welford Road, Leicester

LIST OF CONTENTS

Acknowledgements

Introduction

CHAPTERS

1	Lord Carlisle's Waggonway	1
2	Developments under James Thompson	7
3	Lord Carlisle's link to the Newcastle & Carlisle Railway	17
4	Lord Carlisle's attitude to the Newcastle & Carlisle Railway	25
5	Developments on Lord Carlisle's Railways	35
6	Thompsons of Kirkhouse	53
7	Thompsons' successors	63
8	The Brampton Dandy	73
9	Reopening schemes	83
10	The Resumption of Passenger Services	95
11	The Locomotives 1836-1953	99
12	The Scene Today	113

Appendices

1	Letter—George Stephenson to J. Ramshay and J. Thompson, 23.8.1834	117
2	Letter—George Stephenson to J. Loch and J. Thompson, 18.11.1825	119
3	Letter—Robert Stephenson to J. Thompson, 17.3.1828	121
4	Letter—J. Loch to J. Thompson, 23.10.1825	122
5	Letter—J. Loch to Nathaniel Clayton, 3.11.1825	123
6	Letter—J. Loch to Messrs. Clayton, 13.11.1825	123
7	Extracts—Benjamin Thompson: Report to Directors of Newcastle & Carlisle Railway, 14.6.1825, 19.2.1828	124
8	Extracts—Letter J. Thompson to J. Loch, 26.2.1828	126

References 127

Index

ACKNOWLEDGEMENTS

The first version of this manuscript consisted of 90,000 words, subsequent rewriting reducing this to the size presented here. The editing, correction and typing of both versions is due to the hard work of Sandra J. C. Tassell without whom the work would have been very different to the result seen here. The writer is indeed very grateful for her interest and assistance. For the considerable technical assistance given in connection with process work and reproduction of maps, plans, and diagrams, the help of Norman Elgey has proved invaluable.

The basis of this book is the material collected from 1962 by a good friend of the writer, the late David A. Gordon of Brampton, an astute Scotsman and an electrical engineer by profession, who had lived at Brampton for many years. His interest in the Brampton Railways developed and he travelled many hundreds of miles researching the subject from both public and private sources. Through the kindness and generosity of Mrs. Joyce Gordon, his material was passed to the writer for use in a study of the Brampton Railways, to which has been added further material to complete the story.

The majority of the data is factual, based on the integrated files, maps, documents and correspondence contained in the Howard of Naworth Muniments, both in public records at Durham University's Department of Palaeography and Diplomatic, and in private hands at Brampton. The assistance of the Records Office of the Cumberland, Westmorland and Carlisle Archives at Carlisle Castle, the County of Northumberland Records Office at Gosforth, Newcastle upon Tyne, and Carlisle Public Libraries, Tullie House, Carlisle, is gratefully acknowledged.

Assistance with locomotive information came from Messrs. Andrew Barclay, Sons & Co. Ltd., Kilmarnock; the Hunslet Engine Co. Ltd., Leeds; G.E.C. Traction Ltd., Newton le Willows; the Mitchell Library of the Corporation of Glasgow; the North Eastern Railway Association, and Geoff Horsman.

Photographic and other assistance was from Harold D. Bowtell, Ken Hoole, Les Charlton, Frank Jones, Fleetwood Shawe, the Locomotive Club of Great Britain, the Historical Model Railway Society, the Industrial Railway Society, M. Halbert, and Sid Barnes.

A special mention is due to W. Deryck Cross of Milton Hill, Brampton for giving generously of his time and local knowledge, and for wholeheartedly supporting the work.

To all of these the writer is very grateful.

INTRODUCTION

The significance of the waggonways and railways of Lord Carlisle has never been fully appreciated, although much has been written and published on the subject over the past seventy or so years. The unfortunate fact is that the majority share one common flaw—their inaccuracy both in text and maps; in the latter case it appears that no comprehensive accurate map has yet been published.

The continuous repetition of these inaccuracies has resulted in many misconceptions which have come to be regarded today as fact.

Perhaps the commonly held belief that no contemporary material of the waggonway, the later railway, and the Naworth coalfield had survived was the main reason for the conjectures and the resulting statements on the subject. The truth of the matter is that much material such as correspondence, reports, surveys, plans, and maps do survive both in institutions, readily available to the public and less so in private hands. From these it is possible to obtain a seventy-five per cent coverage of the subject.

The reason for the apparent obscurity of Lord Carlisle's Railways is due to them never having an Act of Parliament permitting their construction. No permission was required as the vast majority of the system was built on Lord Carlisle's own lands.

Over its 155 years' history, Lord Carlisle's waggonway and the later railways, often termed the "Brampton Railway" or "Brampton and Hartleyburn Railway"—although no name can be regarded as their official title due to the system being privately built over their owner's estate—have several claims to fame and historical importance. The waggonway was not the first in Cumberland, but it was the first of its kind in that it was later developed and extended, then converted into Cumberland's first "mainline standard" railway. It was opened in 1799 with wooden rails but changed rapidly for by 1808 it had been relaid in both cast iron and wrought malleable iron rails, being the first successful application of the latter type of rail in a day-to-day commercial way. Although experiments with wrought iron rails continued elsewhere, it was not until the 1820's that it was finally accepted, indeed even by George Stephenson, as the only rail suitable for the locomotive-operated railways of the future.

Much of the credit for the development of Lord Carlisle's Railways is due to James Thompson (1794-1851), Lord Carlisle's colliery agent, and subsequent lessee of the Naworth collieries and rail system. Thompson had a great faith in railways and forecast the universal adoption of the steam locomotive many years prior to its event. He was later a close friend of George Stephenson and through this he built his 1828-9 extension of the waggonway as a proper railway to Midgeholme and to the Stephenson gauge of 4ft. 8½in., soon converting the waggonway to the same gauge afterwards. This was possibly the first non-Stephenson railway to adopt this rail gauge and the waggonway the first conversion to this gauge. Thompson's action was based on his statement that all railways should be made of the same rail gauge to enable subsequent linking-up of railways and the operation of through traffic.

The previously-unacknowledged effect of the firm demands of Lord Carlisle and James Thompson on the route of the western section of the Newcastle & Carlisle Railway, and its rail gauge, is very important. It ensured a route permitting operation initially by horses, but also in due course by locomotives, this being attained even though the Newcastle & Carlisle Railway Act itself forbade the use of locomotives.

The rail gauge adopted by the N. & C.R. was 4ft. 8½in. due to the insistence of James Thompson and Lord Carlisle's representatives.

This was the first application of such a gauge to an important railway not engineered by Stephenson. The fact that the N. & C.R. was the first railway to cross England makes its importance doubly so.

In 1836 the "new railway" of Lord Carlisle opened to replace the waggonway, the result of the joint efforts of Thompson and Stephenson; both Lord Carlisle's and the N. & C. railways opening officially under steam traction.

From 1837 the "Rocket" operated on Lord Carlisle's railway, while between 1838 and 1866 the colliery workshops under the influence of Thompson built their own locomotives. Although primarily a mineral railway, the colliery railway was from 1836 to operate a public passenger service, horse-drawn until 1881, but steam-worked afterwards, and to end in the hands of the North Eastern Railway in 1923.

From this it can be seen that Lord Carlisle's railway warrants much more than a cursory glance from the railway historian.

BRIAN WEBB

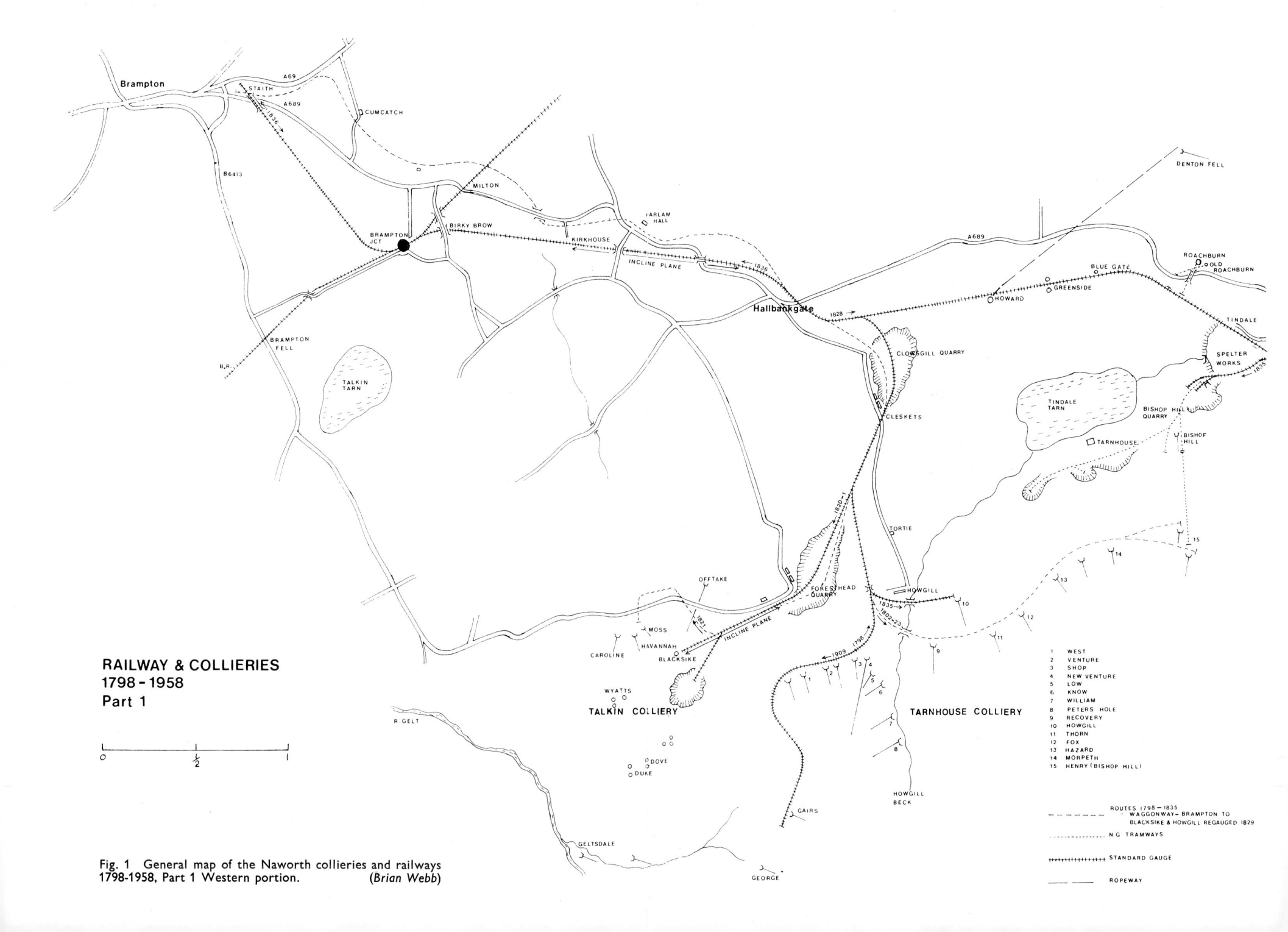

Fig. 1 General map of the Naworth collieries and railways 1798-1958, Part 1 Western portion. *(Brian Webb)*

MAP of RAILWAYS and COLLIERIES 1798–1958

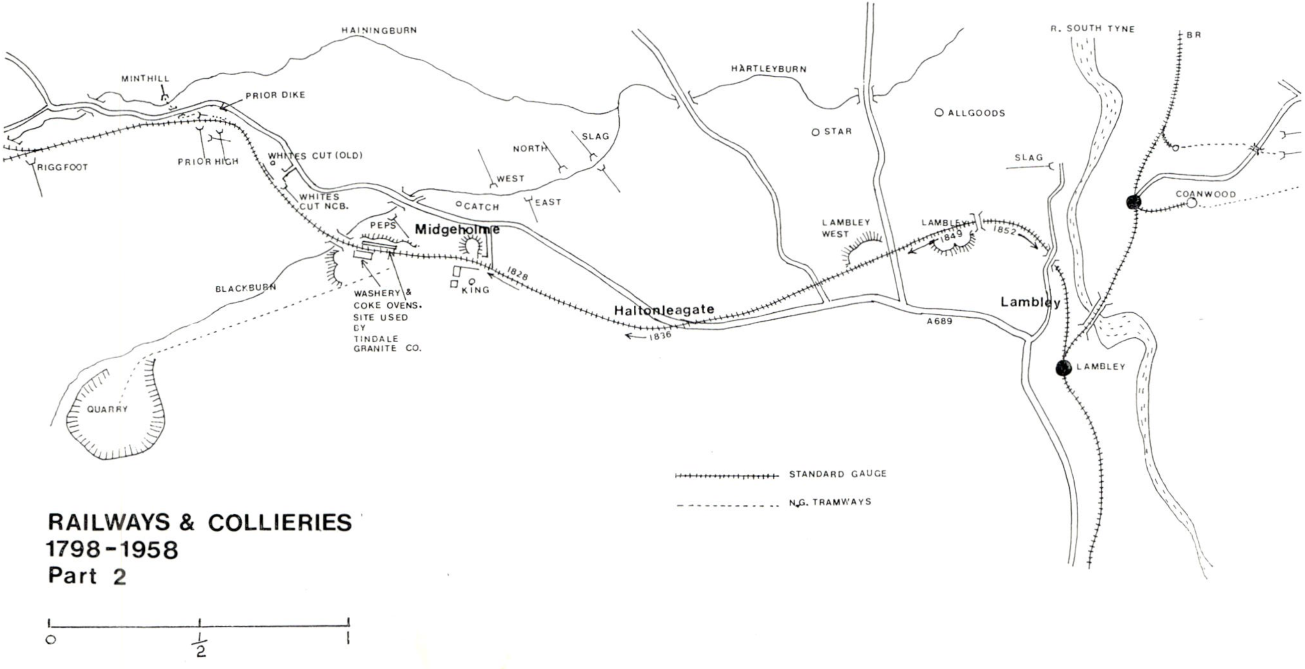

RAILWAYS & COLLIERIES
1798-1958
Part 2

Fig. 2 General map of Naworth collieries and railways 1798-1958, Part 2 Eastern portion.

(Brian Webb)

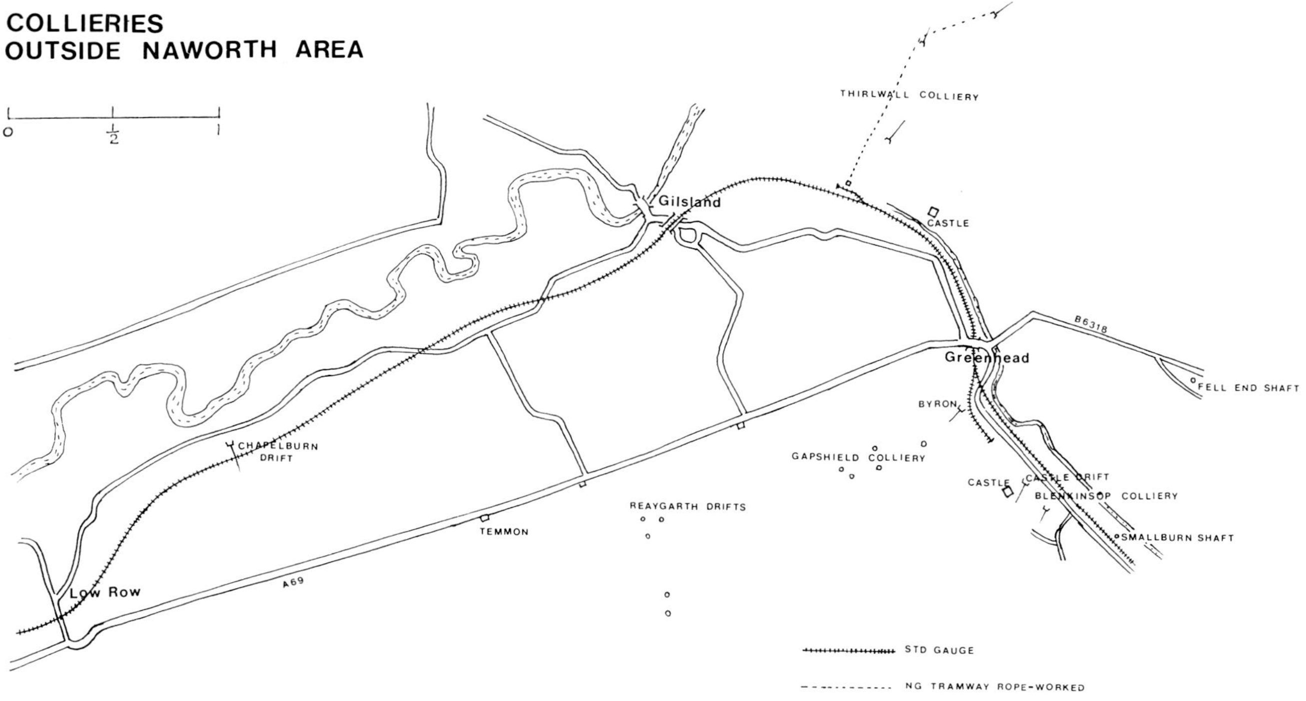

Fig. 3 General map of collieries worked by various lessees of the Naworth coalfield but outside the coalfields' railway system. *(Brian Webb)*

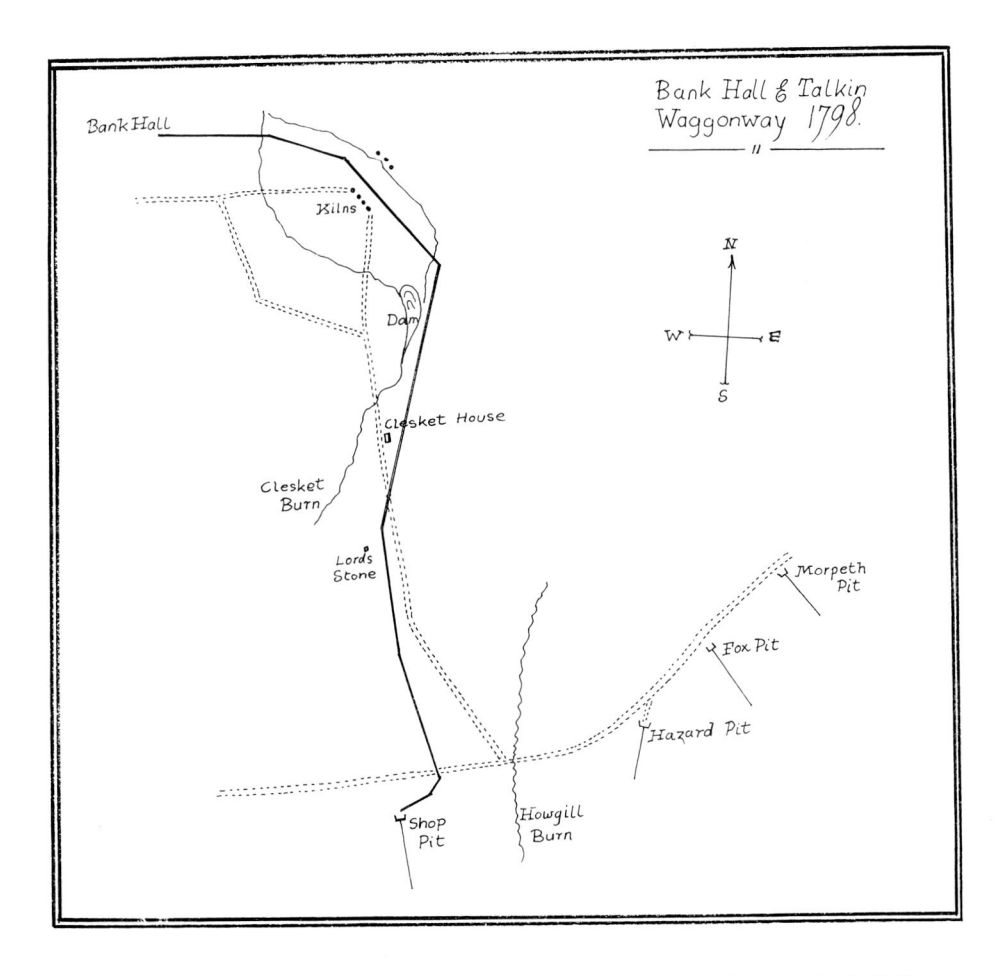

Fig. 4   1798 map showing route of Lord Carlisle's Waggonway between Bank Hall (Hallbankgate) and shop pit in Talkin colliery.   *(Collection of B. Webb)*

Fig. 5 Embankment of Lord Carlisle's Waggonway on south side of Newcastle-Carlisle line east of Milton level crossing at their point of intersection in November 1968.
(Brian Webb)

Fig. 6 1799 Waggonway route now sporting some large trees, east side of A689 road at the point where the "sandy arch" passed under the road. (David A. Gordon)

Fig. 7 Embankment of 1799 Waggonway crossing the field between "sandy arch" and Beck Cottages looking eastwards towards Farlam Hall. August 1972. (Brian Webb)

Fig. 8 View taken on bridge abutments of the 1835 Howgill branch in March 1976. The course of the earlier route of the Waggonway can be clearly seen on Tindale Fell.
(Brian Webb)

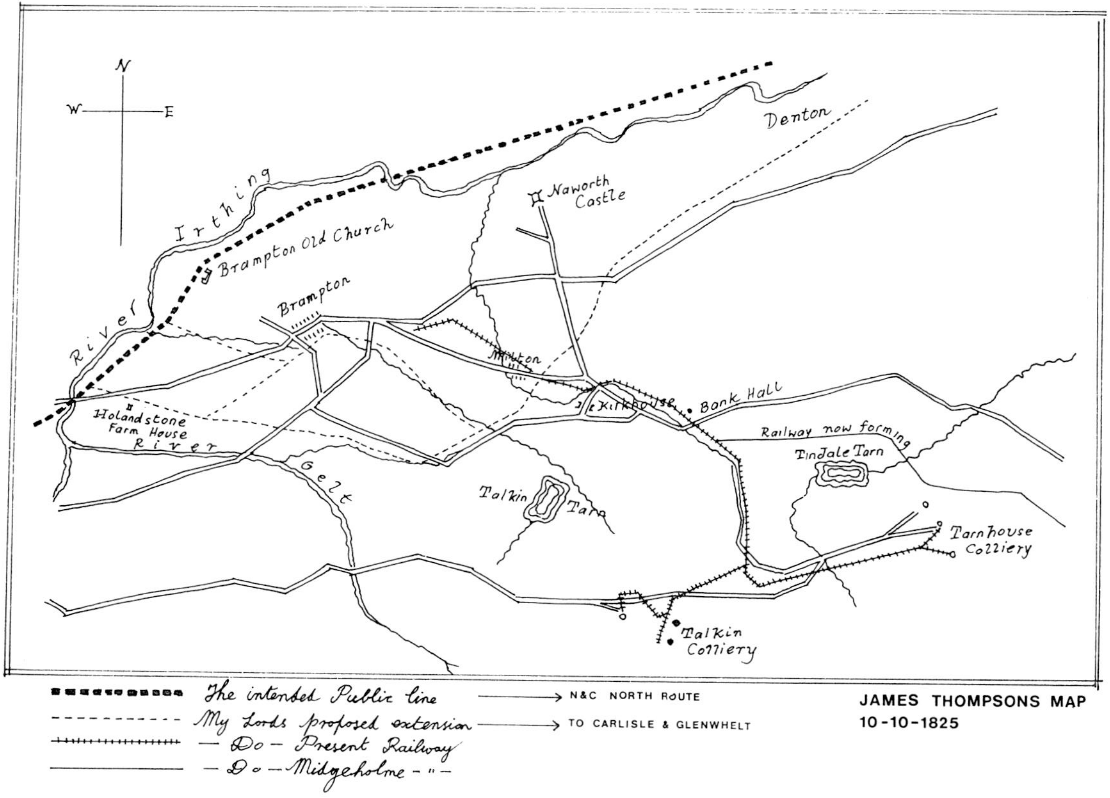

Fig. 9 James Thompson's map of October 1825. Shows proposed N. & C. North route and the earlier proposals as to how the colliery railway should be linked to it.

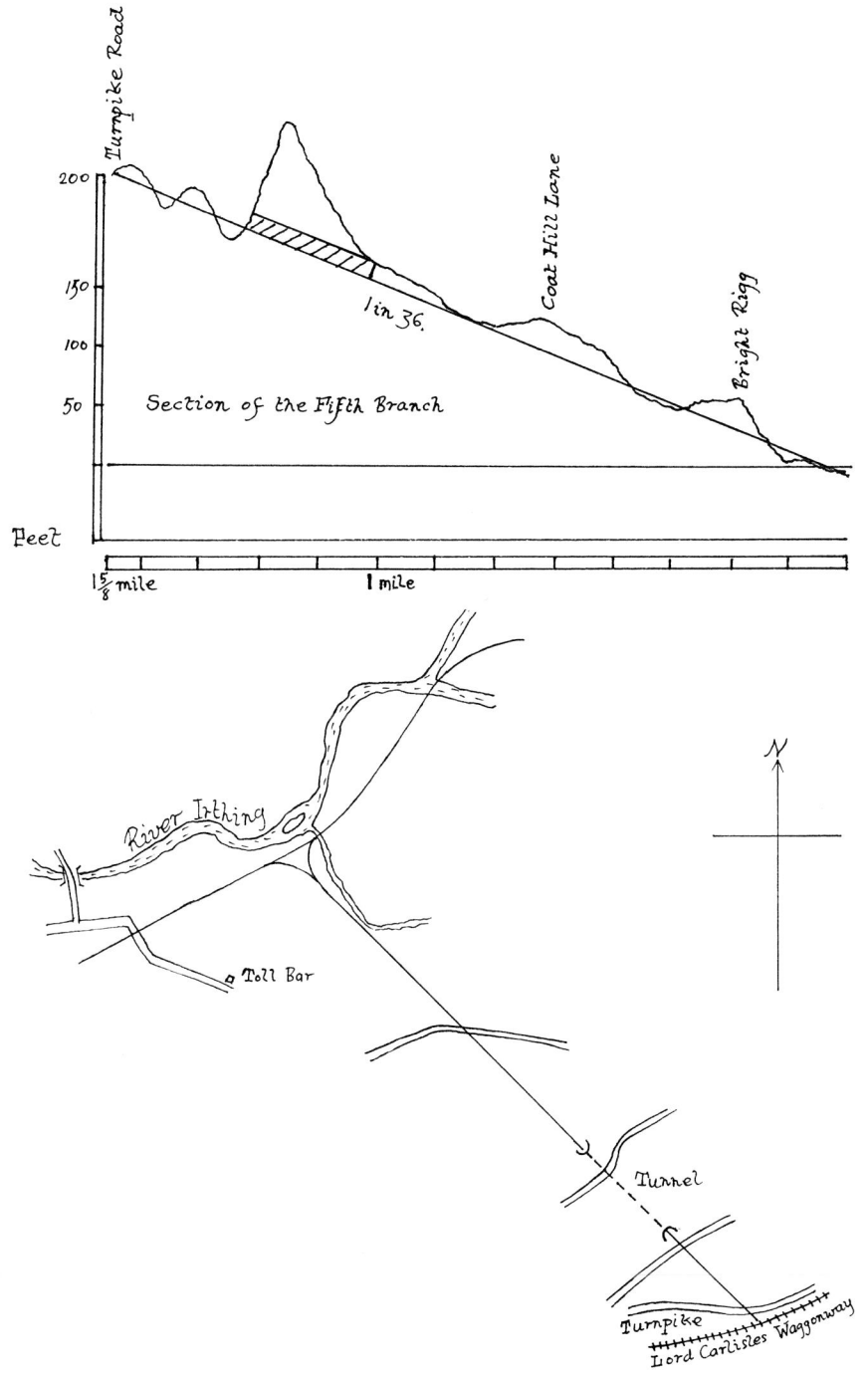

Fig. 10 (1), (2) Gradient profile and plan of the 1825 proposed N. & C. Brampton branch between the North route and the staith on the Waggonway. (*Carlisle Castle Records Office*)

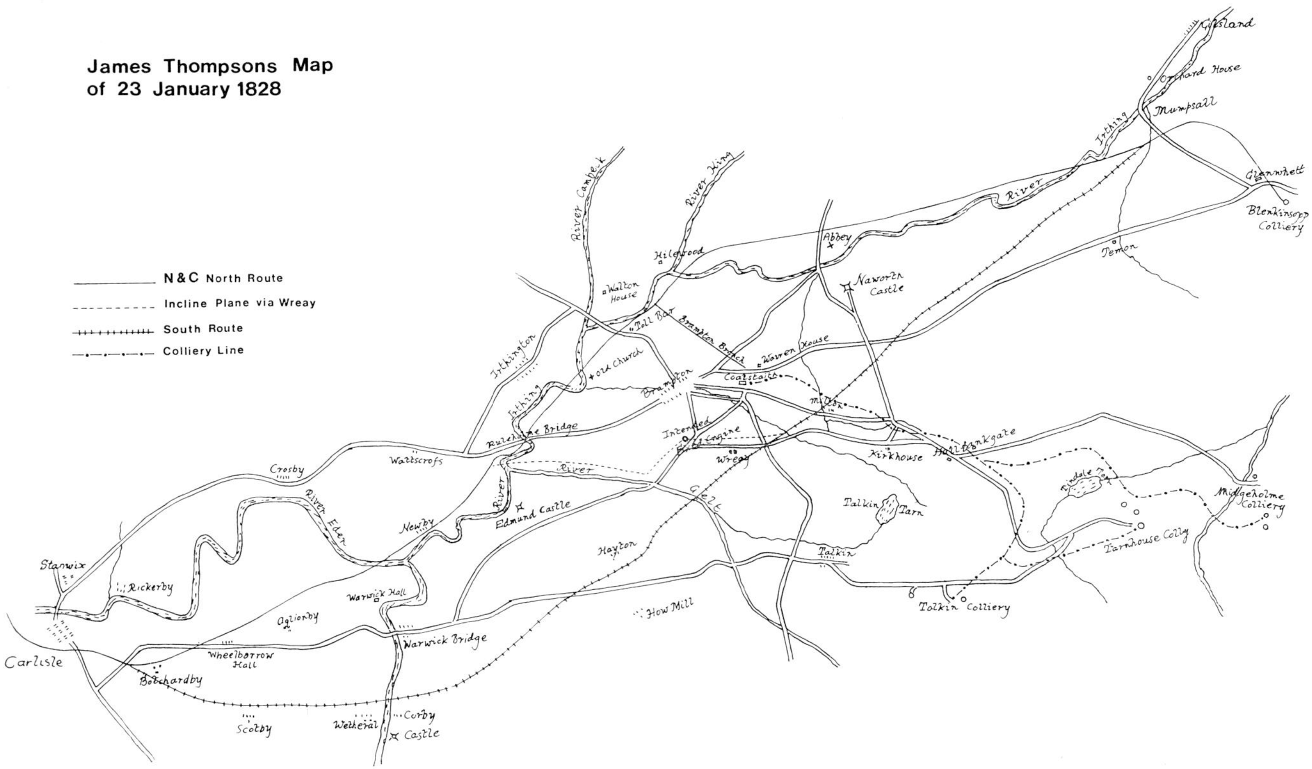

James Thompsons Map
of 23 January 1828

———— N&C North Route
--------- Incline Plane via Wreay
+++++++ South Route
———— Colliery Line

Fig. 11 James Thompson's map of January 1828 showing the N. & C. North route, the then-abandoned South route of the N. & C. following the approximate line of the Carlisle, Brampton & Glenwhelt Railway of Lord Carlisle.

Also shown is the N. & C. Brampton Branch proposal and the controversial incline plane via Wreay as a possible link for the compromise N. & C. North and South route following the problems with Sir Huw Ross at Hayton. (University of Durham)

CHAPTER 1

The Earl of Carlisle's Waggonway

The town of Brampton is situated nine miles east of Carlisle and is a place of some antiquity, a market having been held there for over 700 years. The area around the town is rich in Roman remains, while its close proximity to Scotland brought to it severe fighting and occupation during the wars between Robert the Bruce of Scotland and King Edward II of England.

Its geographical location today is some one-and-a-half miles east of Old Brampton on the banks of the River Irthing, the site being marked by the surviving portion of the parish church of Old Brampton, Brampton Old Church. The fact that the town is located in the bottom of a saucer-shaped dip was, in spite of many other assertions, the principal factor in its lack of access by rail, and it was not until the internal combustion engine arrived on the scene that the problem was overcome.

Lord Carlisle's lands in the district were entitled the Barony of Gilsland and included Brampton, Carlatton, Castle Carrock, Cumrew, Cumwhitton, Nether Denton, Upper Denton, Farlam, Hayton, Irthington and Lanercost. The barony itself descended from ancestor to heir through the De Vallibus, Multon, Dacre and Howard families, the family home in the barony being Naworth Castle.

The successive Earls of Carlisle derive from Lord William Howard, the character "Belted Will" of Scott's "Lay of the Last Minstrel", who inherited Naworth Castle by his marriage to the sister of George, Lord Dacre of Gilsland. Moving on in time we find the fifth Earl, a distinguished literary scholar, incumbent at the inception of the first waggonways in the area. Upon his death in 1825 the waggonway had been a fact for twenty-seven years and the initial expansion of the Naworth coalfield, under James Thompson, was in progress. The sixth Earl, George, was to be the authority behind the most progressive era both for the railways and collieries, his death occurring in 1848. His son succeeded as the seventh Earl, George William Frederick, who died unmarried in 1864. The eighth Earl of Carlisle, the Rev. William George Howard, a Clerk in Holy Orders, spent long periods in a mental home during which time the estate was managed by a Board of Trustees headed by the Duke of Devonshire.

Upon the unfortunate eighth Earl's death in 1889, George Howard became the ninth Earl. Famous in his own right as an artist of the pre-Raphaelite School, a upon the whole idea of the practicability of any public communication across the island . . ." and suggesting that James Thompson might like to write in similar patron of the arts and as a friend of William Morris and his associates, George

1

Howard delegated the management of the estate to his wife. Lady Rosalind, Countess of Carlisle, was very able in business, having gained the confidence and appreciation of the late eighth Earl's Trustees, even though her own opinion of these Trustees and their absent management under Mr. R. du Cane in London, was not high. Lady Carlisle was thus virtually in sole control of the estate, to good effect, calling in only technical advisers as required. Upon her husband's death in 1911, their son, Charles James Stanley, took over as tenth Earl, only to die in 1912 leaving Lady Carlisle once again in control until her death in 1921. The eleventh Earl, George John Howard, continued until 1963, being succeeded by the present twelfth Earl, Charles James Howard.

Going back in time to discuss the industrial history of the Brampton area we find agriculture, forestry, quarrying and coal as the principal economic factors. It is the latter two, namely limestone quarrying and production, and coal, which chiefly concern us here. These two commodities were produced in the area from at least the twelfth century and records survive to prove this, although it is not until the seventeenth, and especially the eighteenth, century that the exploitation of lime and coal grew to larger proportions. Surviving maps of the seventeenth century show drifts into the coal seam on Tindale Fell, while during the eighteenth century mining was also being carried out nearer Hallbankgate at Coal Fell and Templegarth. Further east rich deposits at Midgeholme, Hartleyburn and Lambley were being worked. Further north in the valley of the River Tipple (Tipalt) coal was being worked at Blenkinsopp. Although none of these ventures was very large the combined output was quite large and enjoyed good sales to a wide area, bearing in mind the rural nature of the countryside and the problems of transport in a hilly district.

By the last twenty years of the eighteenth century the major coal mining activity which concerned Lord Carlisle was that on the East Cumberland fells south-east of Brampton where groups of small drifts into the limestone coal seam, known locally as the Tindale Fell seam, were worked as the Talkin Colliery and Tarnhouse Colliery. Talkin Colliery comprised the workings on Brown Fell west of the fault down which the Howgill Beck flows, plus a few slightly south-west on Talkin Fell. The Tarnhouse Colliery consisted of the drifts east of Howgill across the face of Tindale Fell.

The chief source of limestone was the large quarry at Clowsgill, with its lime kilns using local coal, situated about a mile south-east of Hallbankgate. Lime was also obtained from the coal drifts and many small lime kilns were in use all over the district of the collieries in addition to those at Clowsgill.

As intimated, the chief problem faced by the Naworth Collieries was caused by their difficult situation at high elevations, which in itself made working difficult, especially in winter, but more important highly inaccessible from the point of view of transport. There were established coal roads leading to Brampton, Carlisle, Penrith, Alston, etc., but these were becoming increasingly costly to maintain as the greater demand for coal and lime meant an increase in the number of carts using them. Not insignificant to the production of the Naworth Collieries was the cost of cartage which kept the price of coal high, thus restricting increases in sales.

The drifts themselves were operated so that their output was carried to local coal stacks or banks of coal to which the carts would come for their loads, thus in part easing the problem of moving carts to drifts which were up to 1,000 feet above sea level.

The first waggonways, made of wood, were already in use in these drifts by 1770, and the interconnection of different drifts so that coal could be carried by these underground waggonways to lower drifts was a marked improvement. The extension of this to surface waggonways was no doubt considered, but, in spite of assertions in other published accounts to the contrary, no surface rails were laid until 1798. Thus, as may be seen, the Naworth coalfield was an established fact well before the railway era.

The actual area under consideration is the fell country extending eastwards some nine and a half miles and southwards for three miles from Brampton. The main people involved are the colliery agents of Lord Carlisle—notably James Thompson, James Loch his Lordship's London agent, and subsequently George Stephenson.

Local traditions about the waggonways and railways of the locality are varied. Misleading but amusing, one of them states that the monks of Lanercost Abbey mined coal and operated a "bogie line" running from Tindale Fell. Monks mining coal—yes, but using a tramway—no!

In fact we may take the mid-1790's as the basis of the first serious proposals for railways in the area, at a time when a canal was still being debated and planned to link Newcastle with Carlisle.

The need to improve transportation and cheapen the carriage of coal was not to be met by road transport which could not take advantage of the high elevation of the Talkin and Tarnhouse Collieries. It had been observed that the traffic from these collieries was always in a downward direction, no loads being brought to the collieries, therefore an obvious possibility which appealed was the idea of constructing a wooden waggonway down which coal and lime would descend in waggons by gravity, but using horses on the level sections, and to haul back the empty waggons.

With these advantages in mind a waggonway was planned to run from the collieries through Clowsgill Quarry and Hallbankgate to the town of Brampton, where a suitable coal and lime depot would be erected for the sale of such wares to a wide area.

The first actual evidence is to be found in an estimate prepared during 1796 for "Laying a wooden waggonway from the Right Honourable Earl of Carlisle's Tindale Fell Colliery to Brampton". The main points of interest follow:

	£	s.	d.
To laying waggonway with wood and workmanship—5 miles at 3s. 4d. per yard	1466	13	4
Cuttings, embankments, etc., at £60 per mile	300	0	0
Ten coal waggons at £12 each	120	0	0
Building staith near Brampton	300	0	0
Total expense	2186	13	4
Deductions for using wood from Lord Carlisle's plantations	1016	0	0
Total expenditure on waggonway	1170	13	4

The estimate stated that with contingencies the total cost might be £2,500.

An estimate of operating expenses and profit was included, based on the assumption that 20 waggon loads traversed the waggonway each day, each waggon load being equal to 6 cart loads which cost 1s. 6d. per load by road. A profit of £6 0s. 0d. was forecast giving a daily profit to Lord Carlisle of £4 0s. 0d. per day, after paying for the upkeep of the horses and the men's time at 2s. 0d. per waggon per day; from this the waggonway was seen as an attractive proposition and further calculations dated 1799 reinforced this. Again, based on the 20 waggons per day schedule, each holding 16 pit loads, the waggonway would convey 1,920 loads per week for 50 weeks each year. This would give 96,000 loads each year, being carried at 5d. per load at a cost of £2,000 0s. 0d. per year.

The costs of operation and interest charges were put as follows:

	£	s.	d.
10 Waggon horses at £30 each per year (keeping)	300	0	0
10 Waggonway drivers at £25 wages each per year	250	0	0
4 Waggonway Wrights at £30 wages each per year	125	0	0
1 Waggonwright at £30 wages per year	30	0	0
4 Labourers for greasing and repairing the waggonway at £17 10s. 0d. wages each per year	70	0	0
4 Staithmen and labourers at £25 wages each per year ..	100	0	0
Interest upon £2,000 upon money spent on making the waggonway at 5%	100	0	0
	970	0	0
Profit to Lord Carlisle for one year of waggonway	1030	0	0

The laying of the waggonway began in 1798, being laid upon a route requiring only minimal cutting and embanking by the estate's own work force. It ran from a coal and lime depot or staith at the eastern approach to Brampton situated alongside the Brampton to Alston road (A689). The route passed through Milton village, Figs. 5 to 8, Farlam Hall grounds, Hallbankgate, Clowsgill limestone quarry, Clesketts and on to Howgill, where at the foot of the Brown Fell it terminated at one of the drifts of the Talkin Colliery called Shop Pit, Fig. 4. On its route the waggonway had to climb 360ft. in the three and a half miles to Clowsgill, reaching 700ft. at Shop Pit.

The waggonway was laid with wooden rails fastened to wooden bases, using wood obtained presumably from estate sources. The use of wood for this purpose seems surprising in view of the fact that from the mid-1770's both wood and cast iron tramways, and by 1794 wrought iron rails, were in use underground in the collieries. The lack of local or indigenous suppliers for items of ironwork, both for the collieries and the waggonway, necessitated their purchase from Tyneside sources. No doubt the waggon wheels were obtained from Tyneside Founders who had been supplying such items and other ironmongery for underground use.

Construction proceeded through the winter of 1798-9 and the waggonway was officially opened on 15 April 1799 by, according to local press reports, ". . . a band of music and a procession of coal waggons". The waggonway was single track with, later, loops at intervals to allow returning waggons to pass those taking loads to the staith. The waggonway's utility was soon appreciated and extended eastwards, first by serving the drifts on the west side of Howgill Beck, then by a bridge over the beck to reach the more westerly drifts of Tarnhouse Colliery by 1802-3. This easterly extension was extended progressively until it reached an elevation of over 1,000ft., high above Tarn House across the face of Tindale Fell, giving a very steeply graded line which was frequently blocked by snow and thus exceedingly difficult to operate in the winter months.

Within five to six years the waggonway work force was given as 18 waggon drivers to operate the traffic, 7 waggonwaywrights to maintain the waggonway, assisted by a dozen labourers under a foreman. The coal staith had its own staff of 3 staithmen, who possibly shared some of the labourers, the whole operation being supervised by a clerk and his assistant. By the early 1820's the waggonway was serving both Talkin and Tarnhouse Collieries but had not seen further extensions, although the tonnages carried were rising.

Although routes were virtually static we now come to the principal claim for the waggonway, namely, the progressive improvement of its permanent way. Although during 1808 the Tindale Fell extension was being laid with wooden rails, the "main line" of the waggonway was already laid throughout in cast iron bar rails in 3ft. lengths and had been for some years, as surviving records prove. However, this material, although superior to wood, was not satisfactory. In order to overcome the constant fracturing of cast iron rails laid on stone blocks, starting in 1808 some three and a half miles were relaid with wrought iron bar rails of 1½in. square section in 3ft. lengths, which proved vastly superior. After 1808 the wrought iron bar rails were 1½in. square but in 15ft. lengths spiked through to wooden plugs set in stone blocks at 3ft. intervals. The cast iron rails continued on the remainder of the waggonway, failing regularly under the 53cwt. loaded chaldron waggons. The adoption of this rail brought much publicity to this rather obscure waggonway, and visitors were frequent to examine their reliability at first hand. It would seem that Lord Carlisle's waggonway was the first such installation to use successfully in commercial everyday service the wrought iron rail. The importance of this rail was still arousing interest ten years later when the oft-quoted Robert Stevenson of Edinburgh (not to be confused with his illustrious Tyneside namesake) wrote in December 1818 that:

> Three and a half miles of this description of railway have been in use, for about eight years on Lord Carlisle's works, at Tindale Fell in Cumberland, where there are also two miles of cast iron rail; but the malleable iron road is found to answer the purpose in every respect better.

Concurrently to the adoption of new rail forms, during 1808 a youth of 15 years entered the Kirkhouse offices of the Earl of Carlisle's collieries under his Lordship's agent, Thomas Lawson. This was James Thompson, born on 21 August 1794 as the third child and second son of Thomas and Isabella Thompson, who lived at and farmed Farlam Hall. The Thompson family had lived at Farlam Hall since 1716 when they first moved there from Lord Carlisle's Morpeth estate in Northumberland.

James Thompson's keen activity and interest in the progressive development of the Naworth coalfield and waggonway was to stand him in good stead for in 1819 he was to succeed Thomas Lawson and become Lord Carlisle's colliery agent. The granting of this post to Thompson was to prove the turning point for the Naworth coalfield, as will be seen.

CHAPTER 2

Developments under James Thompson

James Thompson with his new authority as Lord Carlisle's agent was soon to establish himself as a well-known figure, initially due to his long-standing faith in the progressive employment of improved forms of rails on the waggonway under his jurisdiction.

During May 1819 he wrote to Bedlington Ironworks on the subject of rails used on the waggonway:

> Our rails are $1\frac{1}{2}$in. square and stand upon stones about 10in. square, and are placed at one yard distance from centre hole to centre hole. Our railway carries four tons weight and has never cost us anything yet, as to the expense of malleable iron, except greasing. The iron I cannot see the least alteration with, although it has now been laid eight years. The cast iron is a daily expense: it is breaking every day.

Thompson's immediate task was to seek further extensions to the collieries, which during 1820 included the multiplicity of drifts forming Talkin and Tarnhouse Collieries served by the waggonway, the Geltsdale Colliery whose George Pit, a drift high on Tarnmonath Fell, supplied coal by road to its associated lime kilns, and to the Penrith district. Both Talkin and Tarnhouse held vast reserves of coal and were ripe for development so Thompson directed his attention towards a field of coal just west of Foresthead at a place called Blacksike. Blacksike Colliery, Naworth's first large-production shaft mine was sunk during 1820-1, going into production during 1822-3 using a steam engine for pumping and coal winding. Always a very wet colliery to operate, Blacksike proved very profitable during its long life of fifty years.

To serve this new colliery a branch was put in from the waggonway south of Clesketts, climbing through Foresthead in a south-westerly direction via a rope-hauled line to reach the bleakly sited colliery, coinciding too with the development of the limestone quarry at Foresthead which was served by the same branch. Subsequently, a short extension of the Blacksike branch was put in to serve the older Talkin drifts near Havannah and some nearby quarries. The Havannah extension was removed by 1827.

Lord Carlisle's practice of acquiring leases on coal outside his barony had commenced by his early lease of the vast coalfield at Blenkinsopp, Greenhead. This coal was owned by John Blenkinsopp Coulson of Blenkinsopp Castle and was taken on a new lease for twenty-one years on 1 January 1814, worked by several shaft and drift mines and proving a lucrative and rich source of coal and lime which was transported by road, for there was to be no rail access until 1836.

During 1822 James Thompson was married to Maria Bell of Brampton, a woman who was later to excel in business affairs after her husband's death.

One of Thompson's chief concerns was the improvement of the waggonway and the mode of transport between the Naworth coalfield and Carlisle. The possibility of discussions being held at Newcastle upon Tyne, resulting in either a canal or a railway to link the east and west coasts was uppermost in his mind, but not as a development to be welcomed. This was due to the twofold effect it was likely to have on the Naworth coalfield, for even though its transit to Carlisle would be improved, so would the transit of coal from Newcastle and its resulting competition for the Carlisle market, then the sole preserve of Lord Carlisle.

There were various methods open to James Thompson to deal with this threat. He could extend and improve the collieries by bringing in new large collieries of greater production potential which, coupled with an improved waggonway, would reduce its price to make Naworth coal more competitive, or he could construct for Lord Carlisle a private railway to link the collieries to Carlisle, an idea greatly favoured by Thompson. All these had one basic problem, that of expense. Nevertheless, Thompson decided to try to obtain sanction from Lord Carlisle to carry out all three, for he saw that even if the cost of his scheme was great it would repay the outlay, as he was to point out in his detailed estimates.

While Thompson was working on his estimates, a proposal for a railway link between the collieries and Carlisle was put forward by R. B. Longridge of Bedlington Ironworks during September 1823. Longridge proposed to construct it and grant sole use to Lord Carlisle, provided Lord Carlisle obtained the way-leave, paid the rental and contracted to send over it not less than 20,000 tons of coal, lime and ironstone annually at an agreed sum. Longridge for his part was to lay and repair the railway and carry over it all goods except coal, lime and ironstone which would be Lord Carlisle's responsibility. Although seemingly attractive, it failed to gain appeal due to doubts about Longridge's honesty held by James Loch, Lord Carlisle's London agent, who had had some experience of double-dealing by Longridge with railway proposals in East Northumberland. This had arisen with plans for a proposed railway to link Lord Carlisle's Netherton Colliery with Blyth during which it was found that the way-leaves for the route were being offered to two parties, the result being an attempt to play one interest against the other.

During 1824, upon Thompson's suggestion, Lord Carlisle took a lease on the coal reserves discovered on the estate of General Wyndham at Croglin. A 21-year lease was taken out for the Guide Pit, a small drift working an extensive but thin seam of low-quality coal. This colliery was ideally placed for the Penrith district and for supplying coal to Lord Carlisle's limeworks at Cumrew, cutting down considerably the cartage mileage.

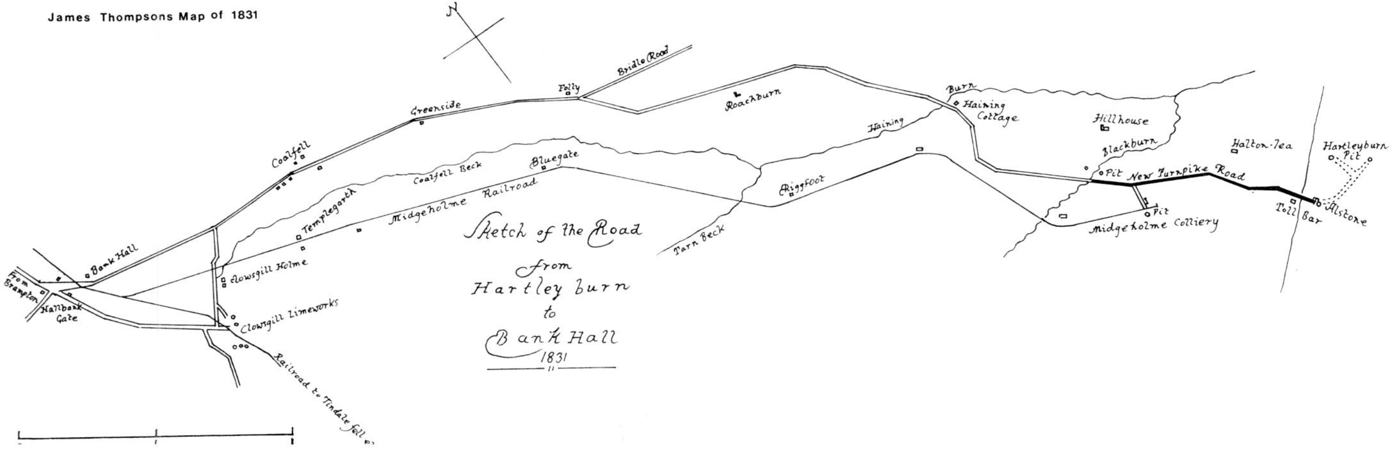

Fig. 12 James Thompson's map of 1831 showing the Midgeholme railway and road to Hartleyburn.   (University of Durham)

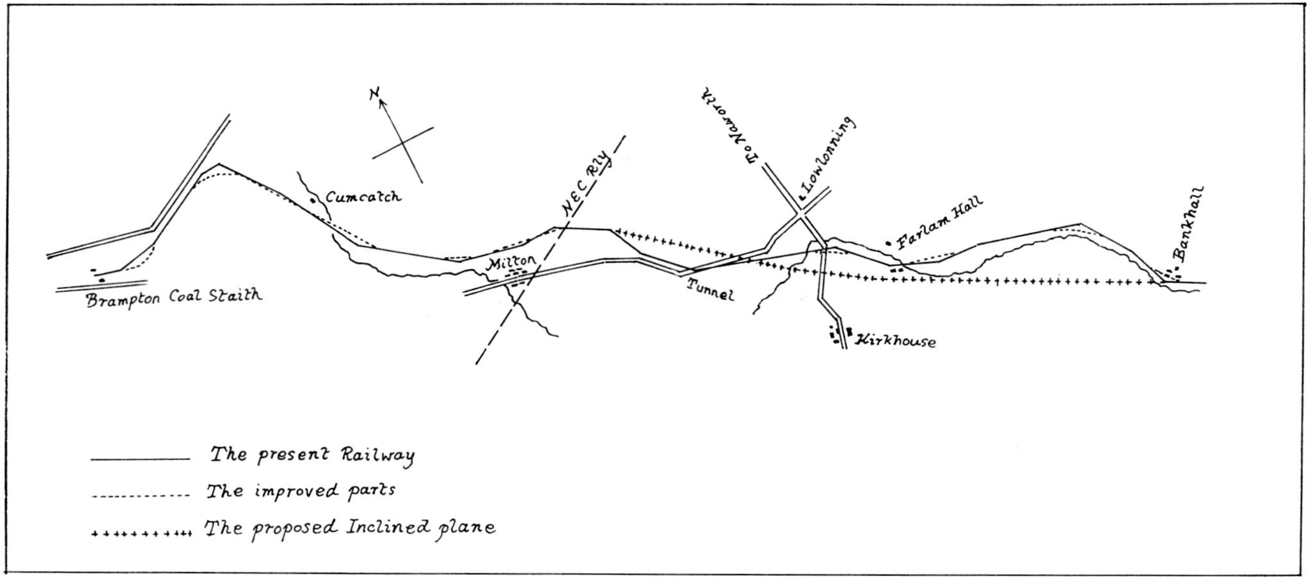

Schemes to improve 1798 waggonway by James Thompson, March 1833.

Fig. 13 Plan by James Thompson showing proposed alterations to improve the 1799 waggonway as an alternative to the new railway proposal. March 1833.
(Estate Records, Brampton)

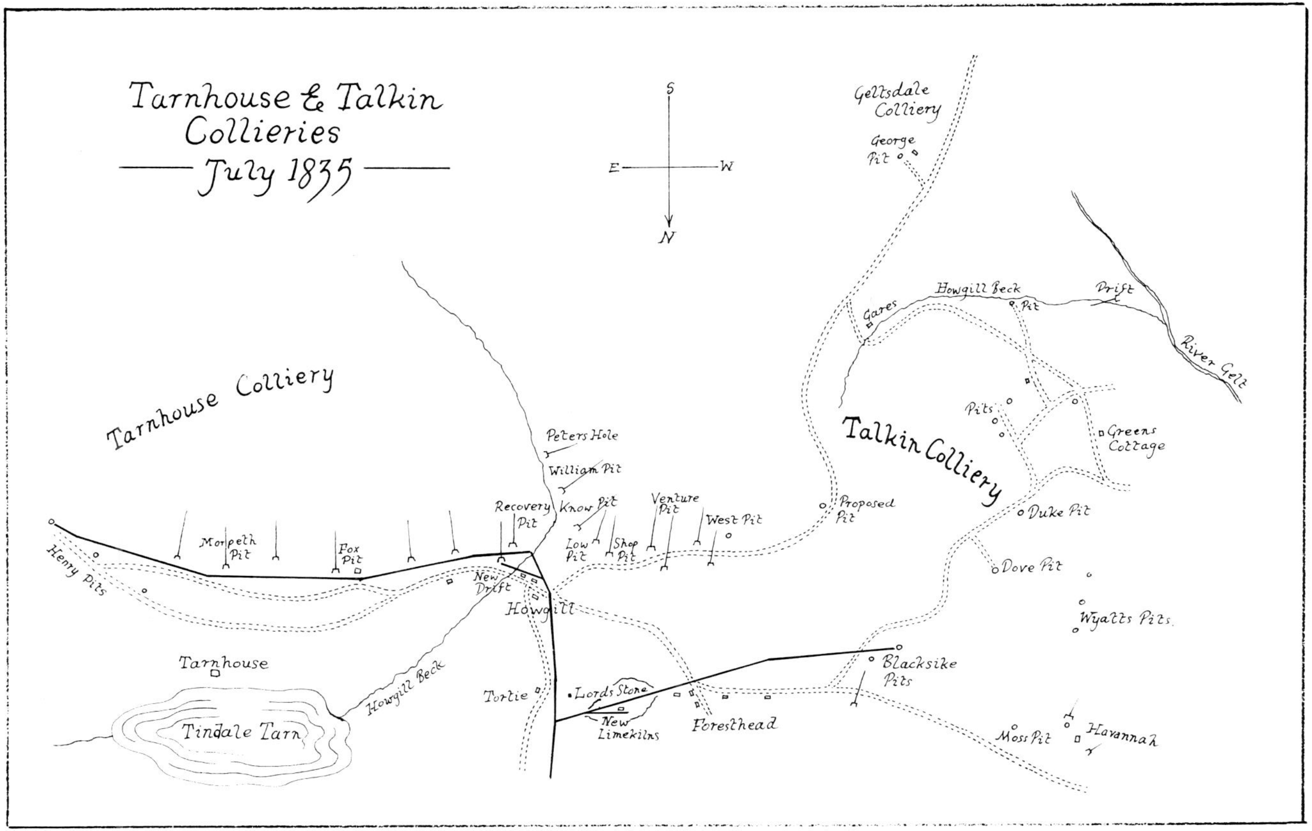

Fig. 14 Map of Tarnhouse and Talkin collieries showing railways and 1835 Howgill branch. July 1835.
(Estate Records, Brampton)

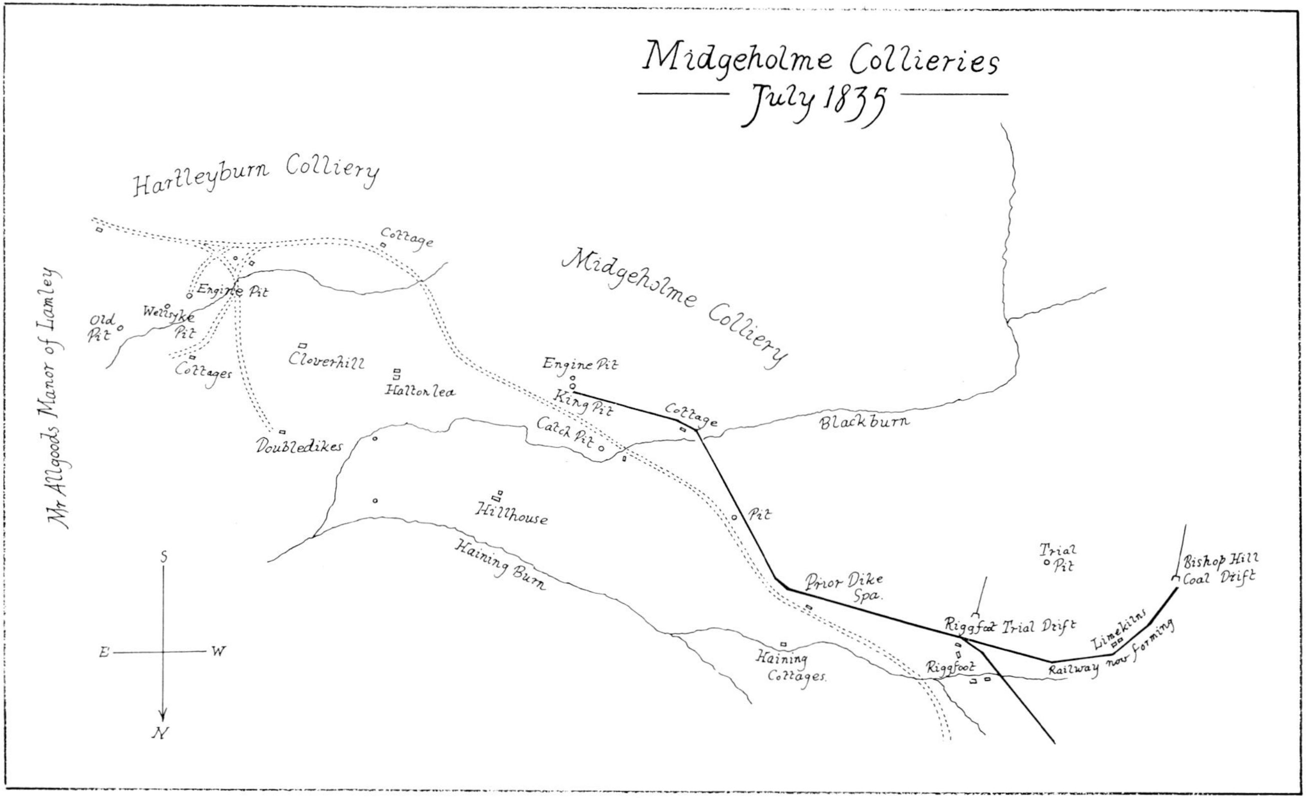

Fig. 15 Midgeholme collieries and railways in July 1835 showing Riggfoot and Bishop Hill branch.
(Estate Records, Brampton)

At the same time Thompson was planning large-scale developments to the collieries further east of Talkin and Tarnhouse at Midgeholme. Since 1821 the Catch Pit had been working there in an attempt to meet the competition of the nearby Hartleyburn Colliery on the land of Mr. Allgood, which had been taking trade from the more westerly collieries of Lord Carlisle, due to its proximity to its users. However, it was to be some years after 1824 before the developments were to be put into operation.

It was during 1824 when James Thompson found the way clear for him to submit proposals for railway development, which by now not only envisaged a private railway to Carlisle but also eastwards to reach the extremity of the barony at Glenwhelt House, Greenhead. Thompson had written to James Loch on 24 April 1824 saying:

> My opinion is that Lord Carlisle should let this line from Carlisle to Brampton, etc., be a public canal or railway, but if possible keep it within himself.

Thompson considered that such a line ought to be built as soon and as quickly as possible to allow the new drift being opened at Blenkinsopp Colliery to be fully exploited, for he knew the vast coal reserves of this colliery, and was also aware of the nearby coalfield at Thirlwall in Lord Carlisle's barony, which would be served by the same railway, both collieries using a common depot.

The attraction to Thompson of a railway from Carlisle to Glenwhelt was that it would be a private line owned by Lord Carlisle but open to the public, so that when it was joined by the line from Newcastle at Glenwhelt they would make a junction with each other. This would result in an interchange of traffic in both directions and bring to Lord Carlisle all the tonnage tolls over his own railway. Hence, a goodly profit from merchandise and passengers and also by carrying competitors' coal to Carlisle. The attraction of getting paid for carrying competitors' coals was most satisfactory to Thompson for he was not used to competition and, indeed, had a great fear of it.

At this time, too, Thompson was trying to obtain sanction for an extension of the colliery waggonway from Hallbankgate eastwards to Midgeholme and Hartleyburn, primarily to gain access to the coalfields in those areas but also to obtain both general merchandise and passenger traffic from these districts, and from Lambley and Alston, for Thompson envisaged traffic from both Carlisle and Newcastle passing over the colliery railway.

Lord Carlisle saw the advantages of Thompson's proposal and was urged by Loch during June 1824 to accept the plan. The result of this was a letter to the promoters of the proposed Newcastle to Carlisle railway on Lord Carlisle's behalf from Loch, which Loch said was written with the view of ". . . discouraging them terms also ". . . without disclosing our own views". On 5 June 1824 Thompson had been asked by Loch to find out the number of way-leaves on the route of his proposed railway to Carlisle from the western boundary of the barony, at the same time noting where bridges would be needed; he was also to prepare a sketch plan of the route.

James Thompson took great care in the planning of the route so that it was kept suitable for operation by horses and ultimately by locomotives when available. Loch, upon inspection of the plan, being neither at all sure of nor in favour of locomotives, and, indeed, failing to appreciate the easily-graded route, said he thought the line should be as straight as possible and operated by employing fixed steam engines and inclined planes, as was, he said, "the modern system". Although Thompson agreed that such a route would, indeed, be shorter, he could not agree at all with Loch's proposed method of operation.

Aware of the urgency, James Thompson set about preparing estimates for the Carlisle, Brampton and Glenwhelt Railway and for the extension of the waggonway to Midgeholme. His directive from Lord Carlisle was that his estimates should show comparative costings for a railway for colliery use only, and one of suitable standard to be able to carry public traffic and allow its subsequent extension to Alston. These, together with Thompson's plans for the renewal of the waggonway between Brampton staith and Hallbankgate to permit its use for general public through traffic, were ready by 15 June 1824:

> An estimate of the expense of laying a malleable iron railway from Carlisle by Brampton to Glenwhelt including a branch from Brampton to Midgeholme, the rails to be sufficiently strong to carry the weight of a locomotive steam engine with a train of Newcastle chaldron waggons loaded with coals, without the risk of breakage.

The estimate went into minute detail but it is not necessary to cover it fully here. The relevant main points were as follows:

	£	s.	d.
The cost of one yard of railway including rails, stone blocks, cuttings, embankments, bridges, laying and ballasting is 14s. per yard.			
The distance from Carlisle to Glenwhelt including loops at 14s. per yard. 38,720 yds.	27104	0	0
Brampton to Bankhall including sidings at 14s. per yard. 6,000 yds.	4200	0	0
Bankhall to Midgeholme at 14s. per yard. 7,000 yds.	4900	0	0
Cost of land, damages, bridges, etc...	8000	0	0
6 Locomotives at £500 each	3000	0	0
100 Coal waggons at £25 each	2500	0	0
Building staiths and the engineering costs	2000	0	0
	51704	0	0
Less £900 for recovery of the old rails of the waggonway between Brampton and Bankhall	50804	0	0

The interest charge on £50,804 for one year at 5% was put at £2,540 4s. 0d., on £25,000 was £1,250 0s. 0d., totalling £3,790, while the cost of three horses and their "furniture" when the line was complete was put at £100. The total first cost of the project was **£54,694 4s. 0d.**

Thompson estimates of the annual traffic likely to be carried on these railways follows:

Blenkinsopp to Carlisle	20,000 tons coal
Midgeholme to Carlisle	10,000 tons coal
Clowsgill to Carlisle	5,000 tons lime
Blenkinsopp and Midgeholme to Carlisle and vice versa all other types of traffic	8,000 tons
From Tarnhouse, Talkin, Midgeholme, Blenkinsopp and Clowsgill to Brampton, Newby and Aglionby	5,000 tons coal
	2,000 tons lime

The annual expense of carrying the above traffic, including the interest on first cost, wear and tear on waggons, locomotives, their fuel, enginemen and boys, and other necessary railway men, clerks and horses, etc., was estimated at **£6,337 14s. 0d.**

The annual revenue broken down into great detail totalled a profit of **£10,087 6s. 0d.**

There then followed a further very detailed estimate for the malleable iron railway from Bankhall to Midgeholme suitable for locomotive operation.

	£	s.	d.
Rails and chairs per double yard		10	6
Stone blocks and sleepers			6
Making cuttings, embankments, carrying materials, laying rails, ballasting, etc.		3	0
Total cost of one double yard		14	0
Whole length of above route 7,000 yards at 14s.	£4,900	0	0

For the same route the cost of a railway to correspond with the existing waggonway between Brampton and Bankhall was estimated as follows:

	£	s.	d.
Rails, chairs, nails per double yard (Cast iron bars 1½in. square)		5	6
Stone block sleepers			6
Making cuttings, etc., carrying materials, laying the way, etc.		3	0
Total cost of one double yard		9	0
Whole length of above route 7,000 yards at 9s.	£3,150	0	0

The detailed nature of the comprehensive estimate included costings for carriage from all the collieries to various places along the proposed railway, showing variations in pit-head prices and staith prices which are too voluminous to go further into here.

On 17 June 1824 Thompson supplied Loch with a list of all the landowners between the western extremity of the barony and Carlisle along the route of his proposed railway which very closely followed that of the British Railways, Carlisle to Newcastle main line of today. Indeed, it followed almost exactly the 1819 route of Chapman's canal proposal.

The railway, Thompson said, must be made strong enough to carry increasing traffic for many years without undue attention or the need to alter it to meet new developments. For James Loch's preference for a straight line using inclined planes and fixed winding engines to surmount the hills, Thompson cared very little. He knew that to construct such a railway would be totally unsound in view of the advancing development of locomotives and the need to provide a clear run as level as possible throughout the railway to allow their introduction. Thompson urged Lord Carlisle to give the scheme his utmost attention in view of its great value when joined to the railway from Newcastle at Glenwhelt. Of the Newcastle railway, Thompson remarked, "I am not so afraid of a railway across the island from Chapman as I would have been from Stephenson had him and his party taken it up". From this we gather that William Chapman was not in favour with Thompson, who also observed that he did not think that Chapman would be in charge of the building of the railway; he was proven correct in this assumption.

During late June 1824 Lord Carlisle agreed to an extension being made from Hallbankgate to Midgeholme suitable for operation by locomotives; in other words, a proper railway was to be built as opposed to the waggonway then in use in the Naworth coalfield. Lord Carlisle did, however, make it clear to Thompson that he could not contemplate the section from Brampton to Hallbankgate being made to the same standard at that time due to the costs involved. One wonders here how much influence James Loch had upon this decision, for Loch was never to be regarded as an ardent supporter of railways, and especially of locomotives.

The question was put to Thompson whether it was worth while to substitute locomotives for horses on a railway which only ran from Brampton to Talkin and Tarnhouse in one direction, and to Midgeholme in another. This questioning of the necessity for improved operation of the colliery railway was again due to the expense involved and no doubt, too, to Loch.

Needless to say, James Thompson said it was a necessity in view of the certainty of the Newcastle railway being built, and the railway from Glenwhelt to Carlisle, observing that a cross-country link would be made whether it was by the Newcastle people or by Lord Carlisle. Thompson said this link would create an increased demand for coal, of which Lord Carlisle would not be in a position to take advantage as the existing waggonway could not hope to carry the increased tonnages he envisaged.

Unable to convince himself of the advantage of Thompson's proposals, Lord Carlisle was advised to seek an independent opinion and George Stephenson was called upon.

Stephenson accepted the task, visited the area and went over carefully the proposals of James Thompson. After the examination Stephenson drafted a report on the findings and sent copies to John Ramshay, Lord Carlisle's steward, with additional copies for James Thompson and James Loch.

The report dated 23 August 1824, sent from Liverpool, can be summarised thus: Stephenson had inspected the country in the vicinity of Brampton, Carlisle and Gilsland and concurred that if a junction with the proposed Newcastle railway was to be made it should be at Glenwhelt in the Vale of Gilsland, as Thompson had suggested. Of Thompson's route he said the summit was at Gilsland and that the route from this point to Carlisle was quite suitable for locomotives hauling fifty tons of goods at four to five miles per hour. The project, Stephenson said, would be of great benefit to the public and local landowners along its route, but would be ". . . almost ruinous to the Lord of Carlisle's coal works . . .'. This was, Stephenson continued, due to the competition from other coalfields on the east and north of Lord Carlisle's, the competition being facilitated by the public railway now proposed which would enable coal to be sent cheaply to Carlisle. He also foresaw that the railway would soon be extended through Carlisle into West Cumberland and gain access to further coalfields whose coal would also be sold at Carlisle, not to mention access to the fine harbours at Whitehaven and Maryport which would be detrimental to the Solway Canal traffic at Carlisle.

Stephenson agreed with Thompson that such events could only be prevented if Lord Carlisle built his own railway, rather than leaving it to the Newcastle promoters, for once this joined Lord Carlisle's railway at Glenwhelt his Lordship would be free to impose tonnage rates on coal as would ". . . ensure him as much profit as though he worked the collieries himself . . .".

Both Stephenson and Thompson were satisfied by their conclusions and then reported on the route under consideration for the improved colliery waggonway and railway. In their opinion it should start in the coalfield east of Tindale Tarn at Midgeholme, passing the tarn in a valley to its north and go through Hallbankgate to the south side of Kirkhouse. From this point some cuttings were considered necessary in order to negotiate the hilly area, but this would be simple due to the route being mostly through sand and gravel, which would be used for the bed of the railway, and, therefore, considered to be no great obstacle. From Kirkhouse the line would run almost straight to Carlisle and be suitable for operation by locomotives, winding engines or horses. The route would permit loaded waggons to run the whole distance by themselves, using locomotives to haul back loads of 20-30 waggons as required. Although the railway did not serve Brampton, it was possible to construct a branch to the town from its south side while the Penrith trade could be served by a depot midway on the route to Carlisle, so shortening considerably the carting distance. After considering the development proposed by Thompson for the coalfield, Stephenson said that if put into effect with the railway Lord Carlisle could probably gain a profit of £20,000 to £30,000 by having the market to himself.

Stephenson said that even if Lord Carlisle decided not to build his own railway to Carlisle he would still require considerable improvement of the waggonway from the coalfield to Brampton. On this theme both Stephenson and Thompson agreed that the solution was to be a completely new line requiring one self-acting inclined plane, and one locomotive to do all the work done on the existing waggonway. Horses would be used for moving and marshalling waggons ready for locomotive haulage.

Of Thompson's estimate for the extension of the railway to Carlisle, Stephenson said he thought it "... very properly drawn up, and I have no doubt of its accuracy ...", concluding by saying "... I think it is only fair to state, in justice to Mr. Thompson, that I have never seen any coal works apparently better conducted than those under his care".

Upon the receipt of the report much high-level discussion followed, but Thompson, ever impatient for a decision, submitted a memo to John Ramshay, which was transmitted to Lord Carlisle in September 1824, restating the principal reasons for building the railway, the main points being that: Possession of the line to Carlisle would (1) give a great advantage for opposing any other railway, public or private over the route, (2) more quickly gain increased profits, (3) give Lord Carlisle an ability to compete with all other collieries.

In order to cost the permanent way materials for the Midgeholme extension enquiries were made to Welsh rail producers and to Bedlington Ironworks, the comparative sums for five yards of railway being as follows:

	£	s.	d.
5 Yards from Longridge's Bedlington, including chairs, etc., at 10s. 6d...	2	12	6
10 Stones at 4d. ...		3	4
	2	15	10

Total cost 11s. 0d. per yard

	£	s.	d.
5 Yards Welsh iron, chairs, etc., of same quality as above ..	2	2	6
10 Stones ..		3	4
10 Chairs and cotteralls ..		9	3
	2	15	1

Total cost 11s. 0d. per yard

On the other hand if cast iron was employed from Welsh sources, it would cost the following:

	£	s.	d.
5 Yards 1½in. square at 7½lbs. per foot is 2cwt. at 11s. 0d. ..	1	2	0
12 Stones at 4d. ..		4	0
12 Chairs at 15s. 0d. per cwt. ..		10	0
Nails and smiths' work ..		1	6
	1	17	6

Total cost per yard 7s. 6d.

These costings when applied to the Midgeholme Railway which required 7,000 yards of track would save 17s. 7d. per yard by using cast iron, a total saving of £1,230 16s. 0d. on the whole line. This was offset, Thompson pointed out, by the additional wear on the waggon wheels and increased maintenance costs.

The outcome when the order was placed was that Bedlington rails were chosen and 150 tons of 28lbs. per yard rail at £19 per ton, delivered at Carlisle, were purchased.

Unfortunately, the Carlisle, Brampton and Glenwhelt Railway was not to be, due to a deep concern on Lord Carlisle's part about the risk to and consequent reduction of his financial resources, and to the hope that the problem might be settled to mutual satisfaction between Lord Carlisle and the Newcastle Railway.

James Thompson had thus to be content with the new railway to Midgeholme which was to bring a railway of main-line standard to the colliery railway system, much superior in every respect to the 1799 waggonway.

Construction of the extension to Midgeholme started in late 1824 and, although a short line, work of some magnitude was necessary, especially on its embankments and cuttings.

CHAPTER 3

Lord Carlisle's Link to the Newcastle & Carlisle Railway

The detailed history of the Newcastle & Carlisle Railway is not our concern here. Nevertheless, the western portion of this railway was to have considerable effect on Lord Carlisle and the Naworth coalfield, hence our interest. As we shall see, it was finally built at its Western end, entirely to suit Lord Carlisle's, or rather James Thompson's requirements.

An east to west cross-country link had been under discussion for some fifty years by 1820 but the first realistic report was probably the canal by William Chapman, the engineer in 1795/6. His plan was presented to a committee of Northumberland subscribers, but it was not until after a further thirty years that Chapman and Josias Jessop prepared surveys and estimates, it being realised that a canal route was also suitable for a railway.

The route chosen at the western end was by Upper Denton, Chapelburn, Low Row, Denton Hall and south of Naworth Castle. The route continued south of Brampton, west of Talkin Tarn and on to Carlisle. The route became almost impossible for a canal near the River Gelt as it had to fall 247ft. in one and three-quarter miles, requiring a staircase of locks.

Briefly, this was the problem of the canal and why it was never put into effect.

Agitation for a cross-country link, either canal or railway, persisted from 1796 until during 1824 Chapman took his observations to the Duke of Northumberland, Lord Carlisle and a number of other leading interests. This was the time when James Thompson's own railway plans were under preparation, since he knew that the canal was quite out of the question, and so did Chapman, for by 10 May 1824 he had decided his route was more suitable for a railway. Chapman observed in his communications to the leading interests that his route was level for the first thirty-one miles from Newcastle, while the remaining thirty-three and a half miles to Carlisle were more difficult but passed close to Lord Carlisle's collieries. Chapman said he would operate the whole system without horses, in other words, by using fixed steam winding engines and inclined planes.

The plan obviously appealed once Lord Carlisle's objection to the line passing through Naworth Park was resolved by re-routing to the south, and Thomas

Telford was appointed to re-check the proposal with Chapman, and report back by mid-1825.

James Thompson was not pleased with the idea of using fixed engines and inclined planes and informed both James Loch and Lord Carlisle of this. However, Lord Carlisle's interest in the public railway project was seen as a solution to the link that Thompson wanted Lord Carlisle to build as a private venture, so saving his large capital outlay. The Chapman and Telford report was completed on time and passed to Benjamin Thompson, who was to be the Newcastle and Carlisle Railway's engineer, for his examination.

The coincidence of two Thompsons at this stage has posed problems to previous writers, in that it has been assumed that James and Benjamin were related or even brothers. This is not so, for Benjamin Thompson was born in 1779 when James Thompson's parents were 14 (father) and 10 (mother)! As James Thompson had forecast, Chapman was not to be the engineer of the proposed Newcastle & Carlisle Railway (N. & C.R.) owing to his conservative ideas, a position not greatly exceeded by his successor, for Benjamin Thompson certainly was not a man of vision, as we shall see. Benjamin Thompson presented his findings on Chapman's report to the N. & C.R. Directors on 14 June 1825. He agreed with the route proposed by Chapman as far as Greenhead, but from this point he proposed a quite different route to avoid using inclined planes, and to permit the whole railway to be operated by horse power so as not to impede traffic flow. Benjamin Thompson had a dislike of locomotives, as did many many landowners across whose land the railway would run, so he insisted that their use be specifically forbidden by the N. & C.R. Directors in their application for an Act of Parliament for the railway.

In order to obtain his objective, Benjamin Thompson decided to take the railway to Gilsland and along the valley of the River Irthing, mainly on its north side, to pass north of Brampton, veering south-west at Brampton Old Church and thence via Ruleholme, Newby, etc., to Carlisle, in the process of which it entirely missed any junction with Lord Carlisle's colliery railway.

It was now clear that the southerly route of Chapman origin had not been retained, due to Benjamin Thompson's aversion and in order to keep a level route to enable horse traction to be employed, although James Thompson knew a southerly route which would also suit horse traction was still practicable. However, a north route was, it seemed, to be the case so James Thompson set about planning how Lord Carlisle would be able to form a junction with it which would be a practicable proposition. He soon came forward with his plan together with an estimate, dated 14 July 1825. The plan was for a four-mile extension from Hallbankgate to the N. & C.R. serving Brampton en route. It was planned to be compatible in standard with the Midgeholme Railway and would replace the waggonway between Hallbankgate and Brampton. The cost of the branch was put at £8,000 or £8,280 with interest charges. The annual expense of it was put as follows:

	£	s.	d.
Interest at 3½% on £8,280	289	16	0
Repairing railway and agency at £50 per mile per year ..	200	0	0
	489	16	0
Deduct the toll for merchandise conveyed, say 4,000 tons at 1d.	66	13	4
Total expenses..	423	2	8

The idea of expending £8,000 on a branch railway did not for a moment appeal to James Loch who, no doubt, influenced Lord Carlisle to the same conclusion, neither of them appreciating the position correctly. The matter was a main topic for discussion for some time until during early October 1825 Loch wrote to James Thompson on the matter. Loch said that the N. & C.R. north route was "a grievous burden" to Lord Carlisle, especially on top of the sum being spent on the Midgeholme Railway, as it required a four-mile branch line for which he had not bargained. Loch put forward three proposals—that Lord Carlisle should oppose the N. & C.R. route by withdrawing his support, that he should try to get the N. & C.R. to construct the four-mile branch themselves, or at least to pay part of the expense.

The first proposal appealed to James Thompson, but of the others he said that the four-mile branch must be built and owned by Lord Carlisle, for if it was an N. & C.R. branch Lord Carlisle would have to pay a toll to use it, which would be in addition to the toll payable on the main line, thus increasing further the price of Lord Carlisle's coal at Carlisle. Thompson said that if the line conveyed 5,000 tons at 1d. per ton per mile toll it would bring in £493 10s. 8d. and pay the branch line's first cost in sixteen years, from which time it would give a profit of that sum, ample reason from Thompson's viewpoint for Lord Carlisle to construct the branch.

Thompson said that in his opinion the N. & C.R. toll for the branch would probably be 2d. per ton per mile which would soon offset any savings Lord Carlisle expected from getting the N. & C.R. to construct and operate the branch. Furthermore, Thompson said that a public branch would permit competitors' coal and lime to be sold at Brampton losing Lord Carlisle his monopoly there, and Lord Carlisle would have to pay the N. & C.R. to carry his coal to Brampton! The possibility of through traffic to Alston over Lord Carlisle's railway from and to the public railway would lose a considerable sum of toll money if four miles of the route were owned by the N. & C.R. Thompson urged Lord Carlisle to reconsider the branch and to use all his influence in getting the N. & C.R. to remain at Brampton Old Church and not to let them construct the branch. Fig. 9.

In order to arrange some semblance of standardisation of rail gauge before the N. & C.R. decided on theirs, James Thompson wrote to James Loch on 10 October 1825 to say that he had recently met Colonel Coulson, who was on the committee representing the interests of the western section supporters of the N. & C.R., and had asked him to ". . . lay before them, the width within the rails of our railway . . ." at the next Directors' meeting at Newcastle. This was the first instance of Lord Carlisle's wishes that the N. & C.R. be made to a specified rail gauge, in this case Stephenson gauge, the gauge of 4ft. 8in. chosen for the Midgeholme extension of the colliery railway by James Thompson.

The outcome of this request was that Benjamin Thompson wrote to James Thompson who informed Loch that he had received a letter ". . . from a Mr. Thompson near Newcastle who appears to have taken the most active part in the engineering, to meet him at Hexham . . . so that the matters named by Colonel Coulson should have attention", indicating again that at that time Benjamin Thompson was not known to James Thompson.

James Thompson, anxious to obtain some decision on the branch to the N. & C.R., suggested to Loch that it would be a good idea to call in George Stephenson to examine the proposals for the branch, since he thought that the hilly nature of the land might necessitate an inclined plane and Stephenson would clear up the matter.

On 14 October Loch told James Thompson that he had suggested to Lord Carlisle that Telford or Rennie might be more suitable advisers due to Stephenson not being held in ". . . such estimation by the more eminent engineers, and that his opinion will not have the weight with Chapman and Jessop, as Telford and Rennie would have". Loch's fears about Stephenson were based on his opinion that he (Stephenson) carried his cutting and embankment work too far in order to obtain level routes. Mentioning the recent failure of Stephenson's engineering on the Manchester Railway, Loch continued by saying, however, that in this case Stephenson ". . . has the benefit of your accuracy and correction and has only to apply his experience". Loch did agree to put Stephenson's name forward as well to Lord Carlisle and let him decide the matter.

Sometime between 14 and 20 October 1825 James Thompson met Benjamin Thompson at Newcastle to discuss the proposed route of the N. & C.R. and their plans on a branch to serve Brampton. This branch, the fifth on the railway's route from Newcastle, was to run from the north route of that railway by a two-way junction near Breconhill, to the north of Brampton, pass through Oakwood, then through a tunnel driven under Brampton Ridge to emerge and cross the main Newcastle to Carlisle road (A69) and join Lord Carlisle's waggonway near Warren House, only a short distance east of the Brampton coal staith. This left the staith under Lord Carlisle's control, but as Thompson was quick to observe, did not prevent the N. & C.R. from setting up their own staith. However, the intention to operate the whole of this branch by a fixed winding engine, due to its great inclination, was not at all in line with James Thompson's ideas. Fig. 10.

Unfortunately, the scheme appealed to Loch and Lord Carlisle, provided certain assurances were obtained, such as limitation of tonnage tolls to 1d. on the railway and 1½d. on the inclined plane per ton per mile, and that the railway was built to "... the same width as Lord Carlisle's". This news, and the authorisation to call in George Stephenson, were contained in a letter from Loch to James Thompson dated 23 October 1825. The instructions were quite explicit, in that Lord Carlisle and Loch thought the vast amount of money required to improve the waggonway was too much, Loch continuing:

> What I wish you and Stephenson to do is this, sit down and consider well what is the cheapest and best way of connecting the Midgeholme and Warren House Railways, taking advantage of the present line between Hall Bank and the staith. And state your reasons where you depart from the present line ...

Loch concluded by saying that the money Lord Carlisle would obtain from the N. & C.R. passing over his lands could be applied to the alterations which would be necessary to the colliery railway. In order to gain time, suggestions which might delay the progress of the N. & C.R. planners included ones in which Lord Carlisle could insist on the use of locomotives on the railway, and the problem of rail gauge, as yet not finalised. The latter course resulted in a letter dated 3 November 1825 which Loch sent to Newcastle stating bluntly that the N. & C.R. must be made to 4ft. 8in. gauge, or in other words, like the Midgeholme extension, which was the same gauge as the Stockton & Darlington Railway.

George Stephenson completed his report, dated 18 November 1825, and made the following points:

He had examined the problem with James Thompson starting with the north route of the N. & C.R. where it passed through the barony, and also their proposed Brampton branch, to ascertain its suitability, or otherwise, to meet the interests of Lord Carlisle. He found it was impossible to make a junction with the north route which would enable Lord Carlisle's coal traffic to be conveyed as cheaply as that of other coal owners and, that a much more suitable branch might be made to serve Lord Carlisle's interests. Although a more economic branch was possible, Stephenson observed that due to Lord Carlisle's coalfields being 200-300ft. higher in elevation than his competitors', quoting Blenkinsopp as an example, he said that the distance from the market was the same, but owing to the poor quality of Lord Carlisle's waggonway the horses were limited in haulage capacity. Blenkinsopp coal, on the other hand, was able, due to the colliery being alongside the N. & C.R. line, to use that railway for sending its coal to Carlisle, enabling a horse to haul 10-12 tons of coal on the line. On the contrary, Lord Carlisle would only be able to haul half that load by his horses on the waggonway, but 10-12 tons like Blenkinsopp on the main line. He pointed out that the Midgeholme Railway would, when finished, permit an equal load to the main line to travel over it.

21

Stephenson said that James Thompson's improvements to the waggonway between Bankhall and Brampton might be done to great advantage, suggesting one inclined plane near Kirkhouse Farm from where a line could be made permitting a horse to haul a double load to Carlisle, but not by the proposed N. & C.R. Brampton branch with its inclined plane. He said that even if a toll of $\frac{1}{2}$d. per ton per mile was charged Lord Carlisle for using the N. & C.R. Brampton branch, he would still not be competitive with Blenkinsopp, adding that accidents on the inclined plane must be taken into account as a further expense to Lord Carlisle. Stephenson said:

> I beg to be understood, that it is not my wish to advise you to attempt preventing the public's obtaining such a benefit: for the same benefit could be given them, if the line was laid out to His Lordship's best interest.
>
> If the intended Bill can be deferred until another year, I think by a plan which Mr. Thompson has suggested to me, His Lordship's interest might be protected. I mean by extending a line into Scotland as far as Annan (by way of Longtown), at which place I understand there is a good harbour; and a branch could be taken off this line to Carlisle.
>
> It would certainly be a great advantage to Lord Carlisle, if the N. & C.R. should not extend to Brampton, as it would then leave the whole market to himself; and if he wishes to favour the public with low-priced coals, he could do it with more honour this way than to be compelled by his competitors.

So here we have reinforcement of James Thompson's proposals and it was now up to Lord Carlisle to decide his course of action.

In the meantime, while Stephenson's report was under preparation, Loch had gotten the agreement of the N. & C.R. that they would build their Brampton branch, and either construct their rails to 4ft. 8in. gauge (or no more than 5ft.) or convert Lord Carlisle's railway and its rolling stock free of charge, in return for Lord Carlisle's support of the N. & C.R. Bill during its passage through Parliament. The N. & C.R. Directors said, however, that they could not give Lord Carlisle special concessions on tonnage rates over their Brampton branch as it would be unfair to other users, but said that it might depend upon the tonnages Lord Carlisle proposed to send over the branch per year which, if of sufficiently high quantity, might permit some agreement.

The N. & C.R. Directors held a meeting at Newcastle on 3 December 1825 at which the north route of the western section of their railway was described in detail. The Brampton branch was described as the fifth branch and was ". . . to serve Brampton and on to Lord Carlisle's collieries . . . and be united with the Earl of Carlisle's new railroad (Midgeholme extension) and be an important medium of communication with Alston Moor". It was stated that a horse would be able to haul a load of 16 tons throughout the route planned allowing for the summit near

Gilsland, and that the directors were very pleased at being able to have a line ". . . exempt from inclined planes, and of easy performance by animal power . . .".

At this time the N. & C.R. had not the intention of being carriers themselves; users of the railway would carry their own goods in their own waggons, or contractors would do this for them, each load being under the sole responsibility of the driver throughout its journey. The Directors' report continued to say ". . . The Directors reflect with great pleasure . . . without sacrificing the interests of the public to give up the idea of using locomotive engines . . .". In fact, a prohibitory clause was to be included in the N. & C.R. Act of Parliament to ". . . forever, preclude the introduction of such machines". This lack of foresight was due, in part, to the insistence of landowners along the railway's route who did not wish to have their peaceful residences disturbed by locomotives, and to Benjamin Thompson who said horses and locomotives would not operate side by side and that the rails would be more costly if made to take the weight of locomotives. He himself had little faith in locomotives, and in this respect, together with his alteration of route, he was to regret these conservative attitudes later, as will be seen.

Meanwhile, construction of the Midgeholme extension of the colliery railway had been proceeding slowly. By mid-1825 the contractors involved, Macadams, were predicting that the line would be in operation by July 1826. However, James Thompson knew this would not be so, as it was stated in his report to Lord Carlisle in August 1825 to be well behind schedule.

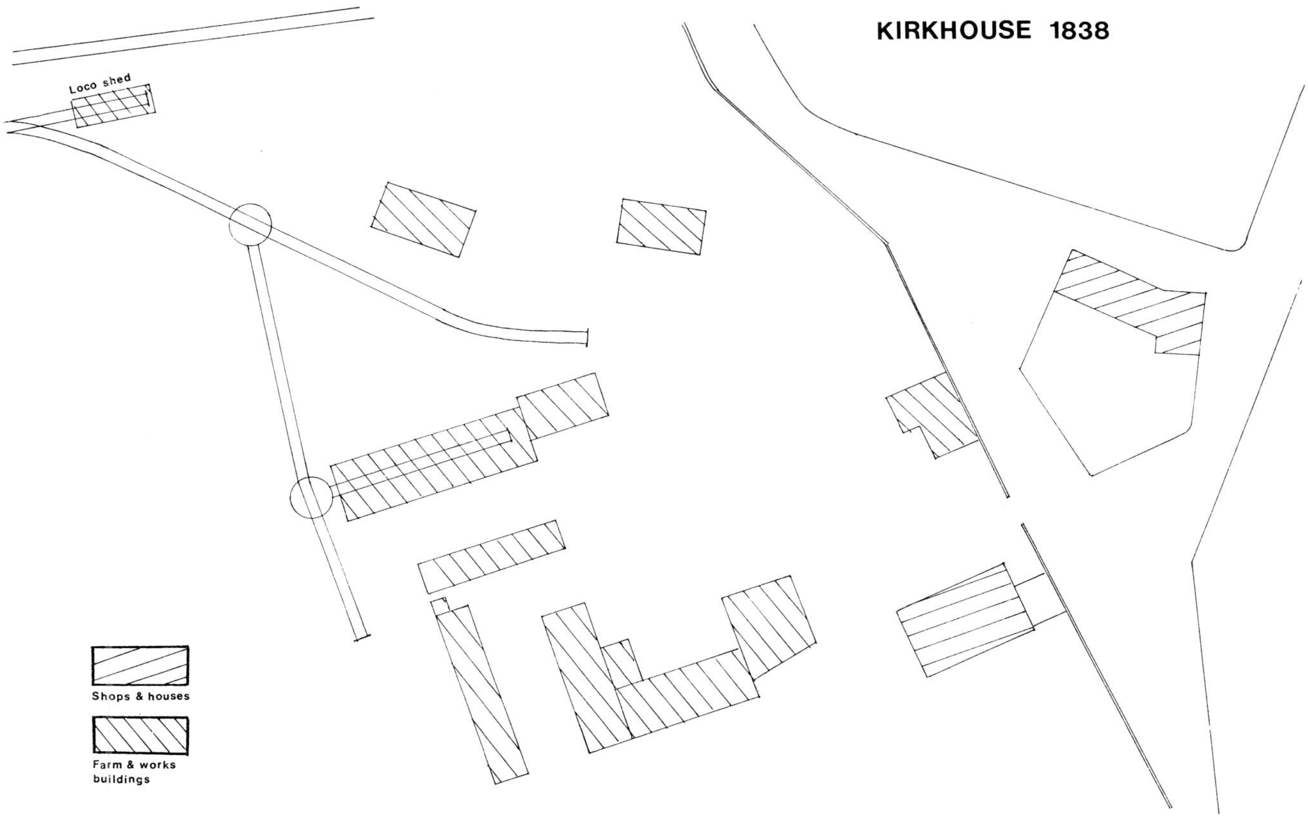

KIRKHOUSE 1838

Loco shed

Shops & houses

Farm & works buildings

Fig. 16 Plan of May 1838 showing the workshops and farm area at Kirkhouse.

(University of Durham)

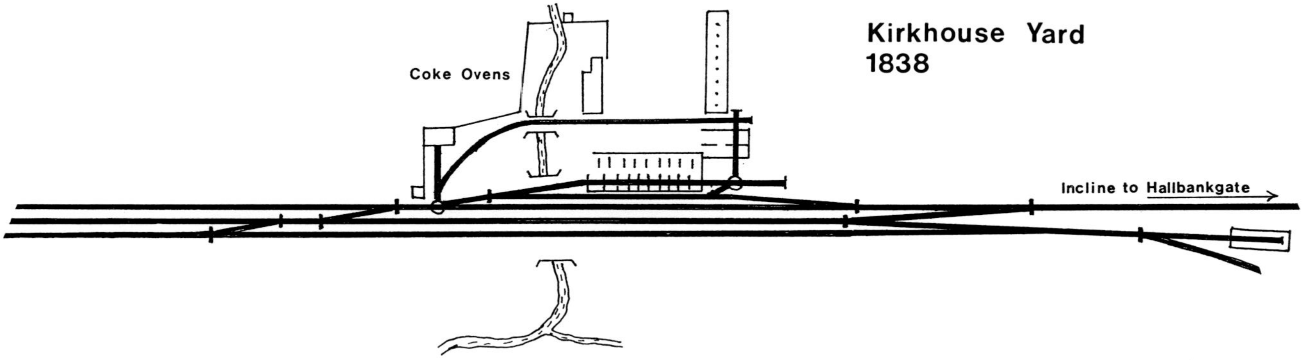

Kirkhouse Yard 1838

Incline to Hallbankgate

Coke Ovens

(University of Durham)

Fig. 17 Kirkhouse sidings and coke ovens in May 1838.

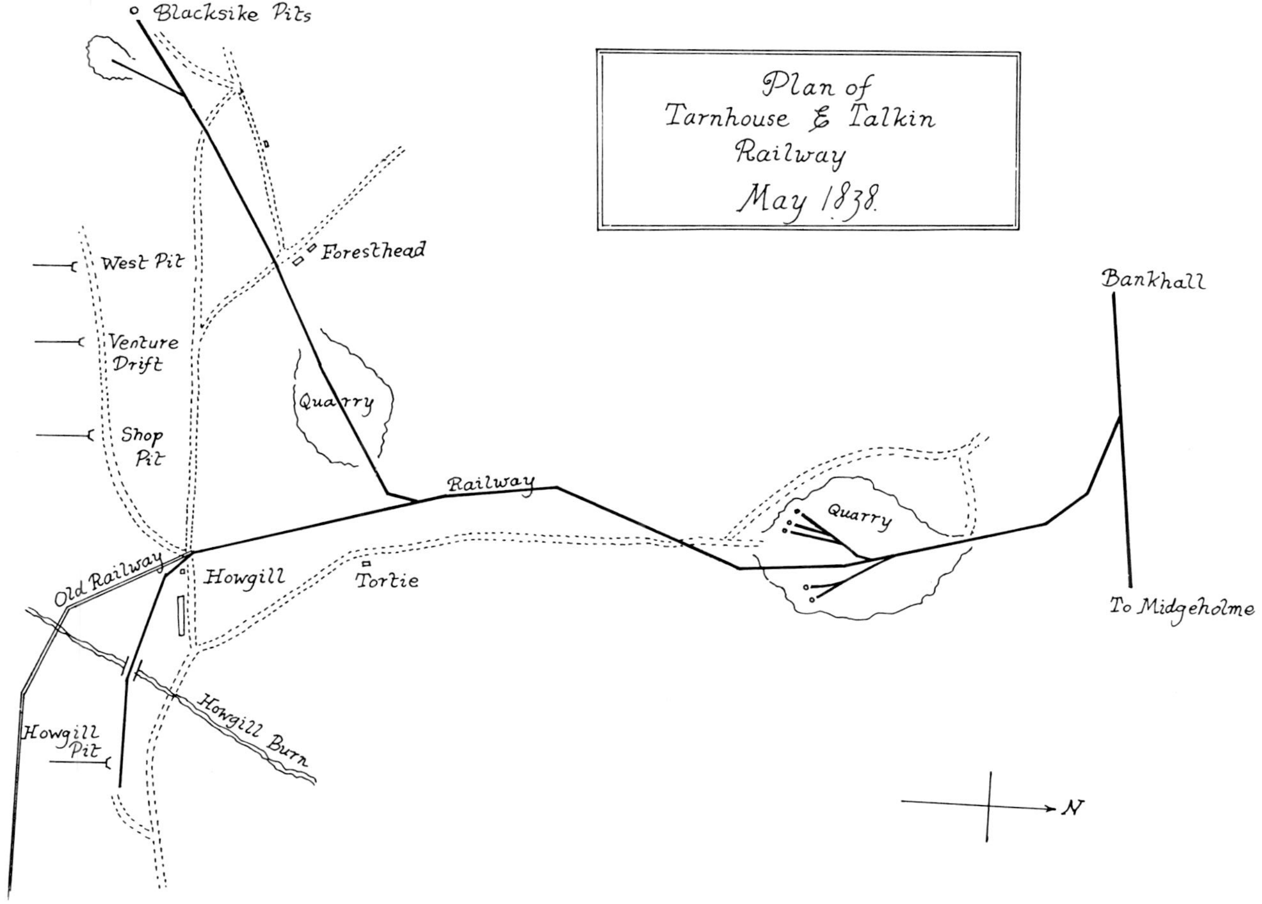

Fig. 18 Map showing railways to Tarnhouse and Talkin collieries in May 1838.

(University of Durham)

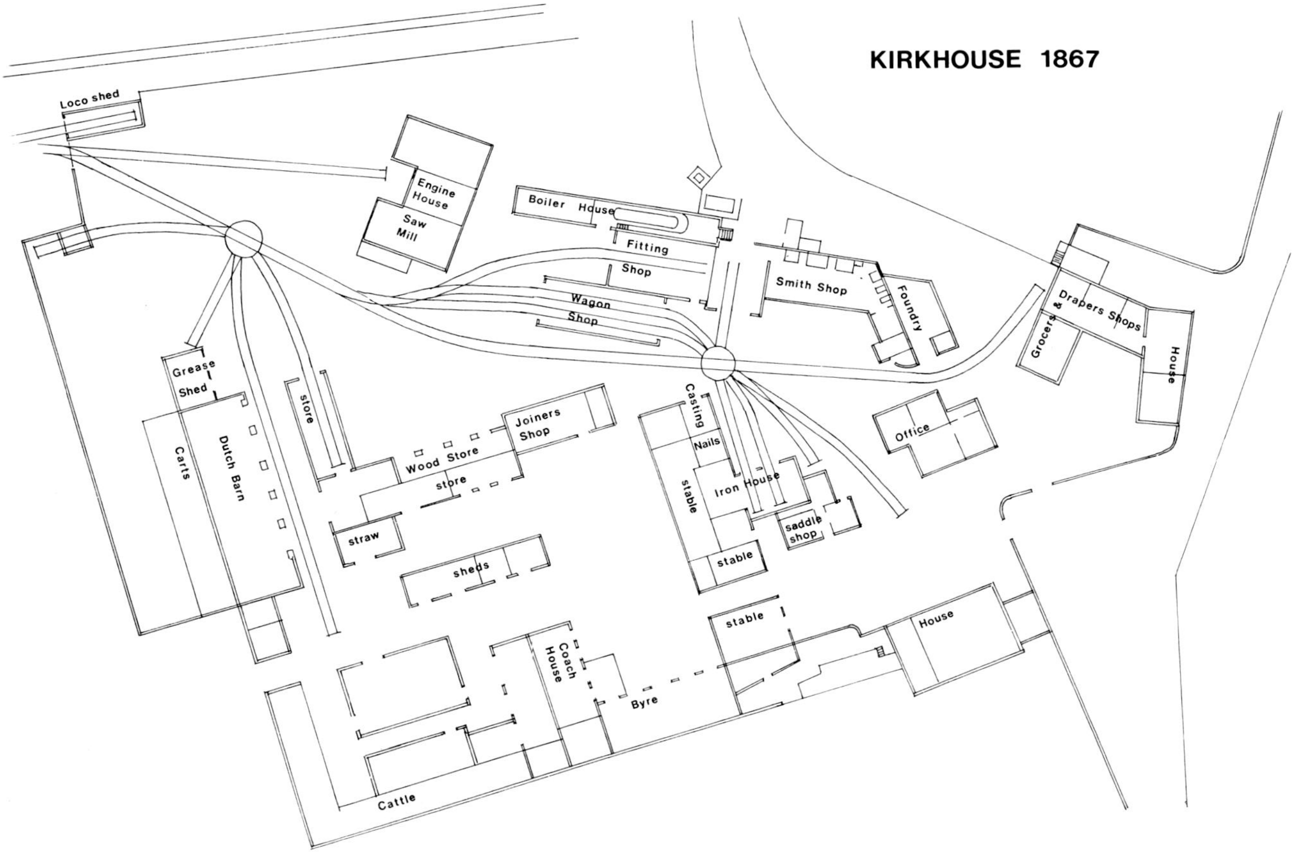

Fig. 19 Detailed plan of Kirkhouse workshops and farm at the zenith of its career in 1867. (University of Durham)

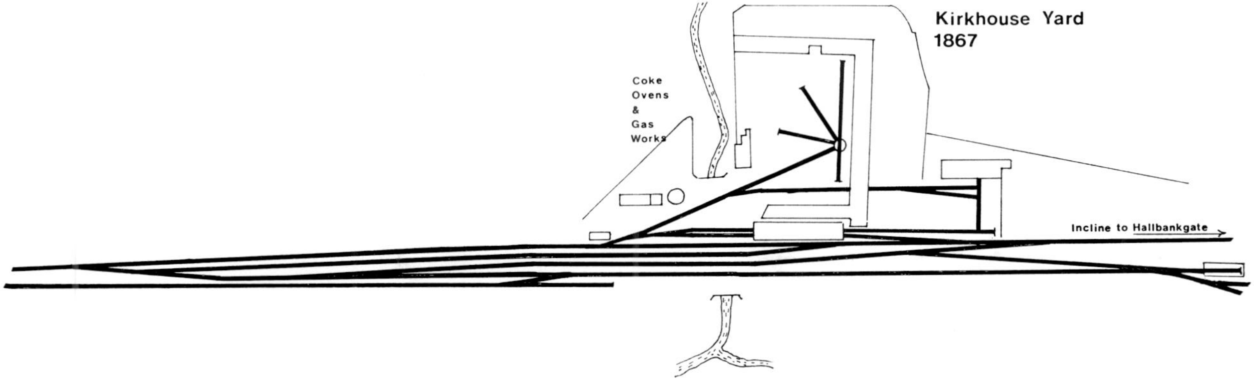

Fig. 20 Kirkhouse sidings, coke ovens and gasworks in 1867.
(Collection of B. Webb)

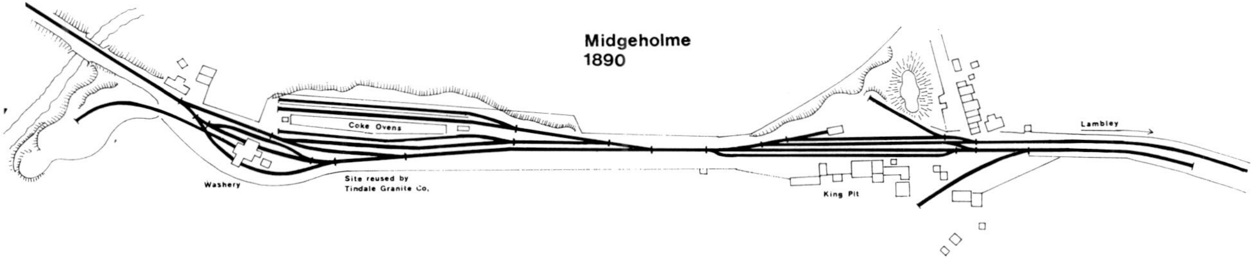

Fig. 21 Plan of the layout at High Midgeholme about 1890, showing washery, coke ovens and the King pit.
(Collection of B. Webb)

Roachburn
1900

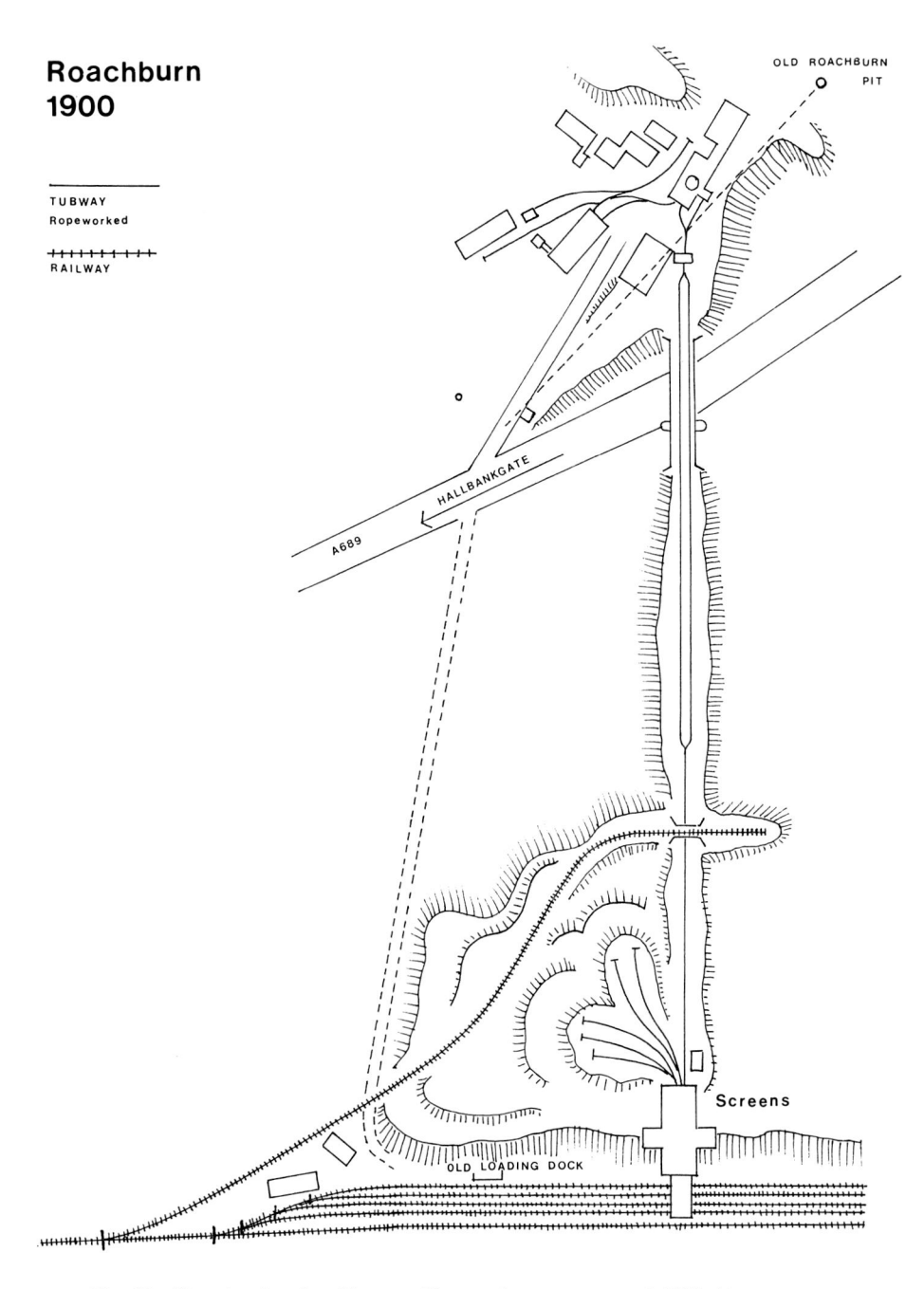

TUBWAY
Ropeworked

++++++++
RAILWAY

Fig. 22 Plan showing Roachburn colliery and screens around 1900. Note access to railway by rope-hauled narrow-gauge tubway. *(Collection of B. Webb)*

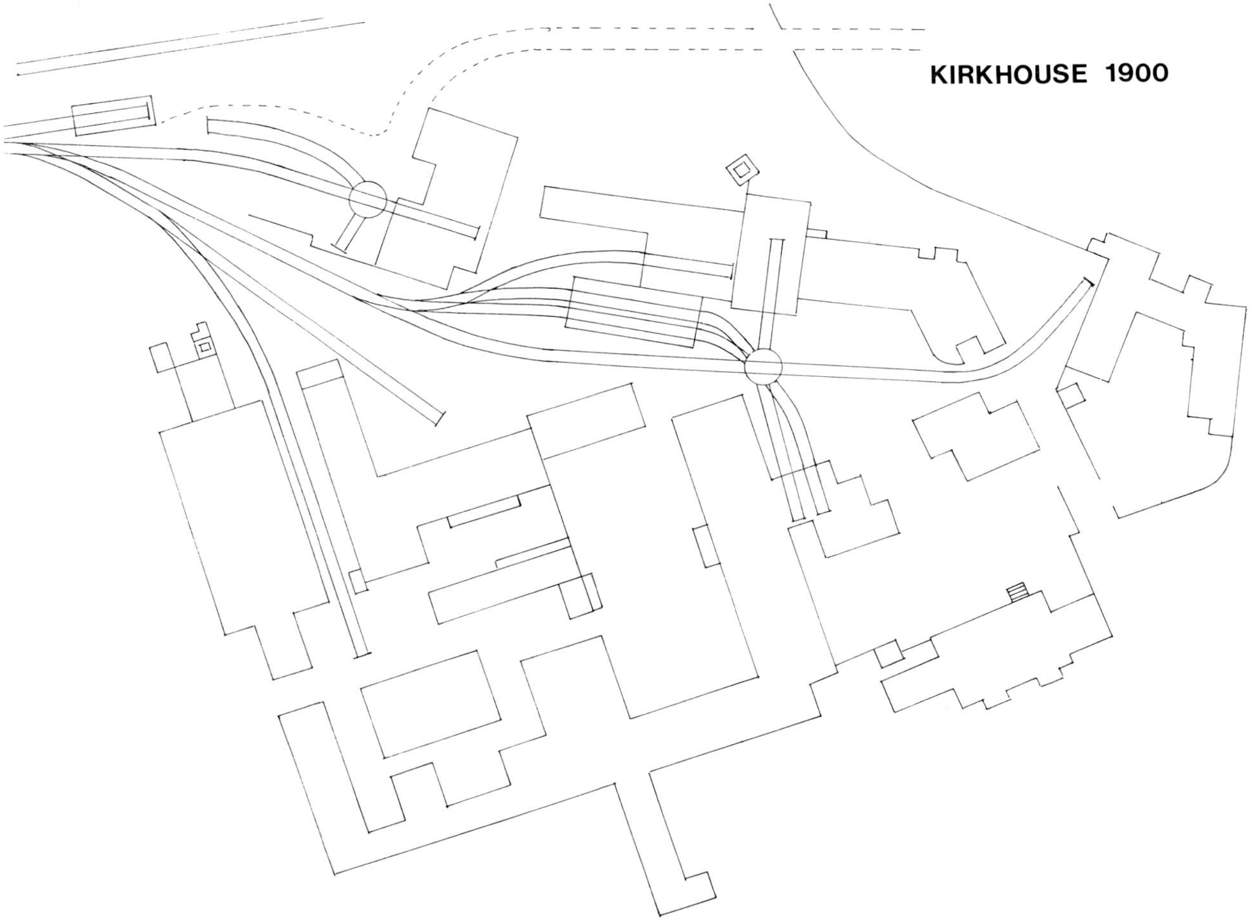

KIRKHOUSE 1900

(Collection of B. Webb)

Fig. 23 Kirkhouse workshops in 1900.

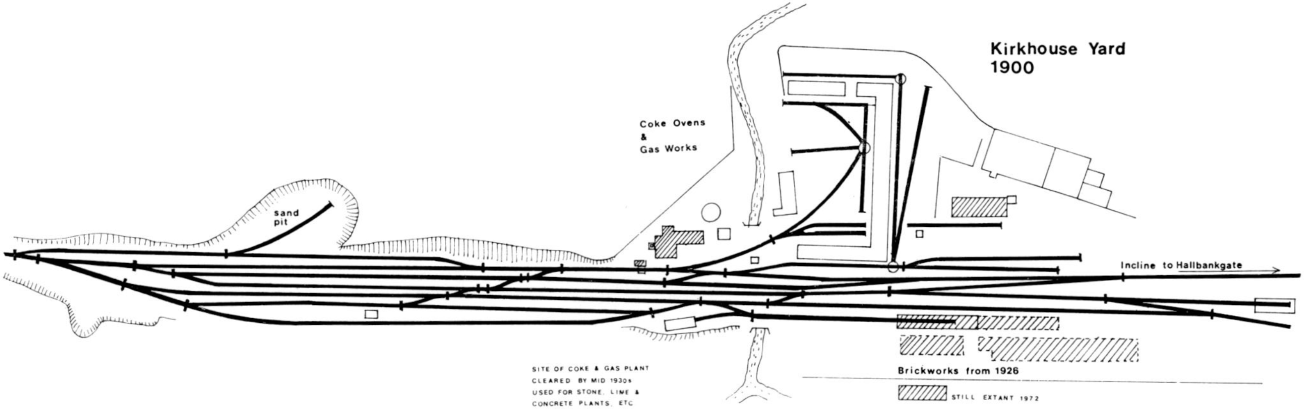

Fig. 24 Kirkhouse sidings, coke ovens and gasworks in 1900.

(Collection of B. Webb)

CHAPTER 4

Lord Carlisle's Attitude to the Newcastle & Carlisle Railway

The result of George Stephenson's comments on the unsuitability of any branch from the N. & C.R. meeting Lord Carlisle's requirements caused much consideration to be given to the subject. Lord Carlisle could not, in all honesty, oppose outright the N. & C.R., but he could, as was suggested by James Thompson, gain the same effect by adopting an attitude of complete neutrality. Such a strategy would introduce a sense of doubt into the N. & C.R. Directors' thoughts who would then be uncertain whether, in fact, they had Lord Carlisle's support or not.

James Thompson knew that no satisfactory connection with the N. & C.R. was possible while they persisted with the north route for the western section main line, and conveyed this to Loch and Lord Carlisle who decided to adopt a neutral attitude which soon had the desired effect. The neutrality of Lord Carlisle put doubts in the minds not only of the N. & C.R. Directors, but also those of a number of the railway's subscribers; somewhat perturbed by this, the N. & C.R. Directors wrote to Loch to say that they could not understand Lord Carlisle's attitude in view of their ". . . earnest endeavours to meet the wishes and guard the interests of the Earl of Carlisle".

The question of the N. & C.R. Brampton branch was to fall into Lord Carlisle's hands when the landowner whose land the proposed branch was to cross said he was in opposition to it. The landowner, Mr. Johnson, had agreed to the route across his land previously, not realising that it would be built, but now, once it seemed likely to become a reality, and to divide his land, he changed his mind. This forced Benjamin Thompson to inform Lord Carlisle of this volte-face of Johnson in January 1826, saying that if the opposition continued they would not be able to build the Brampton branch at all, asking Lord Carlisle to try to reason with Johnson over the matter.

Lord Carlisle had no intention of entering the argument, nor to be seen to abandon his neutrality and, through Loch, reminded the Directors of the N. & C.R. of their pledges of 3 and 9 November 1825 to build the branch. The breaking of these pledges was seen by Loch as Lord Carlisle's lever to withdraw his support from the N. & C.R. and thus emerge from neutrality into actual opposition.

The impasse was to continue, with frequent exchanges of letters, for almost a year, during which Lord Carlisle retained his neutrality but had been persuaded by James Thompson that the only satisfactory solution was to work towards the abandonment of the north route and instead urge the N. & C.R. to adopt the route passing south of Brampton which was convenient for the colliery railway and Lord Carlisle's interests.

During 1826 the Midgeholme Railway proceeded very slowly, being considerably behind schedule. In August James Thompson reported that work was in progress on the Hallbankgate to Tindale section with very little embankment work as yet carried out, although some work on the large cutting just north-west of Tindale village was under way.

Towards the end of 1826 it was obvious that the N. & C.R. Directors had to find some solution to the problems of the western section of the railway in an endeavour to meet the wishes of Lord Carlisle. The Directors, therefore, decided to go against the advice of Benjamin Thompson and see if a suitable route south of Brampton could be adopted. The Directors agreed that provided they could still obtain a railway capable of horse operation and which would not be against the public interest, there was no reason why the change should not be made. How Benjamin Thompson felt about having to revert to Chapman's route, which he had already decided was unsuitable except for operation by inclined planes, is left to conjecture.

As James Thompson had known for some time, Benjamin Thompson found the route entirely suitable for horse traction, and reported this fact to his Directors. During late February 1827 at a Directors' meeting at Newcastle it was noted with pleasure that the adoption of the south route had rendered superfluous the need for an N. & C.R. branch to Brampton, thus saving a sum of £10,000, and had at last overcome the problem of Lord Carlisle, without whose support the whole scheme would have failed. The south route was approved and some relief expressed at the prospect of the project now being undertaken without any further difficulties.

Unfortunately, this was not to be the case because within a few weeks another obstacle emerged in the form of a gentleman at Hayton, west of Brampton, named Sir Hew Dalrymple Ross. He lived at Stone House, Hayton, and objected strongly to the south route being adopted, and its crossing his estate or, indeed, passing within sight of his house. The south route was chosen carefully to make it easy to operate and construct, but in so doing embittered Sir Hew, who went to great lengths to try to obtain considerable sums of money from the N. & C.R. for crossing his property. All this would seem to be of no concern to Lord Carlisle, but in order to obviate paying Sir Hew Ross what he demanded, it was resolved yet again to divert the route of the railway.

Benjamin Thompson at once suggested a return to his north route which passed well clear of Hayton, but in view of the agreement with Lord Carlisle this was now no longer possible. A compromise solution was proposed by Benjamin Thompson and he set this out during late 1827. The route now being considered was to follow the agreed south route, allowing a junction with Lord Carlisle's railway but then heading north-west to climb past the western side of Brampton via an inclined plane to a point near Brampton Old Church, where the north route via Newby to Carlisle was to be re-adopted. In the view of the N. & C.R., the alteration completely met the requirements of Lord Carlisle and alleviated the necessity to pay Sir Hew Ross' demands.

The situation was to continue as such for some twelve months; meanwhile, work continued on the Midgeholme Railway, now greatly behind schedule. During August 1827 James Loch, John Ramshay and James Thompson reported that they had ridden in a waggon from Hallbankgate along the first one and three-quarter miles of the new line, from which point the rails were being laid towards Tindale embankment. This embankment, frequently called by Thompson the "Great Battery", was at this date being filled up to one-third of its intended height and work was in progress from both sides to raise it to its full height. From Tindale eastward the cuttings past Prior Dyke as far as Whites Cut, Low Midgeholme were completed but the embankment thence to High Midgeholme across the valley of the River Blackburn, was not started.

By the autumn of 1827 James Thompson had convinced Lord Carlisle that the compromise north-south route of the N. & C.R. was not in his Lordship's best interest. Thompson explained the situation in detail, saying that after passing the south side of Brampton and the junction with his Lordship's railway, it then turned north-west and climbed via Capon Tree and a stationary engine-worked, inclined plane to reach Brampton Old Church. Thompson said that the inclined plane was even worse for the interests of Lord Carlisle and the N. & C.R. in its new position than when intended for the Brampton branch. He said it would have to be negotiated now by all traffic using the N. & C.R., increasing costs, impeding traffic flow, and, most serious of all in Thompson's view, prohibiting the introduction of locomotives.

James Thompson knew, too, that a south route between Brampton and Carlisle was still practicable and would avoid the problem of Sir Hew Ross at Hayton by being moved further south to pass through Townhead. By January 1828, Fig. 11, he had prepared plans of this proposal which was backed by the survey carried out by the N. & C.R. western section's surveyor, John Studholme, of Carlisle and Thompson's own survey for his Carlisle, Brampton & Glenwhelt Railway proposal of 1824. Duly, in January 1828, James Loch wrote to the N. & C.R. Directors expressing Lord Carlisle's pleasure that the N. & C.R. had found a route suitable to Sir Hew Ross by moving the line further north, but then pointed out that Lord Carlisle was entirely against the revision due to its effect on his interests, writing again in February stating further disapproval ". . . of the line now proposed and of any other line that should have the effect of interposing an inclined plane between His Lordship's works and Carlisle".

The Directors of the N. & C.R. did not appreciate this attitude at all, and through their Chairman, James Losh, said Lord Carlisle should remember the efforts already taken to meet his wishes, pointing out that the north route as originally proposed obviated inclined planes but was not suitable to Lord Carlisle, while the new route passing close to Lord Carlisle's collieries was adopted to meet his wishes and was now also found unacceptable. He said Lord Carlisle was still served by the route chosen to avoid Hayton, and could not understand why this mutually agreeable route was not satisfactory.

James Thompson set out his thoughts on the matter to Lord Carlisle thus: The south route he said would permit a horse to work its loaded waggons to Carlisle and return with the empties in one working day, the whole operation being based and operated from Kirkhouse. The compromise route, on the other hand, with its inclined plane would require horses to work from Kirkhouse to the plane and further horses from the plane to Carlisle, giving a two-stage journey and needing two bases of operation, at Kirkhouse and the inclined plane foot. Obtaining a south route unfettered by incline planes would enable one base both for stabling, waggon repair and exchange, with consequent economy, and the whole operation would be under the direct control of Lord Carlisle's agent. He envisaged the second sets of horses working on the colliery railway east of Kirkhouse bringing the loaded waggons from the collieries for despatch to Carlisle, and returning with the empties. This system on a day-to-day basis would ensure that full waggons were always ready at Kirkhouse for the working to Carlisle.

The inclined plane route with its fixed engine would not only break the journey and require further facilities, but the route thence would only permit a horse to take four waggons to Carlisle as opposed to six waggons on the south route, since a horse was always limited by the number of empty waggons it could draw back.

Unfortunately, it was not evident to the N. & C.R. Directors, who were influenced too much by opinions of so-called "formidable engineers" on the merits of inclined planes. In their view, the only objection to the inclined plane was its interruption of through passenger traffic, claiming that heavy goods and mineral traffic would actually be facilitated in transit by the plane which fell at 1,300 yards at $1\frac{1}{2}$in. to the yard; hence their continued mystification and anger at the neutrality of Lord Carlisle. They informed Lord Carlisle that they were quite satisfied with the opinions of "eminent engineers" and decided in February 1828 that if the support of Lord Carlisle could not be obtained the whole project might be dropped.

James Loch replied saying that on no account could Lord Carlisle support the route as it now stood, due to the increase in time and transit costs and the expense of increasing his establishment, and pointed out that James Thompson felt that a route suitable to all parties, passing south of Hayton, was still possible.

On 20 February 1828 James Losh for the N. & C.R. said he appreciated Lord Carlisle's fears, intimating that James Thompson had little experience of inclined planes and was not, therefore, qualified to express an opinion on their advantages or disadvantages! Losh suggested that if Lord Carlisle would submit the problem to "... competent persons conversant with such subjects he would at the conclusion find that his interests will be promoted by it".

In furtherance of his claim, Losh enclosed a report by his engineer, Benjamin Thompson, whom he said "... has had more experience on this subject than any individual I know of ..." suggesting that Lord Carlisle, too, should call for an independent opinion.

The report was dated 19 February 1828 and said substantially that the distance from where Lord Carlisle's railway joined the N. & C.R. to the turnpike on the Penrith road into Carlisle was ten miles and was the only route free of inclined planes, but was affected by the attitude of Sir Hew Ross, and consequently abandoned. The other route with the inclined plane was only nine and a half miles to Carlisle and its fall of 170ft. in three-quarters of a mile was made easy to operate in both directions by the fixed winding engine on the plane. Benjamin Thompson said that, in his opinion, a horse would haul a quarter more weight on this route than on the south route and the route would provide "... nothing but accommodation ..." to Lord Carlisle, pointing out that Lord Carlisle's proposed new colliery line would have an inclined plane too. Of the inclined plane's operation, he envisaged the horses and men would walk it while their loads traversed it by the engine, and collect their loads at the foot or at the head of the plane as the case might be. He added that the town of Brampton could be served by another inclined plane, shorter but operated by the same engine, which would lower Lord Carlisle's coal to Brampton "... thereby dispensing with His Lordship's present very defective and almost impassable railway between Kirkhouse and Brampton ...".

James Loch replied to Losh in defence of James Thompson, saying that he had complete faith in his opinions and would, if necessary, call for a further independent opinion from an eminent civil engineer. In order to show fairness, the report was studied by James Thompson and some re-planting of trees on the route of the inclined plane postponed until the argument was resolved.

On 20 February 1828 James Thompson told Loch that Benjamin Thompson's report and findings were very different from his own assessment based on the survey of John Studholme, and on his own knowledge of the country, adding that the south route would allow heavier loads to go to Carlisle than the north route which was too level. Of the plane, he said it was an inconvenience not only for its cost and time wastage but also due to the danger of accidents, saying that even if horses did walk up and down some time would elapse before the last horse got his load to the top of the plane. With typical adeptness of thought, he drew attention to the N. & C.R. report of 3 December 1825, showing their, and Benjamin Thompson's, aversion to the use of inclined planes, while the additional plane to serve Brampton would only increase still further the cost of coal. Referring to his lack of experience with inclined planes, James Thompson agreed that his namesake had more, so suggested to Loch that the advice of George Stephenson again be sought to decide which route could be operated with the greatest advantage. His final statement was

"I confidently look forward to some great improvement in locomotive engines . . . and their general adoption on railways. In that case this inclined plane would be an awkward thing between Kirkhouse and Carlisle".

Duly, George Stephenson's advice was sought, and in due course, in the absence of his father, Robert Stephenson replied on 17 March 1828 in a letter to James Thompson. Upon his examination of the proposed routes he found that the superiority of the south route proved beyond doubt that this was the one to adopt as it was the only one capable of operation with one form of motive power, in this case horses. He further observed that it could operate without interruption caused by the transfer of goods from horse to rope haulage and back again, the loss of time and likelihood of accidents, and the wear and tear on rollers and ropes inevitable on a route with an inclined plane. The south route was of uniform grade which would allow a horse to take almost any load to Carlisle, being limited only by the number of waggons it could haul back again. Stephenson said he thought a horse would be able to bring back five empty waggons weighing a total of $5\frac{1}{2}$-6 tons which would have conveyed 10-12 tons of goods to Carlisle. On the north route with its four miles of ascending line, the horse would haul exactly the same load as the south route, both ways, but the inclined plane was the problem and should be avoided if possible. The letter was read and approved by George Stephenson before despatch.

So there was little to choose between the two routes according to the Stephensons, except for their obvious dislike of the inclined plane. James Thompson again commented that in his opinion a horse would take six waggons on the south route as opposed to five on the north route, basing his calculations on his own knowledge of the country and on the survey of John Studholme, informing Loch of his opinion on 19 March 1828.

Stephenson had agreed that the inclined plane was a nuisance so James Thompson was pleased in that respect in that it proved his faith in the south route to be correct. Thompson knew that the south route would equally well meet the requirements of both Lord Carlisle and the N. & C.R., and indeed cover a better area for trading, serving Brampton by a short level branch, the Penrith district from Wetheral, or by a branch to Penrith via Cumwhitton along the valley of the River Petteril, all of which would be impossible if the north route was adopted. He observed, too, that the north trade could be served equally well from the south route by a branch to Longtown.

While this was under consideration the N. & C.R. were still arguing with Sir Hew Ross who had quoted a figure for crossing his estate which was more than the total value of the estate. By the end of March 1828 the matter was left in abeyance after the breakdown of negotiations, and there was talk of not building the N. & C.R. at all, together with threats either to terminate it at Haydon Bridge or head north to reach Annan via Longtown, missing Carlisle completely.

On Tuesday, 8 April 1828 the N. & C.R. Directors decided at a meeting in Newcastle, in spite of the extra costs involved, to construct the Brampton to Carlisle section of their railway by the south route. The additional cost was due to a deviation, to be well clear of Hayton and Sir Hew Ross, which would entail crossing the Cowran Hills by a tunnel (later abandoned for a cutting) but give an open road to Carlisle free from inclined planes. The news was well received by Lord Carlisle and James Thompson, who none the less kept their delight private as it was not yet opportune to abandon the neutral attitude which had proved such a wise move on the Naworth side. The new survey for the N. & C.R. started on 9 April 1828 at both ends and was due for completion by August.

By mid-summer 1828 Henry Howard of Corby Castle was becoming somewhat perturbed by the continued neutrality of Lord Carlisle, being at a loss to understand why this attitude should continue since it seemed apparent to all that the route of the N. & C.R. was to be built exactly to suit Lord Carlisle's wishes and interests. He feared that the scheme might fail due to the uncertainty of Lord Carlisle's attitude, and said that it would be most unfortunate, in view of the great advantages offered by the railway to the countryside and inhabitants along its route. His feeling was that Lord Carlisle's attitude was prompted by the desire to retain for himself all the local markets for his coal and lime, which he stood to lose, in part at least, once the N. & C.R. opened. He wrote and asked Lord Carlisle to declare his intentions which he thought quite unjustifiable in view of the adoption of the south route.

To some extent Henry Howard was probably right in his assumptions for James Thompson's great fear of competition had no doubt permeated the thinking of James Loch and Lord Carlisle. James Thompson's fear was engendered by his lack of experience for the Naworth coalfield in its isolated position had always been protected from such commercial intrusion. However, at this time he said that if the N. & C.R. was abandoned Lord Carlisle could build his own railway from Brampton ". . . in such a direction as would prevent all competition of other coal owners, etc., and at the same time be equally beneficial to Carlisle and the public". This was a resurrection of his Carlisle, Brampton and Glenwhelt scheme of 1824.

All this failed to amuse the N. & C.R. Directors who were once more faced with what was from their standpoint a volte-face by Lord Carlisle, and indeed accused him of this. When advice on the accusation was sought and all correspondence carefully examined, Sir James Graham, Lord Carlisle's legal adviser, said that as far as he could see Lord Carlisle had never pledged his support to the N. & C.R. and quoted on 10 July 1828 the only two references ever directly made to the matter. One was by Loch on Lord Carlisle's behalf, "I do not wish to conceal that the line that is conceived most calculated to meet Lord Carlisle is that which passes most to the south to avoid Sir Hew Ross". The second indicated the fairness of Lord Carlisle, ". . . The line proposed by the Directors is likewise objectionable to a certain degree from the manner it cuts up the enclosures between Brampton and the River Irthing"—this quote referring to the north route was followed, Sir James said, by a decision to stop plantation work on the route, even though it was not a route suitable to Lord Carlisle. With Sir James Graham's favourable opinion all was settled in the minds of Loch, Thompson and Lord Carlisle.

James Thompson's obsessive fear of competition took a new turn at this time when it was learned that once Lord Carlisle's lease terminated on the Blenkinsopp Colliery at Greenhead, it would be re-let to new lessees. Thompson knew that a great field of coal lay at this colliery and that its close proximity to the N. & C.R. main line would greatly assist its competitive state for the Carlisle market. His suspicions were not helped when he found that a proposed new company with several N. & C.R. Directors interested in it was likely to be set up ready to take over upon the expiry of Lord Carlisle's lease. Thompson became convinced that the new Blenkinsopp company was specifically arranged to annoy Lord Carlisle, and voiced this opinion many times. One example was when a toll-gate was set up near Temmon on the Greenhead to Brampton road to exact tolls from traffic using the road, including Lord Carlisle's coal carts from Blenkinsopp and Gapshields Collieries. The fact that a group of landowners opposed to the N. & C.R. had got their solicitor, who was Clerk to the Commissioner of the road, to take this action in an attempt to annoy Lord Carlisle and thereby bring him into opposition rather than neutrality to the N. & C.R. The toll-gate, coupled with the knowledge that already Blenkinsopp coal purchasers were being found in Carlisle for when Lord Carlisle's Blenkinsopp lease ended, prompted James Thompson to complain to Loch over the matter. James Thompson urged Loch to write saying that it was all part of a conspiracy arranged by the N. & C.R. to destroy Lord Carlisle's interests; this he did. Needless to say, the N. & C.R. Directors, somewhat mystified by the accusations, said that they knew nothing of the toll-gate and had nothing to do with the Blenkinsopp company, but if individual directors were privately interested in Blenkinsopp Colliery there was nothing the N. & C.R. could do, adding it was hardly up to them to instruct them how to conduct their affairs.

By summer 1828 it was obvious that some further contact between the N. & C.R. and Lord Carlisle was necessary, so James Losh invited his Lordship to the July Directors' meeting at Newcastle. James Loch was delegated to attend for Lord Carlisle but could not manage to go during July, suggesting a meeting at Naworth Castle to which the Directors were invited during September. Loch assured Losh that Lord Carlisle ". . . will not oppose the measure, provided it is conducted in the direction which appears to him least objectionable, and which will interfere the least with his residence . . . and be most convenient for his existing works and interest". The letter also went on to describe the route Lord Carlisle had decided was most suitable, stating it ". . . must pass near Denton Hall, to the eastward of Scarrow Hill and the village of Milton, and near to where Hell Beck joins the Gelt; . . . ". In addition to these demands Loch insisted that Lord Carlisle should have sufficient influence ". . . in the direction as his interest in the measure demand, in the event of the railway being proceeded with". There is now no doubt as to who decided the route of the western portion of the N. & C.R.!

How the N. & C.R. Directors took this directive is left to conjecture. The Naworth Castle meeting took place on Sunday, 7 September 1828 and all points were agreed by the N. & C.R. in return for Lord Carlisle's support of the N. & C.R. Act in its passage through Parliament, but, as before, neutrality in other matters was to be maintained. Apart from various attempts to draw Lord Carlisle from his neutral stance, all proceeded smoothly, the N. & C.R. Act receiving the royal assent on 22 May 1829.

CHAPTER 5

Developments on Lord Carlisle's Railways

James Thompson reported that during late June 1828 the work on the Midgeholme Railway was nearing completion, work on the "Great Battery"—the Tindale embankment—having proceeded so that the two ends had met and the widening of the top ready for the trackbed was under way. By August the railway was laid and in use between Midgeholme and Hallbankgate by 10-12 waggons of coal daily. The cost of the Midgeholme extension was estimated as £4,900 in 1825, but after completion in 1828, James Thompson reported to James Loch in his letter of 17 December that ". . . the Midgeholme railway cost near £13,000 . . .". Due to the break of gauge at Hallbankgate (the 1799 waggonway was still of sub-standard gauge) it was necessary to tranship the coal into the old waggons, a time consuming and laborious operation which could not be tolerated for long, but bearing in mind the small tonnages involved and the other expenses of Lord Carlisle, Thompson opined that there was no need to ". . . extend or widen our old railway till next season".

On the colliery side at this time, both Tarnhouse and Talkin Collieries were still in operation, the latter's Blacksike Pit especially proving a good supplier of excellent coal in increasing quantity. The Geltsdale Colliery continued at the George drift, supplying coal to the Penrith district.

The troublesome waggonway serving the Tindale Fell drifts comprising Tarnhouse Colliery was a great problem to James Thompson, being of such a gradient as to make its operation difficult, not to say hazardous, and almost impassable during the winter due to its high altitude. The fact that it was often blocked by snow set Thompson searching for coal at the eastern end of the fell so that access could probably be gained from a short branch made from the Midgeholme Railway at Tindale village, thus permitting abandonment of the Tindale Fell waggonway.

To this end explorations at Riggfoot, near Tindale, during 1826 had found low-quality coal but had left it for further exploration until the Midgeholme Railway opened; by 1830 it was in production of limeburning coal.

In July 1830 James Thompson proposed that Lord Carlisle should construct a number of new railways, one of which was to serve Riggfoot drift and the Tarnfoot quarry behind Tarn House at the foot of Tindale Fell. This would eliminate the Tindale Fell waggonway and enable extensions in due course to tap a field of coal near Bishop Hill below Henry Pit at the eastern end of the fell, a development which was to prove of great value in terms of coal production on a long-term life span.

At the western end of Tindale Fell explorations had discovered a large tract of coal on the lower slopes near Howgill and investigations to ascertain its size and quality were under way, leading eventually to the driving of the Howgill drift and a new branch railway to serve it.

Although coal had been produced from Midgeholme for many years and conveyed by carts, it was necessary to consider a new exploitation which would supplement the existing drifts and the Catch Pit at Low Midgeholme. Plans were, therefore, drawn up for a new mine at High Midgeholme at the end of the new railway then under construction. This Colliery, the King Pit, was sunk in 1827-8 and was in full production by 1829, making full use of the new railway. Fig. 12.

Other collieries operated by Lord Carlisle in 1828 were outside the barony and leased to his Lordship. These were the Guide Pit, a drift on the fells at Croglin which worked intermittently between 1825 and 1840; the Blenkinsopp drifts were to be worked out on the areas exploited, to coincide with the termination of the lease in 1835. Yet another leased colliery was the Star Pit at Hartleyburn east of Midgeholme. This had been leased since 1827 and was drained by an adjoining colliery of another lessee of Mr. Allgood, and had a good production potential, Thompson urging Lord Carlisle to extend the Midgeholme Railway to Halton Lea Gate to serve it.

Explorations for coal near Thirlwall Castle, Greenhead, on the Baron House and War Carr estates of Lord Carlisle were successful in locating workable seams. Drifts were put in ready to commence production upon the termination of the Blenkinsopp lease, the men being transferred at the same time. Yet another area near Greenhead was the Gapshield drifts on Lord Carlisle's Gapshields Farm, high above Blenkinsopp on Blenkinsopp Common. These drifts commenced small-scale production in 1833-4.

We may here mention briefly the plans and calculations made by James Thompson while the N. & C.R. was held up by its problems, for in 1827-8 he was again urging Lord Carlisle to make his own railway to Carlisle via the south route.

The proposals were backed by voluminous calculations on tonnages and profits; an abbreviated coverage of some of the more interesting items follows:

The quantity of coal sold at Brampton staith in 1827		21,748 tons
Lime sold at staith 1827		7,000 tons
	Total	28,748 tons
On a railway to Carlisle the tonnage might be increased to	Coal	30,000 tons
	Lime	10,000 tons
	Total	40,000 tons

The expense of carriage from Brampton to Carlisle will be
7s. per ton

	£	s.	d.
Railway dues and truckage per ton		1	8
Savings to people in Carlisle		2	10
Profit to Lord Carlisle		2	6
Total expense		7	0

At 40,000 tons, the 2s. 6d. profit would yield £5,000.
Price of coal at Carlisle will then be 13s. 2d. per ton.

	£	s.	d.
Present price at Brampton		9	0
Railway dues, etc.		1	8
Lord Carlisle's profit		2	6
Total cost		13	2

By using the N. & C.R. to transport 40,000 tons, of which Blenkinsopp might send 8,000 tons, reducing Lord Carlisle's profit to £4,000 and sales to 32,000 tons, his Lordship stood to lose large sums over a period of years, while there was no guarantee that the coal would remain at 13s. 2d. per ton, James Thompson observed. He continued that, bearing in mind Blenkinsopp's direct access to the N. & C.R., they had no transport problems and were, therefore, likely to sell their coal at a lower price than Lord Carlisle at Carlisle. On his own experience at Blenkinsopp, Thompson did the following brief calculation:

	£	s.	d.
Blenkinsopp price for working 1 ton of coal		3	0
Carriage to Carlisle via N. & C.R.		3	4
Rental, supposing their output doubles to 16,000 tons		1	10
Selling price at Carlisle		8	2

In spite of the uncertainty of the prospects of the N. & C.R. ever being built nothing came of James Thompson's plan, although its potential prosperity for Lord Carlisle was not doubted.

The cost of the scheme was its doom but the decision to construct the N. & C.R. by the south route influenced Lord Carlisle shortly afterwards in his decision not to proceed with a scheme of such high capital expenditure.

By the time the N. & C.R. south route was definitely on, that is by September 1828, it was obvious that something would have to be done to improve the 1799 waggonway. This was now totally inadequate for the economic working of traffic of the density and tonnage expected once the N. & C.R. opened. During December 1828 James Thompson, supported by Nicholas Wood, Lord Carlisle's colliery viewer, following their investigations made to plan expansion of the Naworth coalfield, suggested to Lord Carlisle that an improved railway was an absolute necessity to its future prosperity.

Initially, the scheme was to convert the waggonway to the same gauge as the Midgeholme Railway to allow through running. As we have seen, this was readily agreed to, Thompson stating at the end of September 1829 that he proposed to start ". . . to widen or extend the rails of the Brampton and Talkin Railway to the same width as Midgeholme so that waggons of the same length of axles may be used on both". This was completed by early 1830, although how it was accomplished considering the old waggonway was all single track, apart from passing loops, and in the winter months when one would expect coal traffic to be at a peak, is not apparent.

Satisfied with this achievement for the moment, James Thompson knew it was not the final solution, due to the line's severe gradients and curvature, especially between Hallbankgate and Brampton. It was to be almost three years before Thompson's pressure on Lord Carlisle to make further improvements to the waggonway bore fruit, he being authorised in late 1832 to commence a survey of the 1799 waggonway which he reported was in progress during March 1833.

By this period in time the N. & C.R. was under construction but proceeding slowly, being constantly under the eye of James Thompson who suggested that if, as he expected, work on some nearby sections was suspended, Lord Carlisle would be able to take advantage of the contractors and their work-force to build his own new railway since they would have all the tools almost on the doorstep.

Thompson was in possession of this kind of information since he was a member of the advisory team to the N. & C.R. Directors. This team was reporting to the Directors on the work to proceed first and on the quality of the work in progress. Obviously James Thompson's suggestions were directed to the benefit of Lord Carlisle's interests.

Thompson said it would be ". . . a good opportunity of getting it done cheap . . .". Spurred on by this thought, he completed his survey of the waggonway and presented it to Lord Carlisle on 15 March 1833. Fig. 13.

The survey was virtually a compromise with that put forward by Stephenson and Thompson on 23 August 1824. From Brampton the route was to be from the staith to Milton where it would cross the route of the N. & C.R., being little altered except for easing of curves and gradients from the 1799 route. Once across the N. & C.R. main line it soon adopted a new course, completely straight, cutting out the tunnel under the Brampton to Alston road (A689) "The Sandy Arch", crossing this road instead on the level, then ascending by an inclined plane, crossing the rough track to Kirkhouse Farm, the Kirkhouse road, and thence along the south side of the A689 road opposite Farlam Hall to Hallbankgate. By the time the latter point was reached the route had climbed 370ft., of which some 160ft. had been achieved by the inclined plane. Thompson said that compared with the existing working this scheme would mean a saving of 3 men and 3 horses per year without the inclined plane, or 5 men and horses per year with the plane. The plane would add expense to construction, but the cost would then be static. If tonnages doubled there would be a saving of 10 horses and men annually. The improvement would enable each horse to take his load from the foot of the inclined plane to Carlisle without separating the waggons at Milton, one horse doing twice the work between Kirkhouse and Brampton than hitherto.

Looking ahead, Thompson said that a good quantity of passenger and general merchandise traffic between Alston, Hartleyburn and Carlisle was a distinct possibility, giving further remuneration to Lord Carlisle by way of fares and tolls charged for use of his private railway, the same applying to the section from Brampton to Milton. Of the present waggonway, he said that it was entirely unfit and was, in fact, dangerous ". . . for any commercial business upon it", urging Lord Carlisle to consider the proposal very seriously.

During August 1833 Thompson again suggested extending the Midgeholme Railway to Hartleyburn, saying that the work would not be expensive. He suggested a terminus on the south side of the Alston road (A689) opposite the colliery, the coal being brought to the railway by an inclined plane operated by a stationary engine. This scheme did not receive sanction for since 1831 the main turnpike road between Hallbankgate and Lambley had been improved and was thus easier for cart traffic, a fact also appreciated by the lessees of Allgood's Hartleyburn Colliery, who were proving serious competitors.

James Thompson's railway planning did not cease on rebuttal for he immediately suggested another railway about three miles in length from near Cowran on the N. & C.R. to Carlatton Mill, gaining access to the Penrith area and Cumrew, Croglin, Melmerby, Ainstable, Kirkoswald, etc. This plan, though revived periodically, was never approved.

By mid-1833 the position of the collieries was that the end of the Tarnhouse and Talkin Collieries, with their multiplicity of small drifts, was near apart from the larger drift at Howgill, and of course the shaft mine at Blacksike. The isolated Geltsdale Colliery, the George drift, was yet assured of some years' production to serve the Penrith trade. At the eastern end of Tindale Fell the Henry Pits were active, together with one or two drifts, while the leased collieries at Croglin, Hartleyburn and Blenkinsopp, together with Gapshields on Lord Carlisle's property adjoining the latter, were active.

By autumn 1833, James Thompson was more than ever convinced that the interim improvement scheme of the previous March for the waggonway would not meet the requirements of a railway connection to the N. & C.R., the outcome being that he set about re-working the joint report which George Stephenson and he had drawn up as long ago as November 1825, and submitted his findings to James Loch during November 1833:

Estimate of the expense of making a new railway from Bankhall to Brampton by way of Kirkhouse and Milton.

	£	s.	d.
Inclined plane to Kirkhouse	2150	0	0
Railway from Kirkhouse to N. & C.R. at Milton	1400	0	0
Railway from Milton to Brampton staith	1950	0	0
	5500	0	0

Estimate of a line from Bankhall to Brampton by way of Beckgate Fields and Rowbank.

	£	s.	d.
Inclined plane to Kirkhouse	2150	0	0
Railway from Kirkhouse to N. & C.R. at Beckgate Farm	1100	0	0
Railway from N. & C.R. to Brampton staith	2650	0	0
	5900	0	0

Thompson pointed out that it would be possible to deduct £900 for the value of the rails from the old waggonway which might be re-used on both schemes, reducing the costs to £4,600 and £5,000 respectively. He said the railway had to be improved sooner or later, and was in favour of the second scheme. Thompson intended that the section from the N. & C.R. (at a point near Rowbank some three-quarters of a mile west of the village of Milton) into Brampton be used as a public branch line, carrying passengers and merchandise in addition to Lord Carlisle's lime and coal. This would, Thompson said, be the only branch line to Brampton as the N. & C.R. had now no plans to construct one, while the present waggonway into Brampton was totally unfit for such usage by public traffic.

Thompson said that he thought one horse working from the proposed inclined plane foot to Brampton would replace the eight presently used between Hallbankgate and Brampton on the waggonway route, and that if the scheme were approved, it should be arranged for completion to coincide with the opening of the N. & C.R. so that the redundant horses and men could then be put to work taking coal to Carlisle.

Fig. 25 View of Kirkhouse wagon shop in October 1952. (L. G. Charlton)

Fig. 26 View of one of the oldest still surviving buildings at Kirkhouse, the old saw mill built prior to 1838.
Photographed in October 1952—note repaired colliery tubs outside. (L. G. Charlton)

Fig. 27 Hallbankgate locomotive shed in early 1952. (*J. W. Armstrong*)

Fig. 28 A "Dandy Coach" at Brampton coal staith. (*Collection of Fleetwood Shawe*)

Fig. 29 Open Dandy coach in derelict condition at Kirkhouse about 1930. Loco wheels in foreground are probably from *Naworth No. 6*.

(*Locomotive & General Railway Photographs*)

Fig. 30 1836 masonry-built Skew arch over Brampton-Alston road. This was demolished in 1912 and replaced by a steel girder bridge. *(Collection of B. Webb)*

Fig. 31   1836 skew arch photographed between 1908 and 1912 with 0-6-0T *Belted Will* standing on the bridge.   (*Tassell Carlisle photograph from collection of Fleetwood Shawe*)

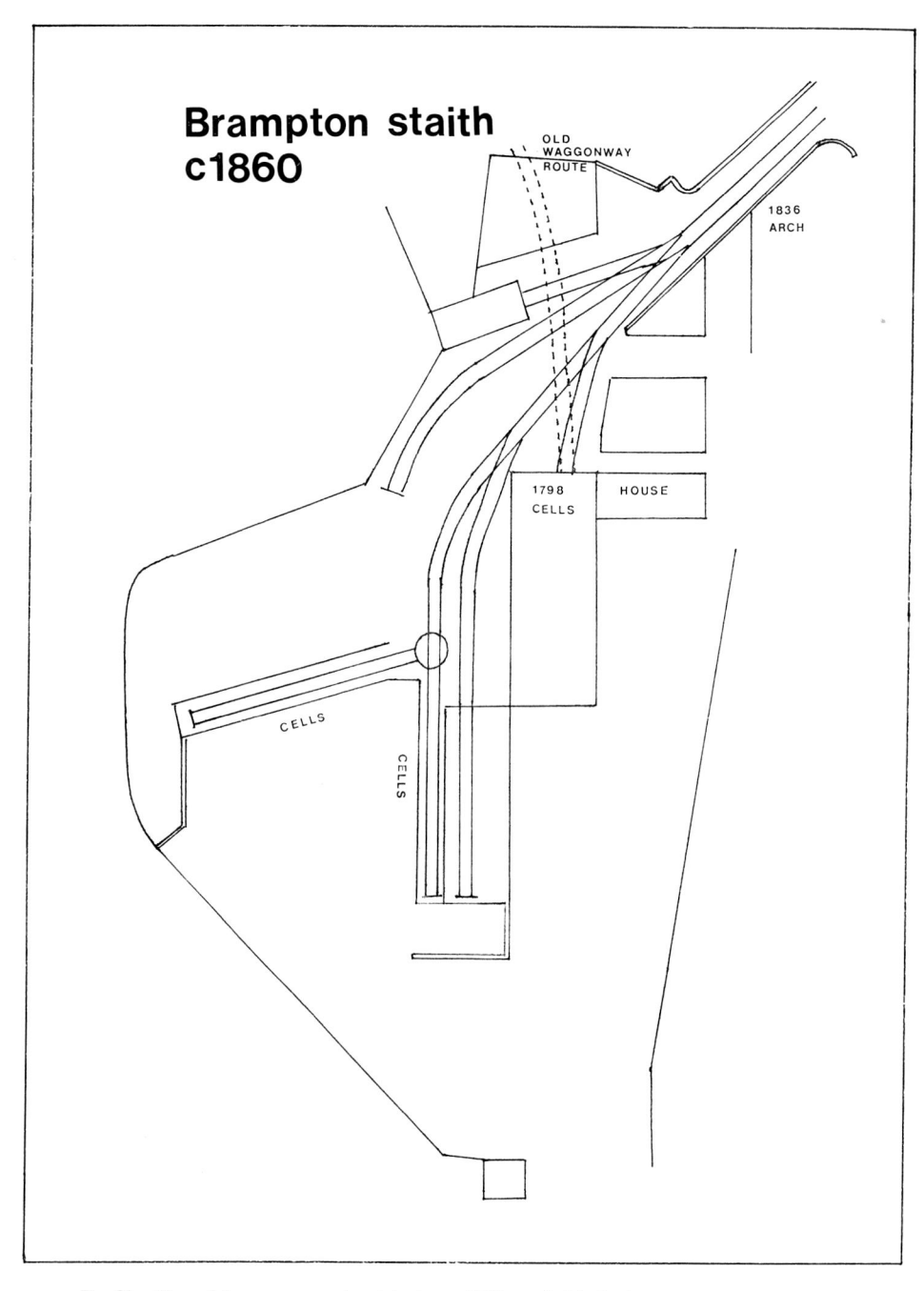

Fig. 32 Plan of Brampton coal staith about 1860, probably little changed since 1836.
(*Collection of B. Webb*)

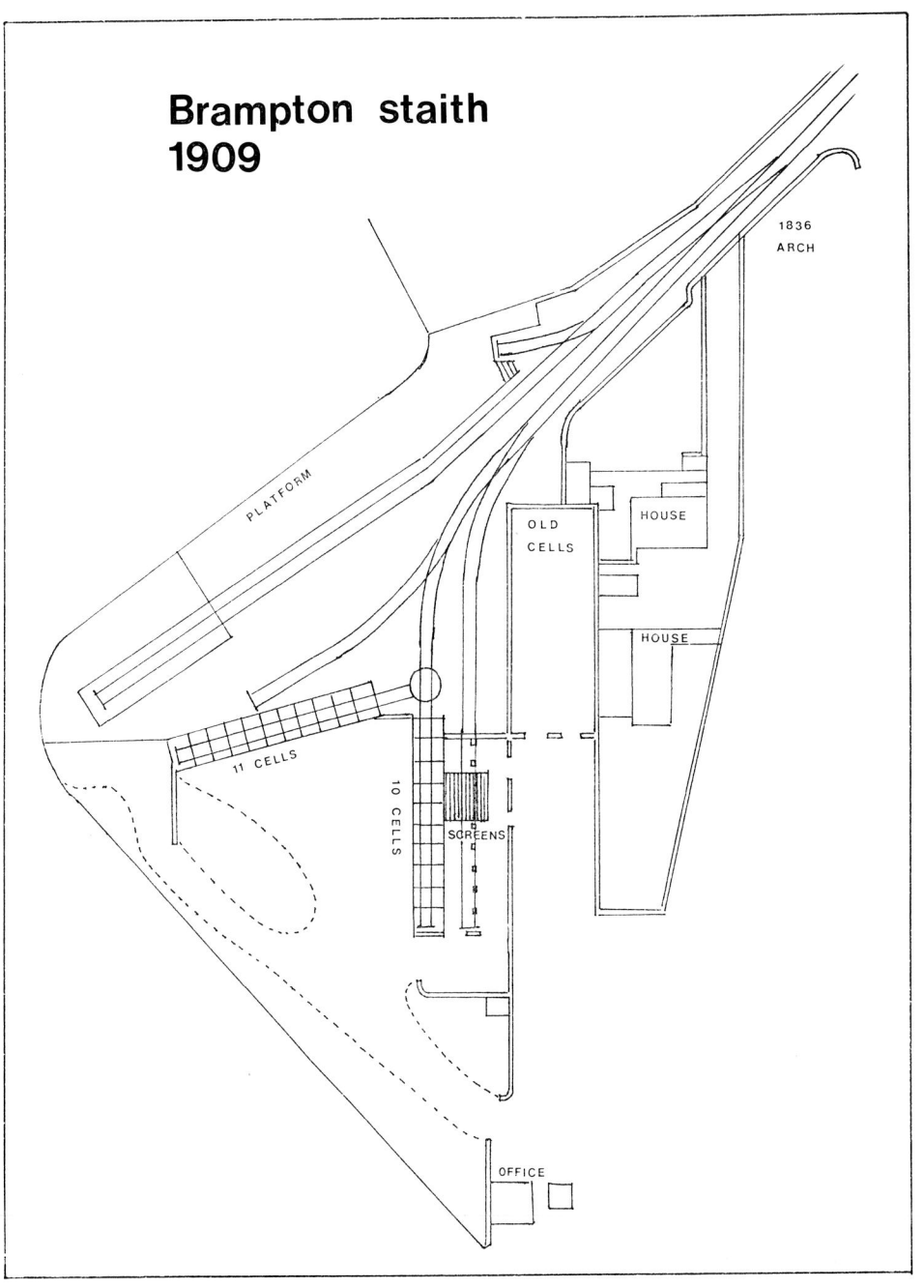

Fig. 33 Detailed plan of Brampton coal staith in 1909 in the condition in which it was leased to the N.E.R., and as altered by Messrs. Thompsons in 1880/1.
(Collection of B. Webb)

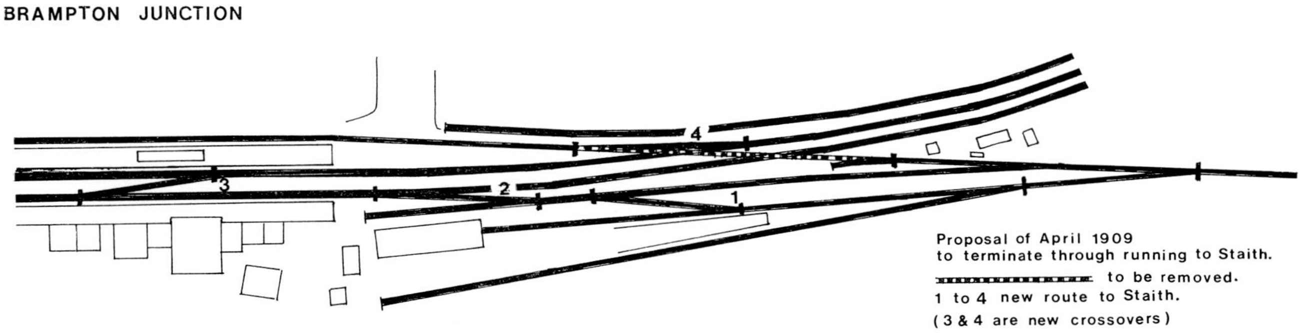

BRAMPTON JUNCTION

Proposal of April 1909 to terminate through running to Staith.
━━━━━ to be removed.
1 to 4 new route to Staith.
(3 & 4 are new crossovers)

Fig. 34 Brampton Junction station in 1909 showing the through crossover right of way held by Lord Carlisle across the N.E.R. N. & C. line, and the proposals to replace this before the N.E.R. would take over the Brampton branch.
(Collection of B. Webb)

The necessity of this route as a scheme to improve commercial viability is obvious but it did not appear so to Lord Carlisle whose fears of the expense involved were only partly allayed by Thompson winning a contract to supply 96,000 stone sleeper blocks to the N. & C.R. to raise £1,000 towards the cost of the improved colliery railway's access to Brampton and the N. & C.R. The problem of convincing Lord Carlisle that his outlay of money would be repaid continued, his Lordship stating that he thought Thompson was ". . . trying to do things on too grand a scale, than anyone else would think of doing".

In order to gain Lord Carlisle's approval for his proposals, Thompson, urged by James Loch, set about preparing a very full report with detailed estimates, presenting it to Lord Carlisle on 17 December 1833. The opinion of Nicholas Wood was again sought and after his approval Thompson said that the scheme was not "too grand" but was designed to enable all increases in traffic to be accommodated without need to incur further expenditure on improvements at all. The railway would be made suitable for all the foreseeable requirements, including the introduction of locomotives.

James Thompson based his scheme on an annual tonnage of 50,000 tons of traffic between Hallbankgate and the N. & C.R., whence it would go either to Brampton or to Carlisle. He said there were 300 working days annually and that an average daily tonnage would be 166 tons. To handle this the old waggonway would cost:

	£	s.	d.
7 horses and their maintenance per year	350	0	0
7 men to drive the horses	210	0	0
1 man and 1 lad for maintaining the waggonway	60	0	0
Materials for repairing waggonway and wear and tear of horses	40	0	0
Waggons—wear and tear—same for both lines	—	—	—
Mileage differences, old waggonway ½ mile further from Carlisle, 50,000 tons at ¾d. per ton	156	0	0
Total	816	0	0

The same quantity by the inclined plane would cost:

	£	s.	d.
Wear and tear of rope	40	0	0
2 men working the plane	70	0	0
Repairing and maintenance of the way	40	0	0
Total	150	0	0

On the basis of an annual sale at Brampton of 18,000 tons or 60 tons per day, the old waggonway would require:

	£	s.	d.
4 horses and maintenance	200	0	0
4 men for driving horses	120	0	0
1 man for maintaining the way	40	0	0
Materials for repairing the way and wear and tear of horses	25	0	0
Total	385	0	0

The same quantity by inclined plane and new railway, same rope wear and plane men:

	£	s.	d.
1 horse	50	0	0
1 man	30	0	0
Wear of horse	6	0	0
Repairing the way	30	0	0
Total	116	0	0

On the new railway a horse and driver would do one-third more work: Comparisons of old and new lines:

	£	s.	d.
Carriage by old waggonway to Carlisle	816	0	0
Carriage by old waggonway to Brampton	385	0	0
Total	1201	0	0
Carriage by new railway to Carlisle	150	0	0
Carriage by new railway to Brampton	116	0	0
Total	266	0	0
Annual saving by new railway	935	0	0

The above totals and costs did not, Thompson said, include general merchandise traffic over the line, of which "There would be a good amount, and passenger traffic too, both from Alston and Carlisle, the east and west and in both directions".

He observed that if Lord Carlisle did not make a proper line to Brampton, a public branch would be demanded by the townspeople with the loss of his coal sales, until now his own preserve, while if no waggons could be taken to Brampton they would be left at the public railway for the townspeople to load and unload, and allowing competitors such as Blenkinsopp to supply coal to the Brampton people. The Blenkinsopp company, Thompson pointed out, were waiting for such a chance, for they were relying on Lord Carlisle's unsuitable waggonway and its expensive operation to keep Naworth coal at a higher price than theirs.

Summing up, he said that it was largely due to the success of the Midgeholme Railway that coal production from Midgeholme had increased and made Lord Carlisle's profits more regular. With such an account (abbreviated here) who could refuse Thompson his railway!

During early 1834 Lord Carlisle agreed at last to the proposed new railway between Hallbankgate and Brampton, including the inclined plane from Hallbankgate to Kirkhouse—Kirkhouse's first access by rail and the harbinger of great achievements soon to be attained there.

On 3 April 1834 the contract for forming the railway from Brampton staith to Kirkhouse was signed by John McKay, the successful tenderer. Interesting items from the contract follow:

> The contractor to find all sleepers, rails, waggons, workgear, tools, of all kinds for completing the work; to remove the soil from the cuttings and relay it on the slopes, the cuttings to be 14ft. wide at the bottom with the sides graded at 1: to 1:; embankments similarly, but 14ft. or 16ft. wide on top, sloping at $1\frac{1}{2}$: to 1: on the sides.

Special instructions for storing the soil were given, and gravel was to be stacked and paid for at 3d. per cubic yard. The contract price for the work was £2,100 and the completion date 1 March 1835.

In May 1834 Thompson was again urging Lord Carlisle to allow him to construct further railways. These were a half mile branch to Bishop Hill from Riggfoot to serve the drift and permit lime kilns to be provided there, while at Howgill the old waggonway route from Clesketts needed some improvement and a new branch was required from this to serve Howgill drift, then being proved for coal. Both these schemes were set out in an estimate dated July 1834:

	£	s.	d.
The Riggfoot branch, including culverts, laying, etc., 1,000 yards at 3s.	150	0	0
Improvement to Tindale Fell or Howgill Railway, consisting of a piece of new railway, altering the old part, and a timber bridge over Howgill Burn	100	0	0
Total	250	0	0

Both these schemes were approved and the railways in use by mid-1835, Figs. 14, 15, but to a proposal reviving the idea of a railway to serve Carlatton Mill from Cowran, no approval was given.

In order to meet the opening of the N. & C.R., Thompson gave an estimate for a railway to serve Baronhouse Colliery at Thirlwall, which was to be put into production upon the end of the Blenkinsopp lease:

	£	s.	d.
Barronhouse—opening Railway forming, laying, etc., 1,700 yards at 3s.	250	0	0

(A road would cost a little less).

The question of a railway to serve the Hartleyburn Colliery from Midgeholme was reintroduced; Thompson said it should be in use by the time the N. & C.R. opened. This extension would re-use the rails removed from the waggonway, and together with culverts, forming and laying, would be 2,100 yards at ¾d. per yard:

	£	s.	d.
2,100 yards using old rails at 3d. per yard	350	0	0

(If new rails were used it would add £400).

On the question of using new rails, Thompson opined that it might be wise to use them only on that part of the Hartleyburn Railway which was within Lord Carlisle's barony, and use the old rails on the section over Mr. Allgood's land, so reducing the cost of new rails to £200. He further observed, that the railway could not be completed until the rails from the waggonway had been recovered, and doubted then if there would be sufficient for the task.

The total cost for railway improvements to meet the opening of the N. & C.R., not including the new railway from Hallbankgate, to Brampton, was put at £850.

Other improvements proposed simultaneously included Lord Carlisle's coal depots on the N. & C.R., which at that time were expected to total six in number at an estimated cost of £50 each.

The railway proposals were all approved by Lord Carlisle, and Thompson's schedule was for work to be carried out first on the Hartleyburn extension, on the Riggfoot branch in spring 1835 and the Howgill branch in summer 1835.

These schedules were not strictly adhered to since Thompson reported in August 1835 that track laying was in progress on the Riggfoot and Howgill branches, and that the track bed was in progress on the Hartleyburn extension.

At the same time work was well under way on the new railway from Hallbankgate to Brampton, the inclined plane being, in fact, completed and in regular use to Kirkhouse. In spite of many assertions to the contrary, no railway ever served Kirkhouse until this one in August 1835, as surviving plans by James Thompson prove. The track bed was ready for rail laying from the plane foot to the N. & C.R., where a junction and through crossover were planned, together with a railway station built by the N. & C.R. to be called Milton, even though a goodly distance from the village of that name. From Milton to the staith at Brampton work was proceeding at a slower pace to keep expenditure more gradual.

Looking ahead, Thompson said it was probable that a good quantity of goods traffic and also passengers would use the new railway, both to Brampton and to Midgeholme and Hartleyburn, and that some provision should be made to meet this by suitable accommodation and warehouse facilities. Passenger traffic could be generated by encouraging a coach to operate between Midgeholme and Alston to connect with the railway. With typical shrewdness, Thompson enquired if it would be possible to set up a toll-gate at Hallbankgate to control traffic as far as Milton to try to prevent people collecting and delivering their goods directly to the N. & C.R. at Milton Station, in doing so creating more traffic for the railway.

On 8 August 1835 Thompson submitted his summary of expenditure to date on the Hallbankgate-Brampton Railway.

	Expenditure £ s. d.	Estimate £ s. d.	Sum to Expend £ s. d.
Cuttings	1038 15 8	2250 0 0	1211 4 4
Laying rails, masonry, etc.	361 3 3	1300 0 0	938 16 9
Land (not in orig. estimate)	110 0 0	110 0 0	— — —
Iron rails and chairs	1288 10 8½	2350 0 0	1061 9 3½
	2798 9 7½	6010 0 0	3211 10 4½
Amount of estimate	6010 0 0		
Amount to expend	3211 10 4½		

To complete the railway it required:

	£ s. d.
Iron, cuttings, laying the way	1400 0 0
	2150 0 0
	3750 0 0
Amount still to expend	3211 10 4½

Increase of cost of rails due to weights and prices over original estimate £538.

In September 1835 the completion date, it was hoped, would be April 1836 (the sum needed to finish the work was £3,750), one year longer than originally stated in the contract.

45

A report by James Loch on the state of the works, dated 3 September 1835, stated that the Milton-Brampton portion was "... not very advanced but that there is much cutting in progress of execution. From Milton to Kirkhouse plane foot the route is formed and standing very well indeed".

One of the most interesting items in Loch's report was the first account of the inclined plane in operation. The plane was 1,432 yards long, varying in gradient from 1 in 18 to 1 in 28, the empty waggons being raised by full ones descending. Loch and a companion climbed into a waggon and ascended the plane at the rate of 7 m.p.h. Loch said the railway to Midgeholme was also standing well, as were its embankments, while the "... extension of the railway to Hartleyburn meets this road (the new Turnpike road to Alston) at the extremity of Lord Carlisle's estate, and the Alston Moor people are expected and are arranging to travel to this place by omnibus and then travel by the railway to Brampton". One important statement made by Loch in this report was that "The number of people travelling now to market by the railway is considerable", indicating that by September 1835 horse-drawn carriages were in use on Lord Carlisle's railway and waggonway. Although no factual evidence of an earlier date for passenger services has been found, their operation probably dates from 1828-9 when rail-gauge standardisation allowed through running to Brampton staith, carrying people of the estate to Brampton market. In 1835 the three vehicles in use, four-wheel coaches or "Dandies" as they were locally named, operated from Howgill, Foresthead and Midgeholme at fares of 6d., 9d. and 1s. respectively. The vehicles were called *Black Diamond*, *Mountaineer* and *Experiment*.

Returning to James Loch's report which went on to describe future developments in merchandise and passenger traffic, Loch said:

> Thompson has a strong desire to engage in all these concerns. Ramshay on the contrary wisely thought they should all be left to individual enterprise and exertion, and I would let the passengers to the (N. & C.R.) railway company and let them have all the details and trouble of them, the same on the Brampton line.
>
> ... We continued our walk along the face of Tindale Fell to Howgill, there examined the railway extension to this place ... Here we rejoined the railway carriage, and without a horse descended at a rapid pace to Kirkhouse.

The contract for track laying on the Milton to Kirkhouse section was signed by Messrs. Taylor & Worsley, the contractors, on 20 January 1836. They undertook to collect the stone blocks from the appointed quarries, bore them, plug them, bore the plug and seat the chairs, lay the blocks, install the fish-belly rails and key the same, also ballasting the way, all for a total price of 1s. 8d. per yard. The contractors had to finish the work on or before 15 March 1836 to the satisfaction of James Thompson. Soon after signing Thompson reported that rail laying was in progress between Milton and Kirkhouse and would be followed by the Milton to Brampton portion. It was intended to close the old waggonway as soon as possible to enable its rails to be removed for use on the Midgeholme to Hartleyburn extension which had been ready for rail laying since November 1835.

A description of the most interesting aspect of the new railway, the inclined plane, is proper at this point. At Kirkhouse the inclined plane was of single-track format, proceeding as such until it passed under Kirkhouse road in a cutting running to the left of St. Thomas' Church, past which it emerged on to an embankment crossing the Brampton to Alston road (A689) by a stone arch near the parsonage, hence its local title "The Priests' Arch". The plane continued eastwards on an embankment and then into a cutting to reach Hallbankgate. Here at Planehead the plane ended, a coal depot was sited and the control cabin for the self-acting incline machinery. At a point about opposite Farlam Hall Cottages, a passing loop was placed to allow waggons on the plane to pass each other. East of this loop the track layout was formed of three rails, the centre one being used by waggons travelling both ways, and continuing as such until they fanned outwards at Planehead to form two separate tracks, with another track joining their junction. This continued for some 100 yards until linked up again with single track. A two-road siding of limited accommodation was provided at Hallbankgate.

Since 1828 some expansion of coal production had taken place, while further plans were ready to meet the opening of the new colliery railway and the N. & C.R. The main potential output of the Naworth coalfield was to come from Blacksike, Midgeholme King Pit, and Hartleyburn Star Pit. The multiplicity of small drifts in the Talkin Colliery were almost all abandoned by 1828, as were those on Tindale Fell forming Tarnhouse Colliery, the exception being the Henry Pit which ended its production from its lofty position at the eastern end of Tindale Fell during 1838. Just below this pit was the Bishop Hill drift which did not enter full production until 1839 and then only for lime-burning coal. The Howgill drift was being driven during the early 1830's and was to come into use in 1835. The drift at Geltsdale was only in limited use between 1828 and 1838, to all intents being virtually closed after 1838, although not finally officially abandoned until 1850. Outside the area of the Naworth coalfield the Blenkinsopp Colliery was to continue until the expiry of its lease on 1 January 1835 when its men were moved to the nearby Baronhouse and Gapshields Collieries, while the most southerly working, the leased drift at Croglin, was to continue until 1840.

By August 1833 no agreement had been reached between Lord Carlisle and the N. & C.R. in compliance with James Loch's letter of 31 August 1828, stating Lord Carlisle's special requirements in exchange for his "unobjectionable neutrality" to the N. & C.R. Act being passed by Parliament.

These requirements were concerned with some form of control by Lord Carlisle over the coal sales within his barony to protect his interests. To this end the ownership, placing and number of coal depots was considered of prime importance to James Thompson who was continually urging Lord Carlisle to settle the matter with the N. & C.R.

By May 1834 no decision had yet been made, but James Thompson was demanding action as the N. & C.R. had said in March that the railway from Carlisle to Lord Carlisle's railway at Milton should be in general use by about May 1835. He suggested that Lord Carlisle might decide to rent staiths built by the N. & C.R. or perhaps make his own staiths, but was of the opinion that Lord Carlisle should secure the right for only his own coal to be sold in the barony, by preventing landowners and the N. & C.R. having staiths. Although this would require an amendment to the N. & C.R. Act, it would be no problem as application for some amendments had already been made. Thompson said:

> ... It would secure the whole supply of coal and lime in the districts of Brampton, Crosby, Kirklinton, Scaleby, Longtown, etc., . . . it would in itself secure a large annual profit, as well as a means of getting some of the inferior sorts of coal disposed of; which could not be effected where a strong opposition existed.

By May 1835 the N. & C.R. was nowhere near ready to start operation between Carlisle and Milton, and during August, James Thompson informed Lord Carlisle of the position regarding coal depots. He said the N. & C.R. proposed to have three depots for coal in the Barony of Gilsland—at Denton Hall, How Mill and Corby, while it was hoping to lay sidings at Scotby, Carlisle London Road and at Carlisle Canal Basin, and finally at Mumpshall near Gilsland, intending to charge ground rent for the site, the owner erecting his own depot.

Fearing the competition, a direct threat to the Naworth coalfield, Thompson said that some agreement with the N. & C.R. was necessary. Another point was that the N. & C.R. had become carriers, thus preventing the private carrier using the railway to carry his own traffic under his own control. This further volte-face was eclipsed by the opening the previous March, on the 9th in fact, of the Newcastle to Hexham section with locomotive-hauled trains, just as James Thompson had forecast! The troubles which beset the N. & C.R. during the first few weeks due to its introduction of locomotives, in complete disregard of its Parliamentary Act prohibiting their use, is out of the scope of this study. As the carriers the N. & C.R. were to supply locomotives, waggons, etc., and intended to charge $2\frac{1}{2}$d. per ton, per mile for coal and lime traffic using their railway.

It had always been the intention to open both the N. & C.R. western section and the new colliery railway on the same day, but the honours went to Lord Carlisle, who actually commenced using his own railway and sending his coal directly to Carlisle during early July 1836, the traffic being horse and gravity worked, the horses riding behind the waggons on downhill gradients on "Dandy" carts.

The official opening ceremony took place on Friday, 15 July 1836 when Cumberland's first passenger-carrying, steam-hauled train was operated on Lord Carlisle's railway between Kirkhouse and Brampton coal staith. The occasion was observed locally as a public holiday, receiving much publicity at the time.

The inaugural train left Kirkhouse at 11.30 a.m. formed of at least one passenger carriage, lent by the N. & C.R., and a train of coal waggons. The carriage conveyed James Thompson and the official party, the waggons held the workers from Lord Carlisle's collieries.

Everything was suitably decorated, bands played and the train was sent off amidst firing of cannons. The train was drawn by two locomotives named *Atlas* and *Gilsland*. At the coal staith refreshments were provided before the return to Kirkhouse where a large tent had been set up to accommodate the crowd ". . . and an ample supply of provisions was provided". About 1,000 people were reported to have taken part under the Presidency of John Ramshay, ". . . and mirth and good fellowship were kept up to a late hour." The ladies were all entertained in another tent where tea was served, and in the evening a dance took place. All in all, a fitting ceremony for Lord Carlisle's railway, a great credit to James Thompson.

The opening of the western section of the N. & C.R. took place four days later on Tuesday, 19 July 1836 with four locomotives, including those used for the opening of Lord Carlisle's railway, and in addition two N. & C.R. locomotives, *Hercules* built by R. & W. Hawthorn, and *Samson* built by Stephensons. Four trains left London Road Station at Carlisle, from 10.30 a.m. for Greenhead, the terminus of the line's eastern extremity at that time. The happenings on that day were amusing, to say the least, but have been recounted many times before and need not concern us here.

One important point about the opening of the N. & C.R. was that some of its stations and depots were not completed and caused much friction, especially in the winter of 1836-7. In addition, Lord Carlisle, was considerably affected in having to carry his coal by cart from London Road to the Canal Basin owing to the unfinished state of the canal branch railway. James Loch had always contended that the western section should not open until all the work on the railway was completed, and found his opinion reinforced by the troubles being experienced.

The poor surface of London Road yard, together with inefficient weighing machinery added to Lord Carlisle's problems, while the promise of the completion of the canal branch by the end of 1836 seemed unlikely to James Thompson who inspected the work in November, reporting that in his opinion it would not be ready until at least March 1837.

The canal branch opened on 9 March 1837 by a ceremony of three trains, the first carrying passengers hauled by *Hercules*, the second conveying Lord Carlisle's coal, drawn by *Goliath*, and the third conveying coal from Blenkinsopp hauled by *Atlas*.

There were attempts to make political capital at the time by veiled accusations that the N. & C.R. had been built to suit individual landowners as well as by the most difficult route, and these were to be frequently reiterated during the next fifty years or so.

It was not until the autumn of 1836 that Lord Carlisle and the N. & C.R. came to an agreement on the location and operation of coal depots as decided by the amended N. & C.R. Act. The N. & C.R. was free to erect depots outside the Barony of Gilsland and had decided to make them at Carlisle, Scotby and Gilsland. Lord Carlisle was to have three private depots—at Corby, Low Row and How Mill.

Since the opening of the N. & C.R. on 19 July 1836 one of the "Dandy" carriages of Lord Carlisle had been plying between Brampton and Milton Station meeting every train. The story of the Brampton passenger services is not pertinent at this point.

Since the new colliery line opened, rails had been lifted from the old waggonway for use on the extension to Hartleyburn and laying was reported to be in progress by August 1836. On the colliery side of operations the production of the collieries had increased considerably, the improved railway proving itself most useful in handling the traffic which above the inclined plane was still horse-worked. The short period when a locomotive was used between Kirkhouse and Brampton staith, during July 1836, prompted James Thompson to try to interest Lord Carlisle in acquiring a locomotive of his own to work to Midgeholme and Hartleyburn. On consulting James Loch, that worthy told his Lordship, "Thompson thinks there could be a considerable saving made if the coals, etc., were brought down by a locomotive to the top of the inclined plane". Loch said he himself was doubtful of this, but had asked James Thompson to make his calculations which would then be submitted to Nicholas Wood for his opinion, prior to consideration and decision on the matter by Lord Carlisle.

In order to obtain information on locomotives, Loch sent John Ramshay to see Booth & Sinclair, managers of the Liverpool & Manchester and Bolton & Leigh Railways, carrying letters of introduction. Ramshay was to enquire if they had any of their light locomotives for sale and their cost. The report was dated 2 October 1836. Ramshay was delayed on his visit but wrote to Loch on 6 October saying ". . . I shall . . . take Liverpool in the course of a week or so". The result appears to have been found financially satisfactory, the outcome being the purchase, according to Liverpool & Manchester Railway records, of the locomotive *Rocket* on 26 October 1836. On 4 November 1836 James Thompson wrote "I have no doubt at all in my mind but that the locomotive would be a great saving". According to Thompson family tradition, *Rocket* was put to work on the Midgeholme Railway on 15 April 1837.

All was not well, for James Thompson was aware of an acute situation developing between himself, the Naworth coalfield and the new lessees of Col. J. B. Coulson's Blenkinsopp Colliery. The situation was exaggerated in Thompson's thinking, but no doubt there was some hard feeling on the side of Messrs. Foster & Dixon, Blenkinsopp's lessees, who had taken over the colliery at the termination of Lord Carlisle's lease, only to find it almost worked out on the existing workings, a situation apparently specially engineered by James Thompson, who had only opened out enough coal to satisfy the tenure of Lord Carlisle's lease.

The situation at the opening of the N. & C.R. forced Blenkinsopp to publish that they were unable to supply coal but were pushing ahead with their new drifts, hoping to supply coal shortly. The position pleased Thompson because it wiped out the nearest serious rival to Naworth coal, a situation which was to continue until after the opening of the whole of the N. & C.R., for it was not until 1842 that the new Blenkinsopp drifts were completed, and not until 1847 that coal production in quantity was finally achieved.

So it was that continual argument ensued between Thompson and Blenkinsopp over prices and measures of coal and lime, each one trying constantly to undercut the other, although Blenkinsopp denied this.

The sales of Naworth coal had increased since the opening of the N. & C.R., but not to the extent that James Thompson had expected, therefore Thompson and his brother were sent to Ireland in late 1836 to try to find more customers for Naworth coal, which would be shipped from Carlisle via the Solway Canal.

CHAPTER 6

Thompsons of Kirkhouse

During 1837 Lord Carlisle was anxious to lease the collieries and railways provided a capable lessee could be found. This had been under consideration for over ten years and now looked a distinct possibility, both Nicholas Wood and Matthew Liddel supporting the proposal, in that it would provide Lord Carlisle with a steady income unaffected by fluctuations of trade.

On 14 March 1838 Wood and Liddel, who had been carefully investigating further the leasing idea, reported their findings to James Loch. Briefly, they thought the idea good and were in favour of leasing the collieries, railways, farms and quarries. After some discussion on how to obtain a lessee, Loch suggested James Thompson as being suitable.

By 10 May 1838 the valuation of the items to be leased was ready. The eighth and nineteenth clauses contained items on the railways to be leased, while the erections at Kirkhouse were also included. Thompson accepted the opportunity to become lessee, but was forbidden to manufacture iron or sell ironstone without the permission of Lord Carlisle, while the coal produced must all be sold to prevent wastage. Careful rental clauses were included to cover the amount payable to Lord Carlisle for all types of coal.

The twenty-page valuation was entitled:

> Schedule and valuation of the stock of wood, wrought iron, cast iron, lead and associated materials upon the Earl of Carlisle's collieries, railways, depots, and lime kilns as valued by the within named persons. May 11th 1838.

It was signed by John Ramshay and James Loch; the main points of interest may be noted here:

	£	s.	d.
BLACKSIKE PIT			
1 winding condensing steam engine. Cylinder 18in. diameter. With cast iron cistern, boiler and firebars	140	0	0
3,019 yards iron tramway	157	12	6
1 single powered pumping engine. Cylinder 31¼in. diameter. Boiler 21ft. 6in. long by 6ft. diameter. (Engine wants repairs)	180	0	0
HOWGILL PIT			
1,575 yards iron tramway	82	0	0

HARTLEYBURN PIT
1 pumping engine—steam. Cylinder 16in. diameter by 36in. stroke. Boiler 18ft. long by 4ft. diameter 190 0 0

MIDGEHOLME KING PIT
1 high-pressure steam winding engine. Cylinder 20in. diameter by 5ft. stroke. Boiler 26½ft. long by 6ft. diameter .. 380 0 0

COAL WAGGONS
74 coal waggons of different descriptions. 24 ballast and other waggons. 1 luggage waggon coupe with 30in. diameter wheels 797 10 0
1 Mountaineer coach in good repair with springs 15 0 0
1 Experiment coach ditto. 6 old ballast waggons 11 0 0

KIRKHOUSE
1 Black Diamond coach with 4 Losh wheels supported by 6in. iron rails. Frame of fir. Springs for wheels and double iron brakes 25 0 0

MIDGEHOLME KING PIT (Underground)
1,225 yards malleable iron tramway 63 2 3

MACK DOLLS HOLE
1 locomotive engine and tender 150 0 0

The schedule went into minute detail—the last item above is the solitary locomotive owned by Lord Carlisle, namely *Rocket*. This puts an end to the speculation as to who actually owned this locomotive, for it seems unlikely that James Thompson would take over a locomotive he has often been reputed to have personally purchased.

At the time when the valuation for the Thompson lease was prepared, a great variety of rail forms were laid upon the railway system, and in view of the interest attached to this matter it is worthwhile to consider these.

The majority of the main lines, Brampton staith—Milton—Kirkhouse—Hallbankgate—Midgeholme, were laid with patent rails of 28, 30½, 32, 35 and 36lbs. per yard weights. Specific examples being—the inclined plane:

	£	s.	d.
946 yards patent iron rails 30½lb.	233	6	8
244 yards patent iron rail at meetings	62	0	4
961 yards patent iron rail top of plane	244	5	1

Midgeholme Railway:

    1,688 yards patent iron rail from Whites embankment to Rigg-
foot 281lb. 400 18 0

Many of the sidings and less important routes had old rails but Kirkhouse, only rail served since 1835, had patent rails of 28, 30½, and 32lbs. weight. The section from Blacksike junction to Recovery pit had 1,334 yards of 1½in. rails of three types, iron rail of 20lbs., cast iron nail rail of 30lbs. and iron plug rails of 32lbs.

The list for Brampton staith gave infinite variety, for it had 1¼in. and 1½in. square rails of 13 and 20lbs., cast iron nail rails of 30lbs. and cast iron plug rails of 32lbs. in its very few sidings.

Although some of the tracks on Tindale Fell may still have been in situ, none is included in the valuation, so apart from a few cases of wooden check rails, and some wooden tramways laid in some of the collieries underground, at Hartleyburn and Midgeholme, the wooden rail was extinct.

Methods of fixing the rails were listed very briefly at the end of valuation simply as:

    3,2141 stone sleepers good on mainline
    23,956 small wood and stone sleepers on mainline
    32,142 chairs for patent rails on mainline
    1,280 chairs for small rails

In May 1838 prices for rails were quoted as:

    Wrought iron waggon rails 11s. 0d. per cwt.
    Cast iron chairs 7s. 6d.
    Cast iron rails and chairs 8s. 0d.
    The total of the valuation came to £12,191 17s. 7d.

So started the history of Thompson & Sons, Kirkhouse, a period unparalleled in the long history of the Naworth coalfields.

Until Kirkhouse came under the direct control of Thompson it was only lightly developed and of limited capacity, although a plan of June 1838, Figs. 16 and 17, shows that coke ovens were already established, together with a smiths' shop, joiners' shop, smiths' yard, saw mill, etc.

James Thompson announced his intention to develop Kirkhouse into a self-contained industrial centre capable of meeting all the requirements of the estate, its collieries, railways and farms, being offered £200 per year over the first seven years of his lease to carry out the initial developments. In due course he got the allowance which was arranged to be paid to him as he spent it by subtracting it from his rental as Lord Carlisle's lessee.

By 14 November 1838 the books and vouchers of the collieries prior to his lease had been put in order and passed to John Ramshay for safe-keeping at his Naworth office.

On 21 January 1838 Thompson executed the bond of the lease, apart from one clause about the types and prices of coal and how much he should pay Lord Carlisle for these, the problem being resolved by early April.

The expansion and vigour of the Naworth Collieries under their new lessee was most marked, as some surviving tonnage figures prove. During the twelve months of April 1837 to May 1838 the railway carried 70,000 tons of coal. By May 1839 the collieries had produced 104,730 tons of coal in their first year under Thompson, while ten years later in May 1849 122,489 tons had been produced in the previous twelve months.

As to the colliery side of the business, Tarnhouse Colliery on Tindale Fell was being operated only at Howgill by 1838, Fig. 18, continuing until this closed on 3 June 1848. At the eastern end of the fell, Henry Pit closed during 1838 thus enabling the fellside railway to be finally closed. However, Bishop Hill drift on the lower eastern slopes of Tindale Fell was put into operation from 1839 to 1841, closing until 1845, to reopen to coincide with the opening of the long-mooted spelter works of J. H. Attwood at Tindale which was to use most of its output of low-quality coal. The coal was delivered via a self-acting incline put in during 1846 and continuing until the drift closed in 1885. Talkin Colliery still flourished and was to open up new tracts of coal as soon as improved drainage had been obtained by a new level from the River Gelt, thus ensuring a good future for its Blacksike Colliery. During 1843-5 the old Havannah drifts were reopened so that some substantial pillars of coal could be removed, but yielding only 1,662 tons of coal.

Moving east, the early eighteenth-century workings were reopened by a drift alongside the railway at Prior Dyke just west of Whites Cut, but only producing low-quality coal suitable for burning lime or for use at Tindale Spelter Works where most of its coal was sent during its short production period between 1845 and 1849. At Midgeholme, the King Pit was still very active, producing over 57,000 tons of coal in the twelve months ending 12 May 1849.

Collieries in operation not rail-served by the private railway were the Geltsdale Colliery, continuing until 1843, Gapshields until 1868, and Baronhouse until 1840. The leased Croglin Colliery closed in 1840 due to the poor quality of its coal.

Meanwhile, James Thompson's health was failing, there being a widely-held belief that he worked too hard, taking on all the work himself, and was literally "working himself to death" through not sharing the burden with anyone else. As a result he suffered a stroke at Easter 1847 and was never fully to recover from this.

The final extension of the colliery railway took place in the autumn of 1849, after prolonged discussions on the merits of carrying out the extension, conducted between James Loch, Matthew Liddel, the colliery viewer, and James Thompson.

Fig. 35 *Dandie Dinmont* 0-4-0Toc (N 2738/81) built for Thompsons for use specifically on the passenger traffic between Brampton staith and the N. & C. line station at Milton (Brampton Junction). Here it is depicted with its train of ex-L.N.W.R. carriages in **1881** at the staith. *(Collection of B. Webb)*

Fig. 36 A scene in the mid-1880's showing *Dandie Dinmont* climbing away from Brampton coal staith over the 1836 skew arch with a two-coach train for Brampton Junction. (Sid Barnes)

Fig. 37 View of steel girder bridge put in in 1912/3 by N.E.R. to replace 1836 skew arch prior to reopening the Brampton branch for passenger traffic. *(Fleetwood Shawe)*

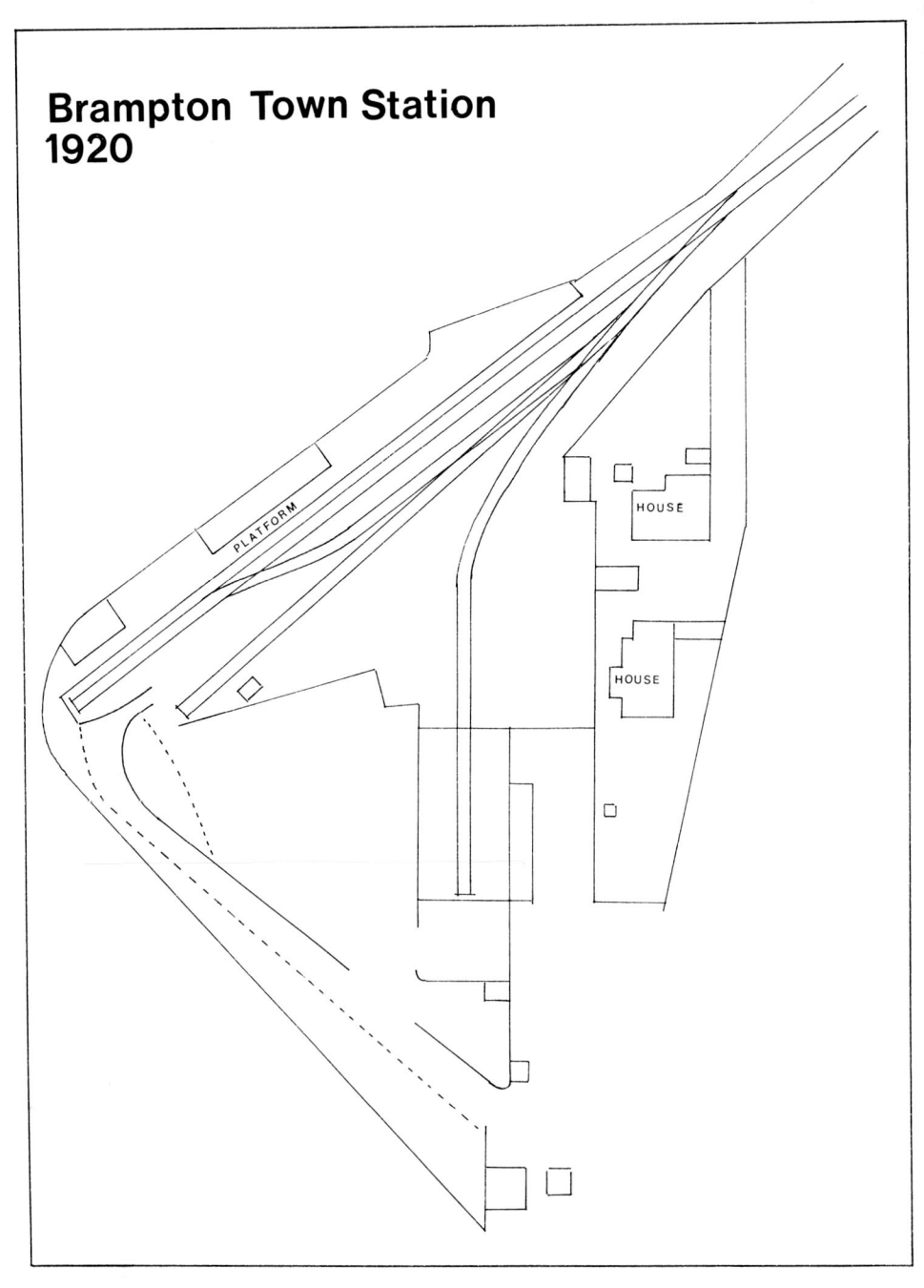

Fig. 38 Plan of Brampton Town station as altered by the N.E.R. in 1912/3.
(Collection of B. Webb)

Fig. 39 Lady Cecilia Roberts unlocks the gate of Brampton Town station on the opening of the N.E.R. passenger service on 31 July 1913. *(Collection of B. Webb)*

Fig. 40 Sightseers at the approach to Brampton Town station on 31 July 1913.
(Collection of B. Webb)

Fig. 41   View of site of Brampton Town station in 1973. *(Brian Webb)*

Fig. 42   The official N.E.R. party at Brampton Junction station on 31 July 1913. Note N.E.R. inspection saloon. *(Collection of B. Webb)*

Fig. 43 Brampton Junction station with auto-train and N.E.R. class BTP 0-4-4T on 31 July 1913.
(Collection of B. Webb)

Fig. 44 Brampton Town N.E.R. station, probably during the period between March 1920 and October 1923. N.E.R. BTP class 0-4-4T No. 60 standing at the platform.
(Collection of M. Halbert)

Fig. 45 View of part of Brampton Town coal cells. (*Fleetwood Shawe*)

Fig. 46 Cleared site of Brampton Town station with platform still *in situ*.
(*Fleetwood Shawe*)

Thompson's poor health and his disablement were making him reticent either to open up new collieries or extend existing ones, while the railway proposal, a short line from Halton Lea Gate to Lambley Colliery, was a veritable anathema to him until the Alston branch of the N. & C.R. was built. Lambley Colliery was taken on lease by Thompson in 1846 and had a very good coal production potential, Liddel forecasting 30,000 tons per year as its minimum output once the railway was laid to it. The extension of the line across Hartleyburn Common required way-leaves over Mr. Ellison's land and eventually these were reluctantly obtained by Thompson, and the railway built and in operation by the late summer of 1849.

Upon the opening of the line to Lambley Colliery, Thompson closed the Star Pit at Hartleyburn and decided to work its coal from Lambley whose production, nevertheless, did not reach Liddel's forecast of 30,000 tons until well after James Thompson's time.

James Thompson continued to hold full reign at Kirkhouse, despite the state of his health and constant urging from friends to delegate some of the work-load to his two elder sons who worked alongside him in the office.

He died on 14 July 1851 at the age of 56, a man who has never been given the recognition he merits as a highly-important railway pioneer of considerable vision. In his time he had forecast and seen the general adoption of the steam locomotive, the adoption of the wrought iron rail (in this respect influencing George Stephenson who was impressed by their performance on Lord Carlisle's railway), had helped to standardise the rail gauge of British and overseas railways to 4ft. $8\frac{1}{2}$in. gauge, and designed and built his own locomotives at the Kirkhouse workshops, Figs. 19 and 20. His development of the Naworth coalfield between 1838 and 1851 set the basis for its unrivalled prosperity.

Although Thompson's two sons were ostensibly left in command upon their father's death, they were not to take over their father's lease, as we shall see.

From 1851 many changes were to take place in the Naworth coalfield, not the least of which was the assumption of control of the collieries' lease by Maria Thompson, James Thompson's widow. The takeover by a woman of such an enterprise is regarded even today as surprising but, considering the restrictions placed on women during the Victorian era, is a feat worthy of some consideration. She took on a new lease from 2 September 1852 and traded as M. Thompson & Sons, being assisted by her two sons, George Africanus Thompson and Thomas Charles Thompson. Her third son, James Hetherington Thompson, had little interest in the family concern, but one of his sons, William B. Thompson, was responsible for a number of early published accounts around the turn of the century about the Brampton Railways and their locomotives—his accuracy in these matters, one might add, left much to be desired.

On the colliery side of the business, the following were at work on 10 May 1851—Blacksike, which produced 32,988 tons in the previous twelve months, Midgeholme King Pit with 48,193 tons, Bishop Hill with 5,337 tons, Gapshields with 2,948 tons and Lambley with 21,949 tons. Both George Pit and Hartleyburn had no recorded production and were abandoned from this date.

The colliery railway had since 1838 sustained no further closures but during June 1848 Howgill drift was closed down, making the railway, from its junction at the Blacksike branch southwards, redundant; it was probably lifted by 1851, although this is not certain. Locomotive sheds existed at Kirkhouse and also at Hallbankgate where a stone-built, two-road shed was erected during the 1840's, the method of locomotive operation being to work the railway in two sections, above and below the inclined plane.

Prior to James Thompson's death and the construction of the Lambley extension in 1849, it was made known that it was the intention to form an easterly exit for Naworth coal via the projected N. & C.R. branch from Haltwhistle to Alston. An earlier plan of 1845 to link Lord Carlisle's railway to the Wear Valley Railway and the Stockton & Darlington Railway via Alston was not pursued due to an agreement between Lord Carlisle and N. & C.R. to link to their Alston branch. The Wear Valley Railway planned to gain access to Carlisle by crossing the lands of Lord Carlisle by a new line to which Lord Carlisle would have full access. Some regrets were expressed when it appeared that the N. & C.R. Alston branch, originally intended to run along the western bank of the River South Tyne to permit an easy junction with Lord Carlisle's railway at Lambley, was to be changed to run along the eastern side of the river.

To this suggestion of November 1847, John Ramshay wrote to Matthew Plummer of the N. & C.R. as follows:

> Dear Sir,
>
> In the paper this week a notice is given by the N. & C.R. for an application to Parliament to alter the line of railway from Haltwhistle to Alston, the effect of this proposed alteration if carried with effect would be entirely to exclude Lord Carlisle's collieries from any connection with the Branch railway from Haltwhistle to Alston. Lord Carlisle can look upon this proceeding in no other light than as a direct attack upon his interests as a coalowner and as a most hostile proceeding, quite contrary to the understanding and arrangement which took place between the Railway Company and Lord Carlisle's agents and colliery lessee in 1846 when the Act for the Alston Branch was obtained.

In a further communication a few days later Ramshay told Plummer:

> You are perhaps aware that the Wear Valley Company in 1845 made repeated attempts to obtain Lord Carlisle's sanction and support in bringing their line to Alston and so on to Milton, and His Lordship was induced to intimate to that Company that he could not support them on the grounds that his countenance would be given to the Branch proposed by the Newcastle & Carlisle Railway.

After heated exchanges the connection was made by the fine stone viaduct across the river at Lambley, and a short branch, the Lambley Fell branch, laid from Lambley Station to Lambley Colliery by the N. & C.R. One point springs to mind here in that, apparently, the Alston branch opened on both sides of the uncompleted Lambley Viaduct. If this was so, how were the trains worked on the section between Lambley and Alston? Did N. & C.R. locomotives travel over Lord Carlisle's railway to reach the isolated section, or did Lord Carlisle's lessee work the traffic for the N. & C.R. ? Perhaps we shall never know. The Alston branch did enable the large coalfield on the eastern side of the river at Coanwood and Featherstone to be opened out and worked continuously from 1856, initially by Thompsons and later by numerous other lessees and sub-lessees until 1944.

New coal reserves in the Naworth area were opened out near the railway between Hallbankgate and Tindale, the first being Roachburn Pit which produced 23,259 tons of coal between 1860 and 1863, its output being loaded into railway waggons from carts at a small tipping dock near, but west of, the later Roachburn screens sidings. The second opening was of the Greenside drift in 1863 which produced 337,000 tons of coal by its closure in 1875, its production being taken over by the Howard Pit the same year. Howard Pit, situated alongside the railway, reached a peak production of over 89,000 tons during 1877. Southwards, further mining was re-started in the province of the old Talkin Colliery by drifting into Brown Fell, west of Howgill, resulting in the Venture drift. This drift operated during 1868-9, and was reopened in 1873 by the nearby new Venture drift situated east of the first Venture, adjacent to the workings of the very old Shop and Low Pits of eighteenth century origin. New Venture closed on 20 July 1875.

By this period in time the large colliery at Greenhead, the Byron drift, which was driven in 1867 and went into production in 1869, was in full production. Byron was situated alongside the old Blenkinsopp Colliery, but quite separate from it due to the presence of a large geological fault separating their workings. Byron Colliery topped a production of 95,000 tons during 1866-7 and was rail-served by a siding from the North Eastern Railway at Blenkinsopp.

By 1889 considerable anxiety was being shown in the future of the Naworth coalfield, for Blacksike Pit, after producing 1,055,426 tons of coal since May 1838, had closed in 1872, close on the heels of Clowsgill limestone quarry and kilns. Midgeholme King Pit, which had produced 2,930,182 tons of coal between May 1838 and May 1888, was said to have only two or three years of coal reserves left in 1889, and closed during 1893, to be followed by Howard Pit two years later.

The picture was not, therefore, very bright unless some expansion on "home ground" could be achieved. The only new development had been the reopening in 1885 of the old Henry Pits, previously closed in 1838, and situated some 1,100ft. up the eastern face of Tindale Fell. The reopening was made possible by extending the Bishop Hill rope-worked incline from that drift, closed in 1885, to serve its successor. Henry Pit's coal was tipped into railway waggons at Tarnfoot, and it continued to operate until 1910. The next loss of production occurred in 1886 when Lambley Colliery's lease expired.

The Thompson lease of the collieries and railways was due to expire in May 1893 and from late 1888 was the subject of much concern to both the lessees and lessors. In March 1889 Messrs. Thompsons told Lord Carlisle that many of the coalfields were drawing to a close, that it was becoming difficult to keep their output up and that profitability had been low for some five years. The lessors were at the same time trying to get Thompsons to relinquish the Brampton branch railway so that they could omit it from the new lease and thus enable the N.E.R. to take it over, but were to prove unsuccessful in their bid.

A more happy event of this period was the Kirkhouse fete of 9 August 1889, which was well publicised in contemporary newspapers, it being only necessary here to note that some 1,600 people attended the fete prompted by the marriage of Charles Lacy Thompson to Catherine Forbes. The crowds were accommodated in large marquees set up in a nearby field, and the event marked by speeches covering the history of the Naworth collieries and railways, followed by tea, entertainments and dancing. People were brought by special trains from Featherstone, Midgeholme, Howgill, Foresthead and Hallbankgate, while free tickets were issued to those travelling on the N.E.R. from Greenhead, Gilsland and Haltwhistle.

The new colliery lease was drafted in May 1890 for forty years and excluded all those areas either worked out or abandoned, the Thirlwall coalfield at Baronhouse, together with an area south of Geltsdale. At this time the Thompsons were operating Howard, Byron, Henry, Midgeholme and Featherstone Collieries, the last having been opened in 1888 and operating until 1904. During 1893 Midgeholme King Pit, Fig. 21, together with its thirty coke ovens, closed, to be followed in 1896 by Howard Pit, but there was some hope due to explorations on Denton Fell.

In 1891 Maria Thompson passed on. The lease was to be seen out by the sons of Thomas Charles Thompson, who had married Gertrude Lacy Thompson in 1856. Their sons were Charles Lacy Thompson (1857-1920) and James Thomas Thompson (1859-1899), the former giving up the lease in 1908 but being survived 42 years by his wife, she passing at the age of 92 in 1962 at Farlam Hall.

The explorations for coal on Denton Fell took much longer than expected, but after some six years a large tract of coal had been found. The result was that, after considerable difficulties, the Roachburn Colliery was sunk and put into operation during 1895. This colliery, a shaft mine, was built on the site of the old Roachburn Pit of 1860-3 and like its predecessor was to prove a very wet pit to operate, though expected to yield 15,000 tons of coal for forty years. The coalfield it worked contained vast reserves of greatly fluctuating quality in very irregular and fault-ridden seams, running mostly in very steep inclinations, while water penetration not only made working conditions atrocious but also made it necessary to pump out 1,200 gallons per minute to prevent flooding. Roachburn was not situated on the colliery railway but alongside the Brampton to Alston road (A689) so that to gain access to the railway it was necessary to construct a 2ft.-gauge tramway which crossed the road by an 80ft.-span lattice-girder bridge. The tramway was operated on an endless rope-haulage system which took the coal-tubs to the screens and refuse tips sited on a small hill overlooking the colliery. The tubs tipped their loads into the screens which in turn fed the coal by chutes into the railway waggons standing in the sidings in the deep cutting. These sidings were put in using the old rails from the Greenside depot and Howard Colliery sidings. A further siding ran to the top of the hill adjacent to the tramway, but was not used for loading coal. Fig. 22.

The persisting difficulties at Roachburn aggravated the Thompsons many times, to the extent of threatening to terminate their lease, while the continuing attempts to get them to give up the Brampton branch railway did not help either. All these problems meant that the new lease was not finally signed until May 1893.

Thompsons gained concessions in their lease to counteract lower production and their problems at Roachburn, which was soon to be their chief source of coal. The advice of Mr. T. E. Forster, the mines adviser, opined that a restricted lease was ideal for both the Thompsons and Lord Carlisle, for it would encourage Thompsons to continue at a reduced rental and obviate the almost impossible task of trying to find a new lessee for the Naworth mines should Thompsons give up their lease.

The outcome was that it was desirable to ensure continuation of the Thompsons' lease and it was finally agreed by all parties that Thompsons continue the collieries at Roachburn, Byron and Henry Pit, while the extensive coalfields at Thirlwall, Midgeholme and Featherstone could be offered to other operators, so from 1904 this was what happened.

In 1905-6 the remaining three Thompson Collieries produced the following tonnages: Roachburn 65,412 tons, Byron 41,716 tons and Henry Pit 2,299 tons, these three continuing until the final blow fell on Tuesday, 28 January 1908. On this fateful day the troublesome Roachburn Colliery flooded due to the roof of workings near the surface giving way under the moorland of Denton Fell. The workings in question, sited in good coal, were very steeply inclined and had been driven to their fullest extent, reaching clay without the adoption of the normal practice of leaving a plug of solid coal to ensure safety.

This practice was usual at Roachburn, although it had not previously given any trouble, but in this case it was in the vicinity of surface water deposits, known locally as the Backstand Ponds, which entered the workings with moss or peat, sand and clay with great rapidity, quickly flooding the affected workings and, subsequently, the majority of the colliery. Three men were imprisoned by the inflow and their bodies never recovered. They were Matthew Hilliard, back overman; Robert Pattinson, deputy overman and James William Wharton, hewer.

Roachburn employed some 300 men underground on its various shifts, producing 290 tons of coal daily and, being linked underground with Byron drift, encompassed a large area of coal. The disaster—not unexpected, according to the miners, who had frequently joked that someday the Backstand Ponds would come in and flood the mine—was subject to an inquiry by Mr. J. B. Atkinson, H.M. Inspector of Mines. His report said that, prior to the inflow, water, clay and mud had been entering the workings through a roof fissure for some eleven hours, which gave way just after eleven o'clock on that fateful day, following the flight of the deputies who were so alarmed by the quantity of material entering that they left the area immediately. Upon reaching the top of a nearby incline they heard a noise like thunder and spread the alarm. The missing men, Pattinson and Hilliard, went to look for Wharton and were apparently trapped by the rising flood.

A subsidence measuring 613ft. by 714ft. and 50ft. deep was visible on Denton Fell, and it was estimated that some 90,000 cubic yards of peat had entered the colliery from the nine-acre subsidence. Attempts to plug the hole with trees, bushes and colliery arch sections failed when they, too, went down the hole. Eventually, it was stopped and a solid concrete plug built into the affected workings. To the most unfortunate loss of life was added the loss of the colliery, and also the Byron drift which flooded too—a serious financial loss to Lord Carlisle, justifying compensation which, although considered, was never claimed. The result of the accident was that Charles Lacy Thompson decided to terminate his lease in May 1909, subsequently altered with great reluctance to 30 June 1908, and regretfully agreed to by Lord Carlisle. Thompson boring on Tarnmonath Fell for the new colliery at Gairs was stopped at the end of June 1908, but other companies were showing interest in Gairs, one being the Coanwood Coal Company.

The lessor of the area in which Byron Colliery had been working, Mr. Joicey, did not wish to re-let the coal at that time, and in any case the serious flooding of Byron was likely to preclude this. The men at Byron would, it seemed likely, find employment at the nearby Thirlwall Colliery just about to be opened in a larger way, but for the men at Roachburn the outlook was bleak, for the small Henry Pit could not take on any more, even if it was reopened by another lessee.

At Kirkhouse the obvious decline of the Thompson empire had left its mark, for by 1908 little work was going on there, apart from waggon repair work. Figs. 23 and 24. The colliery office at Kirkhouse was to close after Thompsons moved out, exactly 100 years after James Thompson had first entered it in 1808.

Charles Lacy Thompson was to live on until 1920 when he died at the age of 63 years.

CHAPTER 7

Thompsons' Successors

The demise of Thompsons, a most serious blow to the prospects of their employees since no alternative work existed, was to be taken very badly by the local population, who were aware of the probable difficulties of finding anyone who would take on the ailing Naworth collieries and so continue their employment.

Over the final fifteen years of their regime, Thompsons had gained many concessions by their repeated threats to discontinue their lease, and it was only through determined effort that a new lessee was, in fact, found.

The efforts were made by Lady Rosalind, Countess of Carlisle, from the date when Thompson gave notice to quit in March 1908, her main task being the continuation of the employment of the miners, and the completion of the driving of the Gairs Colliery high on Tarnmonath Fell. Lady Carlisle conducted lengthy meetings with prospective lessees, finally being successful in finding a company who would take on the coalfield, its collieries and railways. This was the Naworth Coal Company who took on the lease for forty years from 1 July 1908.

The most important aspect of the new lease was that the lessee had agreed to complete the driving of Gairs Colliery which was to prove their main source of coal. This Colliery had a good coal potential but was difficult to reach, requiring a new railway to serve it. The Gairs Railway was put in during 1908-9, and was very steeply graded between Brown Fell and Simmerson Hill. It was laid initially from the junction of the old Foresthead and Blacksike Railway along the formation of the old 1799 waggonway to just west of Howgill. From this point it turned southwest along a new route by a gentle curve to climb away between Brown Fell and Simmerson Hill towards Tarnmonath Fell and the colliery. The severely-graded railway ran directly to its destination—and involved no reversing siding to gain elevation, in spite of the previously-published accounts and popular belief to the contrary!

The first-recorded coal output from Gairs was during the twelve months ending July 1909, of 1,026 tons. Two years later it stood at 40,600 tons, reaching its peak with this lessee during 1916 with a total of 60,500 tons.

The Naworth Coal Co. investigated Byron and Roachburn Collieries to see if pumping would clear the flooding, but found it impossible. They decided in March 1909 that they could continue the latter colliery in a limited way, purchasing the plant in late 1909.

The small drift on Tindale Fell, Henry Pit, continued to operate under the new lessees until 1910 when it closed after producing 3,368 tons of coal for them since take-over.

On 29 June 1912 the Naworth Coal Co. reported that their two collieries were Roachburn, which had produced 21,900 tons, and Gairs with 34,520 tons of coal. This was the last production at Roachburn due to the poor quality of its coal and the impossibility of reaching the better coal. New pumps had been installed, but they had failed to deal with the situation and the lessee announced that they could no longer expend more money at Roachburn and intended to stop drawing coal in 1912. In all it had produced 102,000 tons during their period of operation. Concurrent with Roachburn's closure, the washing and preparation plant at Midgeholme closed too, its sole purpose since 1895 being the washing of coal from that colliery.

In an attempt to find another source of coal, the Naworth Coal Co. asked permission to try the old pre-Thompson workings just west of Midgeholme at Whites Cut. Although this area was outside their lease they were allowed to work it as a separate lot and brought out their first coal in 1913 by working the pillars and ribs of coal left from previous workings. They continued to do so until the end of their lease but reaching a peak output of 23,288 tons in the twelve months ending 29 June 1918.

The colliery railway terminated now at Whites Cut, about a quarter of a mile west of the site of Midgeholme washery, its previous terminus, while the track itself finished at Halton Lea Gate, the section thence to Lambley Colliery having been lifted during 1909—removing forever the eastward exit from the Naworth coalfield. After 1913 the track between Whites Cut and Halton Lea Gate was lifted.

The quest for coal during the war years resulted in further attempts to reopen old workings such as the 1875 Venture drifts near Howgill, which were operated from 1915 until 1924, the output being conveyed on the Gairs Railway. This was followed by an attempt to enter the Howard Pit workings during 1916, but yielding only 225 tons of coal before abandonment, while old heaps of coal at Blacksike were removed producing over 1,300 tons during 1916-17. The final colliery tried by this lessee was the Prior Pit near Prior Dyke which had last been worked by Thompsons during 1846-7 and, situated alongside the railway about a quarter of a mile west of Whites Cut, was worked only during 1923-4 and produced a mere 4,308 tons of low-quality coal.

By the early 1920's the Naworth Coal Co. was in financial difficulties, and the closure of Whites Cut and the failure of Prior Pit left the company with only Gairs and Venture to produce coal, hardly sufficient to pay the tonnage rentals, so that they decided to terminate their lease in 1924. Their final twelve months' coal output figures for Gairs and Venture, dated 28 June 1924, was 46,465 tons, and for Prior and Whites Cut 15,531 tons.

At this point the future of the coalfield again looked very bleak indeed, while the railway seemed completely doomed east of Hallbankgate, as it now appeared that only the Gairs and Foresthead branches would be required by any future lessee.

At Kirkhouse, waggon repair work continued and a small foundry operated in one of the old gas-works buildings, but its future was to be continued decline. Upon the ending of the Naworth Coal Co. lease, the whole system closed down—collieries, railway and all.

During the period of the Naworth Coal Co. other lessees were active at Thirlwall, Featherstone and Gapshields. The Thirlwall coal was leased during 1900 to the Coanwood Coal Co. who gave up the lease in 1907 to a new company trading as the Thirlwall Coal Co. Ltd. They closed in 1912, only to be followed by the Thirlwall Colliery Co. (1913) Ltd. the following year, who were bankrupt by 1917. The final unfortunate operator was the Mickley Coal Co. Ltd. of Newcastle, who tried unsuccessfully to drift into the friable coal seams from 1913 to 1926 when they finally abandoned their attempt.

At Featherstone various areas of coal were worked from 1903 by such lessees as the Coanwood Coal Co.; the Plenmeller Colliery Co. Ltd.; Featherstone Coal Co. Ltd. and Featherstone Colliery Co. Ltd., some large combined outputs resulting.

The old Gapshields drifts, discontinued by Thompson in 1867, were let from 1915 to the Gapshields Colliery Co. Ltd. and, although usually in financial difficulties, they continued to operate the drifts until the mid-1920's.

Yet another small company formed by a family called Woof was obtaining coal from a number of drifts with the name of Lyneholme Burn Colliery, just south of the Kirkhouse Farm and situated along the burn of that name, together with another colliery called High Fell Colliery. These were apparently leased under a royalty called the Bow Bank Wood royalty and operated amid financial difficulties during the 1920's. These small workings were served by road transport.

The desolate spoil heaps of the Tindale spelter works, consisting of vast tonnages accumulated between 1845 and 1900, were from around 1910 attracting attention from companies interested in trying to re-process the waste for reclamation of residues, but apart from some loads being sent away for testing little was done at this time.

The closure of the Naworth coalfield was a problem which proved difficult to resolve due to its limited potential and rundown condition, not to mention the lack of prospective lessees with sufficient capital to carry on the enterprise.

Its resurrection was to be the task of three local families—all beneficiaries under the late Lord Carlisle's will—who held the estates divided between them, the whole being managed by M. R. H. Minerals Ltd. The initials of the Murray and Roberts families, together with that of Lord Henley, provided the company name.

The company took over the collieries and set up the Naworth Collieries Company Ltd., after some initial difficulty in attracting capital which was resolved by the success of the Miners (Industries) Trust Fund Ltd. set up by Mr. Charles Roberts for that purpose.

The new company took over officially in March 1926 and at once set about re-opening the Gairs and Venture Collieries, which by the end of August 1926 had under the new operators produced their first coal outputs of 2,381 and 589 tons respectively.

Although, since 1924, coal production within the Naworth area had been suspended, other lessees were at work. The Mickley Coal Co. had continued to try the difficult Thirlwall coalfield, ceasing work in 1926 and terminating their lease in May 1927—as such the last lessee of this coalfield. The Featherstone Colliery Co. were to continue at Featherstone until 1944 while the adjacent Plenmeller Colliery only ran on until 1932. At Gapshields the Gapshields Colliery Co. were to continue until 1933 when the Naworth Collieries Co. took over the operation. At Midgeholme, the Midgeholme Colliery Co., operated by Messrs. Pepperell and Sarginson, was in business from 1926 to 1932. Their colliery, a drift on the south side of the Brampton to Alston road (A689) on the bank of the River Blackburn, worked towards King Pit, going out of business for financial reasons. This drift was always called locally "Pep's Pit" and was taken over by the Naworth Collieries Co. who operated it from December 1932 until they closed it early in 1939.

The Gairs Colliery was soon in full production, reaching a tonnage of almost 30,000 tons by 1927, but falling steadily from that date to 23,500 tons in 1930-1, down to only 4,200 tons in 1935-6, closing late in 1936 due to declining coal quality and the desire to expend no further capital searching for fresh seams of coal. During its lifetime from 1909 to 1936 Gairs had produced some 778,748 tons of coal.

The Venture drift operated from 1926 to 1928 and again from 1933 to 1939, but then closed down completely, rendering the railway south of the junction of the Foresthead branch redundant. The Gairs Railway was lifted during 1940-1.

Naworth Collieries' first new colliery was driven in 1926-7 into Mint Hill. This was the Mint Hill drift and was situated on the north side of the Haining Burn near the Brampton to Alston road, almost opposite the Prior and Prior Dyke Colliery sites.

Mint Hill went into production in late 1926 and its coal, initially taken away by road, was soon conveyed by a narrow-gauge tramway in tubs across the Haining Burn and under the A689 road, being rope-worked by a haulage engine through the workings of the Prior Pit, to emerge alongside the colliery railway at Prior Dyke. Mint Hill continued in production until 1931-2, reaching its highest output of 40,000 tons during 1929-30.

This new development brought fresh life to the eastern arm of the railway, which was in fact extended eastwards from Whites Cut to reach the Midgeholme King Pit site where the Tindale Granite Co. laid a 2ft.-gauge rope-worked tramway and erected a stone crushing and loading plant on the old washery and coke ovens sites to serve their nearby Dolomite quarry. The railway gained much useful traffic from this source.

Yet another source of traffic was provided by a small drift driven above the railway at Prior Dyke and opened in 1931. This drift was very short-lived, producing in fact very little coal; its short siding was retained for use in later years by a peat extraction scheme.

During 1926-7 expansion came again to Kirkhouse when the Kirkhouse Brick & Tile Co. Ltd. built a brick and tile works on part of the yard opposite the old gasworks site, incorporating the large locomotive shed into its buildings. To meet the demand for shale to make bricks the Foresthead quarry was reopened, together with the old Blacksike branch serving it. The quarry had its own internal 2ft.-gauge rail system using small skips hauled by a "Simplex" petrol locomotive, although for a short time a Kerr Stuart "Wren" class steam locomotive was used.

At about the same time Naworth Limeworks Ltd. were operating a quarry at Bishop Hill, to which the old Riggfoot railway led, this being relaid to serve this new development, to provide a narrow-gauge tramway operated by petrol locos. This traffic, together with that from Midgeholme quarry, provided some quite high tonnages for the railway. A series of attempts to exploit the Tindale spelter works slag heaps held out hope of yet more traffic and although some companies did set up extraction plant, nothing material was gained from this work.

The interest in the vast coalfield under Denton Fell, last worked in 1912 by the Naworth Coal Co. with the ill-fated Roachburn Colliery, was revived during the late 1920's. There was no chance of ever reopening Roachburn, even though a number of shallow ventilation and safety shafts entering the flooded workings existed on the bleak moorland of the Fell. Investigations showed that it was possible to drift into the outcrops of coal in the vicinity of the 1908 subsidence, and in due course during November 1931 the Denton Colliery was opened. This drift, always called locally "The Backstand", produced over 30,000 tons of coal up to its closure, due to water penetration, in March 1934. The inaccessible location of the Denton Colliery was resolved by the installation of an overhead bucket ropeway, purchased second-hand from Ireland, which delivered its coal to a new screening plant built for this purpose on part of the old Howard Colliery site.

The closure of this drift did not mean that all interest in the coal under Denton Fell had faded. On the contrary, the Naworth Collieries Co. instigated a survey by Forster, Raw & Partners of Newcastle, which was dated June 1934. This report said that trials on ways of de-watering the colliery were under way and that, provided sufficient solid coal was left around the inundated Roachburn workings, three areas of coal were available for mining—Part A with 65,000 tons was not sufficient on its own to make working economic, Part B with 380,000 tons of coal, and Part C with several million tons of coal of unknown quality. Forster, Raw & Partners envisaged a second drift capable of producing 300 tons per day to supplement the existing drift with its capacity of 200 tons of coal per day, which in combination would produce enough coal to make a good profit for its operators. They observed that if the water problems were resolved and sufficient time and capital made available, a viable colliery might result, but added "The risk of the speculation, however, is one for your (the Naworth Collieries Co.'s) consideration and decision". No further mining was attempted and the coal remains to this day. The overhead ropeway, "The Roachburn Telfer Line", was subsequently dismantled.

During 1933 the Gapshields Colliery drifts were taken over from their former operators and worked intermittently with some on Reaygarth Farm until the end of the Naworth Collieries Co. in 1946. Another colliery quite near to Gapshields was put into production in 1934. This was the Chapelburn drift, adjacent to the L.N.E.R. Newcastle to Carlisle railway line, and indeed working under it into Denton Mains, tapping the Thirlwall coal seam. On the site of a very old and apparently untraced drift, it was leased to its operators who worked it with little success owing to lack of capital and were absorbed into a new company in partnership with Naworth Collieries Co. during 1936, which ran on until 1946. As with Gapshields and Reaygarth, Chapelburn was served by road transport.

In 1933-4 the coal reserves along the valley of the River Blackburn at Low Midgeholme, north of the A689 road, again attracted attention. Coal had been worked there for many hundreds of years, and records of 1765 with plans of old drifts working under the Blackburn and along both sides of its course still survive. New trials revealed a potential so that in 1935 the East and West drifts were opened, soon to be followed by the Coronation, North and Slag drifts, work continuing on some of these drifts until the end of the Naworth Collieries Co. tenure. Their coal was taken by road to the nearby Whites Cut Colliery site where a tipping dock and sidings were installed, the coal being tipped by the road lorries into waiting railway waggons prior to railing to Howard Screens.

Clouds were by now appearing on the horizon, for by 1937 the Tindale Granite Co. were thinking of switching their stone traffic to road transport, which was implemented in 1939 when Naworth Limeworks Ltd. took over the quarry and stone preparation plant at Midgeholme. At the same time their limestone traffic from Foresthead quarry went over to road transport too, but the shale for brickmaking continued to be rail-borne to Kirkhouse. The railway track between Midgeholme and Whites Cut was again lifted, this time finally, in 1939.

Kirkhouse was by now boasting not only the brickworks, but also a large lime kiln built on the site of the old coke ovens, which towered above its surroundings, surviving the hostilities, to be demolished in the 1950's. Other activities here were restricted to the repair of waggons and colliery tubs.

The final trials for coal made by the Naworth Collieries Co. were near Blue Gate Farm, just west of the Howard Colliery site. This abortive drift, known as Blue Gate, did not prove any workable coal and its life span was only during 1943-4.

By the end of the tenure of this lessee on 31 December 1946 they worked collieries at Chapelburn, Gapshields and Low Midgeholme.

The railway was in use between Brampton junction and Foresthead quarry, and eastwards as far as Whites Cut, the immediate future appearing secure.

The return of a Labour government in 1945 made it necessary to take over by nationalisation a number of key industries of national importance, one of these being the coal mining industry. So, on 1 January 1947 the collieries operated by the Naworth Collieries Co. Ltd. and its railway, together with the Hartleyburn Coal Co. Ltd. and its Lambley West Colliery, were taken over by the National Coal Board (N.C.B.) as their Naworth and Lambley unit.

The Naworth portion took over the Low Midgeholme drifts known as East, West and North drifts (the Slag drift there having closed in 1946) and the Gapshields and Chapelburn drifts.

The N.C.B. simply took on the Naworth lease, not actually owning the mineral rights or the railway and buildings, but purchasing the collieries and equipment, together with the locomotives and waggons, from M.R.H. Minerals who remained the lessors.

The new operator worked the railway from Brampton Junction east to Whites Cut loading dock and south to Foresthead quarry, acting as carriers for shale traffic from the latter point to Kirkhouse brickworks. They also retained the waggon repair shop at Kirkhouse, the engine shed, coal depot and offices at Hallbankgate and the Howard Screens. Figs. 25 to 27.

At the Lambley end the West drift was connected to the L.N.E.R. Alston branch by the short Lambley Fell branch, most of its coal leaving by rail, although some was taken by road to Whites Cut and subsequently to Brampton Junction.

Soon after their takeover the N.C.B., rightly or wrongly, decided to try the Whites Cut area by a new drift alongside the railway. This drift, into an area which had been worked over many years since pre-Thompson days, proved a failure, being said to have produced hardly a waggon load of saleable coal up to its abandonment in 1949.

The drift at Gapshields closed during 1948, to be followed in 1949 by Chapelburn drift. Due to the increase in carriage rates for handling stone and shale traffic between Foresthead and Kirkhouse to meet rising operating costs, the N.C.B. lost this traffic to road transport, and in so doing rendered the southerly arm of the railway from Hallbankgate to Foresthead redundant.

In an endeavour to raise coal production, extensive mechanisation and modernisation had been introduced by the N.C.B., the merits of this being arguable, in that in the opinions of some local people the capacity of the surviving collieries to justify such expense was doubtful.

Another scheme initiated was the exploitation of the coal reserves still extant in the area worked from 1829 to 1893 by the shaft mine at High Midgeholme, which had been a Thompson enterprise. The N.C.B. hoped that modern methods and pumping could enable an efficient colliery to be set up on the old King Pit site, work commencing in 1949.

The site was cleared, the old shaft unsealed, relined and pumping carried out, while new underground roadways were laid out and new pit-head buildings set up to permit opening in 1951. Strangely, the railway was not extended the necessary half-mile from Whites Cut to the new colliery, which was to be served only by road.

Miners for the new King Pit were obtained by transferring men from some of the Low Midgeholme drifts, and by the closure of the East drift there, soon followed by the demise of the West drift, these two closures reducing the railway coal traffic from Whites Cut dock quite considerably.

The sole remaining Low Midgeholme drift, the North drift, continued to operate until in January 1953 it was announced that it would close at the end of March, so finishing the railway once and for all.

Concurrent with the decision to cease mining at Low Midgeholme, the N.C.B. informed Mr. Stanley Walton of M.R.H. Minerals that they wished to terminate the lease for the railway and all buildings, except the office and garage at Hallbankgate, on 31 March 1953. So, after 155 years the railway—one of the oldest in the country—was to cease operation and be sold for scrap.

In preparation of the lists of materials for disposal in July 1953, it was noted that considerable alterations had taken place since 1926 and its assessment for that lease. There were now no sidings at Roachburn, Tindale stores or at Midgeholme washery, but additional sidings had been put in at Kirkhouse, Planehead, on the Foresthead branch, Whites Cut and at the Howard Screens. Of the latter two places it was hoped that the N.C.B. would leave these to replace the three former denuded sites mentioned in the 1926 lease. As it happened, their 2,528 yards of single rail were, in fact, claimed by the N.C.B.

After M.R.H. had got the list finalised the N.C.B. was offered the railway for scrap, but declined the offer. The materials and equipment for disposal were as follows:

Rails, chairs, sleepers, ropes, pulleys and other fixed gear on the railway extending from the road bridge at Birkey Brow (nine yards east of the bridge) near Brampton Junction to the culvert carrying the River Blackburn under the embankment near Midgeholme, including branches to Foresthead, Tortie and the spelter works, sidings at Kirkhouse, Planehead and elsewhere (excluding Howard Screens and Whites Cut Colliery).

Approximately 17,000 yards of 65-90lbs. rails were involved, together with the waggon weighbridge at Hallbankgate and the water tank there.

Various types of tenders were drawn up, but before final tenders for dismantling were accepted, Mr. Walton approached a number of bodies to see if they were interested in any of the fittings or equipment for preservation. His main interest lay in the equipment in the Planehead control cabin, reputed to be unique and of Stephenson design, although probably made at Kirkhouse. Of this equipment, the apparatus for indicating the speed of waggons and their position on the inclined plane was most interesting, no record of similar equipment on other inclined planes having been found. Unfortunately, the value of this apparatus once removed and, therefore, out of context, is debatable; nonetheless they should have been saved and used in conjunction with photographs or models of the cabin and incline. The outcome was quite typical of the times—they were scrapped!

Tenders were received from T. W. Ward Ltd., Sheffield; Cox & Danks Ltd., Salford; Geo. Cohen & Sons Ltd., London; Todd Bros., St. Helens; Robert Frazer Ltd., Hebburn; D. S. Bowran, Gateshead; W. Bush & Son Ltd., Alfreton, and Ellis (Metals) Ltd., Newcastle. George Cohen's tender of £10,500 was accepted on 10 October 1953 and dismantling started soon afterwards, to be completed by early summer 1954.

The N.C.B. dismantled their Low Midgeholme drifts using the railway to take equipment and materials from Whites Cut, and were filling in the drifts in August and September 1953. The Howard Screens were dismantled in July 1953, followed by Whites Cut loading bay.

Although at the end of 1953 all the former Naworth collieries had closed, except for the resuscitated King Pit, enquiries from private people interested in opening up small drifts were afoot, but nothing was to happen until 1954-5. Meanwhile, the N.C.B. had run into difficulties with the King Pit, reasons given being water penetration, faults in the strata and some difficulty in trying to reach lower levels via the old shaft, due to its partial blockage and the impossibility of lowering pumping gear down it.

Therefore it was decided to close their bold King Pit venture in 1955, so ending large-scale coal production in the Naworth coalfield. Great hardship was caused by the loss of employment, only met in part by the transfer of miners to the new collieries further east. The Lambley West drift continued until 1958 when it, too, closed down, resulting in the lifting of the Lambley Fell branch soon after.

The discontinuation of N.C.B. mining activities was not the end of mining in the Naworth area, for during 1955 some miners from King Pit had obtained a licence to try for coal at the old Havannah drift west of Blacksike, working into Talkin Fell. Workable coal was not found so they left to try instead the old Recovery Pit, just east of Howgill on the lower slopes of Tindale Fell. As the Duke Coal Co. they were to operate successfully until the end of September 1971 by removing the pillars of coal left from earlier pre-Thompson workings. By early 1972 another small group of men was again trying the old Havannah drift, hoping to operate it as the Blacksike drift, but a year later had given up the task.

In 1975 interest in the old Howard colliery site alongside the course of the Midgeholme extension near but west of Hallbankgate saw local men start a drift intent on removing supporting pillars under the railway, however the perennial problem of water saw this abandoned. Early 1976 saw their attention attracted again to the fells above Howgill by reopening the old Peters Hole drift on the west side of Howgill beck, a steeply-graded road being put in to give access.

Aware of the coal reserves still remaining within the Naworth areas, the N.C.B. Opencast Executive was boring for coal during 1977, with undisclosed results, but, who knows, perhaps a new future may yet open on the Naworth coalfield?

The only other local coal mining is taking place at the Blenkinsopp Colliery at Greenhead where the 1842 drift under Blenkinsopp Castle is being worked, removing the pillars left from previous operations. Blenkinsopp had been closed in 1888-9 following flooding due to inadequate pumps.

The scene today in the Naworth coalfield still has much to offer the historian. At Brampton much of the coal staith remains as do parts of the Kirkhouse workshop and farm area. One can find remains of both the 1799 and 1836 railway routes between Brampton and Hallbankgate, while the routes southward and eastward are easily traced, together with ample evidence of the very extensive coal workings throughout the area. At Blacksike and Howgill one may still find 15ft. lengths of 1824 wrought iron fish-belly rails lying in the undergrowth! Fig. 26.

Fig. 47 The small locomotive shed at Kirkhouse dating from at least 1838 in roofless condition during October 1952, shortly before demolition. (L. G. Charlton)

Fig. 48 Side elevation of Thompson locomotive *Belted Will* 0-4-0vc built at Kirkhouse in 1838/9, possibly after some rebuilding by Stephensons. (Brian Webb)

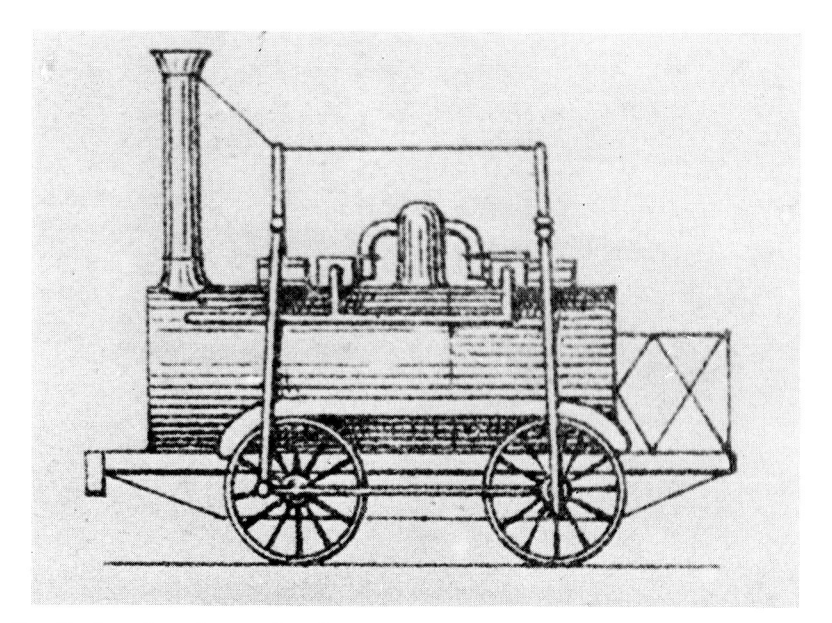

Fig. 49 An enlarged copy of an illustration of *Belted Will* taken from an **1889** engraving and showing great similarity to Fig. 48 in spite of artistic licence. *(Collection of B. Webb)*

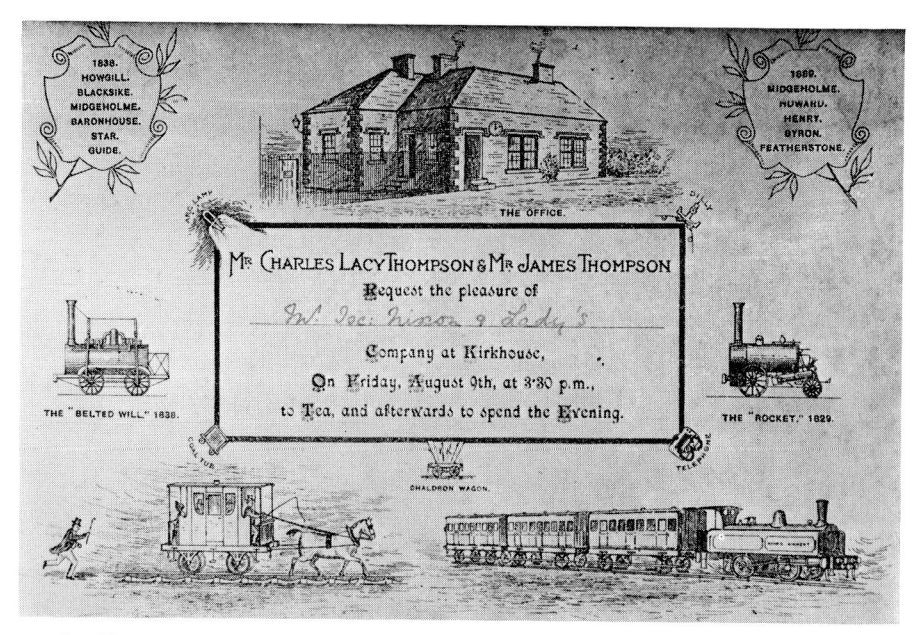

Fig. 50 Invitation card for the Kirkhouse fete of **1889**.   *(Collection of B. Webb)*

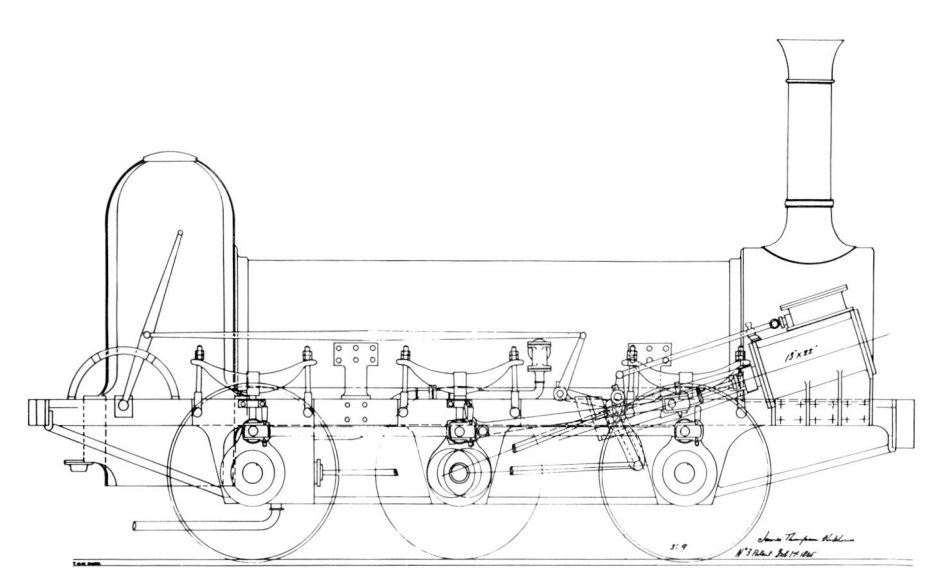

Fig. 51 Diagram of *Loch* 0-6-0c tender engine probably built at Kirkhouse in 1848 to Stephenson No. 3 Patent. The original is signed by James Thompson and dated February 1845. *(Collection of B. Webb)*

Fig. 52 Side elevation of *Loch*. This locomotive was one of the first long-boiler type industrial locomotives. *(Brian Webb)*

Fig. 53 An impression of *Loch* as running in the 1870's fitted with a stovepipe chimney, shunting at Hallbankgate Plane-head sidings.
(Sid Barnes)

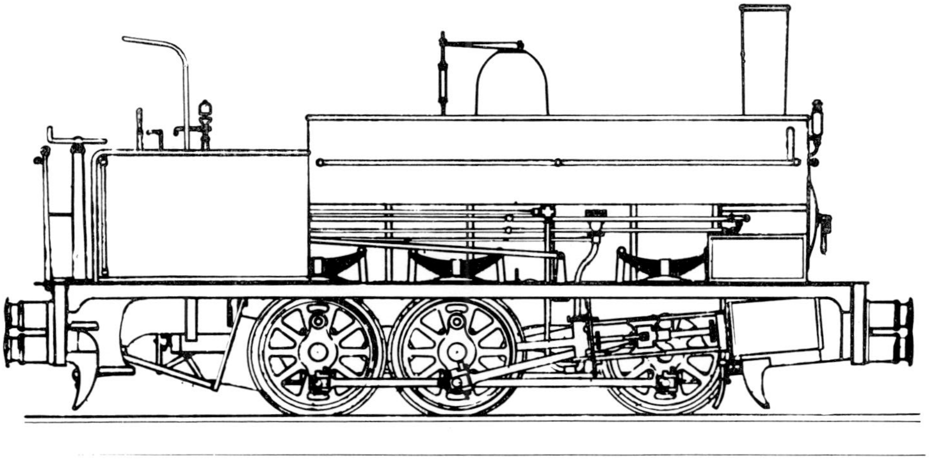

Fig. 54 Side elevation of *Tichborne*, the railway's first tank engine. 0-6-0SToc (RS 2011/72). It was rebuilt as a tender engine in 1879. (Collection of B. Webb)

Fig. 55 A reconstruction of a scene during the 1872-1879 period with *Tichborne* in its original form leaving Hallbankgate en route to the collieries with a train of children wagons

Fig. 56   *Tichborne* in its second form after 1879. Seen here near Hallbankgate loco shed around 1900.
(*Collection of B. Webb*)

Fig. 57   *Tichborne* photographed, it is thought, near Roachburn screens around 1900.
(*Collection of F. Jones*)

Fig. 58 *Belted Will*, the 0-6-0Toc, which resulted from the second rebuilding of *Tichborne* in 1907-1909 period. Seen here at Brampton staith probably just after returning to service.   (*Collection of B. Webb*)

Fig. 59 The railway's only unnamed locomotive—the 0-6-0oc tender engine *No. 5* (RS 2351/78).   (*Collection of F. Jones*)

CHAPTER 8

The Brampton Dandy

Of all the questions concerning Lord Carlisle's railways, perhaps that of "Why has Brampton never had a convenient railway station?" is the most common. The answers have been diverse and often untrue, but the most likely reason, the geographical location of Brampton (since the town lies in a saucer-shaped dip), has not been considered, the cause usually having been related to the people of Brampton's lack of desire for a railway, when actually the reverse was true!

In 1833 James Thompson referred to the district as ". . . being so disadvantageous for railways". This real villain of the piece was not overcome until the road vehicle, with the internal combustion engine, arrived on the scene.

From 1799 Lord Carlisle's waggonway served the town with coal and lime at the coal staith which was situated in the top of a vee formed by two roads, the road to Alston (A689) and to Newcastle (A69). The waggonway operated no passenger services at all, but after conversion to 4ft. 8in. gauge in 1829 a service was possible to enable people to travel to the Brampton market. However, no proof has been found of such a service until 1833 when three horse-drawn "Dandy" carriages, Figs. 28 and 29, were put into use, named *Black Diamond*, *Mountaineer* and *Experiment*. The term "Dandy" seems to be taken to apply to the "Dandy Cart" used to carry horses on waggonways which operated in part by gravity, but it has been suggested that the word "dandy" was popularly applied to any innovation which caught the eye of the public.

No public passenger service operated until the new colliery railway between Hallbankgate and Brampton staith opened officially on 19 July 1836. Although the line had been traversed from Kirkhouse to the staith by a steam passenger train four days previously, this form of traction was not to serve Brampton travellers on a regular basis until forty-five years later.

The passenger service linking the coal staith with Milton Station on the N. & C.R. was introduced on the same day as the N. & C. line opened, and was operated by a horse and one of the aforementioned "Dandy" carriages. The line cut through Milton Hill to reach the staith, crossing the Alston road (A689) by a new stone arch built on the skew, Fig. 30, and was always called, and, indeed, still is, the "old Dandy line".

Black Diamond appears to have initiated the service and by August 1836 James Thompson was able to report:

The new railway from Brampton to Bankhall is finished and now in regular use. A railway carriage runs on that part of the said railway laying between Brampton Staith and Milton Station with passengers to meet each train that passes along the public line, for which 3d. each is charged.

Although two locomotives, *Atlas* and *Gilsland*, worked the first passenger train over the branch, neither locomotive belonged to Lord Carlisle, so unless *Gilsland* continued to operate coal traffic between Kirkhouse, Milton and Brampton, which is doubtful, in the writer's opinion, Lord Carlisle's railway was entirely horse-worked until April 1837, and partly so for some years afterwards.

Nevertheless, the town of Brampton welcomed its new link with the outside world, regardless of its horse haulage or the somewhat unusual method of operation. The practice was to use the horse for the first part of the journey from Milton to the staith, until the final down-graded section was reached. At this point the horse was removed and the carriage allowed to run, under control of its brakesman, gently down to the staith. Fig. 32. No doubt this novel method proved rather disconcerting to those travellers unaccustomed to such operational methods, but it lays forever the ghost of the oft-repeated and published assertion that the carriage was stopped only by a mound of sand or soil at the staith.

The rather long walk for the Bramptonians to the staith soon brought criticism and the suggestion that Messrs. Thompsons should extend the railway nearer the town, the start of a long controversy to last many decades.

The first proposals for a new railway to serve Brampton came, surprisingly, from the north when, during 1846, the Glasgow, Dumfries & Carlisle Railway wanted to head towards Brampton in a line almost parallel to the present Brampton to Longtown road (A6071), but west of it. It was to cross the Brampton to Carlisle road (B6264) west of Brampton, curving towards the town and on to join the railway at the coal staith, from which it continued on the 1799 waggonway route to Milton village and a junction with the N. & C.R. Later in the same year the Caledonian Railway put forward a similar scheme following almost the same route.

Other schemes put forward included one in 1852 by the Glasgow & South Western Railway, again on a similar route, except that in this case it hoped to use Lord Carlisle's Brampton branch to gain access to the N. & C.R. at Milton Station. The final attempt from the north was by the Brampton & Longtown Railway in 1865, again by a very similar route, but hoping to gain access to the N. & C.R. (now the North Eastern Railway—N.E.R.) at Milton Station independent of the colliery railway.

The next proposal was quite unconnected with the others, and was the most interesting, being designed to really serve the town of Brampton. Under the title of the Carlisle, Brampton & Milton Railway it came on the scene in July 1871. This single-track railway was to start at Milton Station (since August 1870 renamed

Brampton) and pass through Rowbank Wood, between Aarons Town and Hemblesgate, crossing the Brampton to Castle Carrock road (B6413) by a 30ft. span bridge, 15ft. high, for which the road was to be lowered by 8ft., continuing to cross Paving Brow just south-west of the crossroad formed by Tree Road, Tarn Road and Crawhall. It then ran parallel to Crawhall, crossing this near the Old Brewery, across Well Meadow, then Moat Side, by a 16ft. high, 40ft. span bridge, heading then north-west and parallel to Union Lane. After this it left the north side of Brampton via St. Michael's Rest, crossing the River Irthing by a bridge near Brampton Old Church. On its way to Carlisle it was to have stations at Irthington, Crosby and Brunstock. The gauge of this railway was to have been 3ft., with light rolling stock, and to have been built on the Fairlie principle, its engineers being Robert Fairlie and Henry Hoggarth. It was to cost no more than £3,500 per mile and the capital of £50,000 would, it was hoped, be raised by £10 shares. The solicitor for this scheme was Mr. George Waugh of London, and even though the Bill for the railway passed parliamentary Standing Orders on 13 February 1872 the cash was not forthcoming, so the project failed.

No matter, the Brampton "Dandy" still plodded its way between the staith and the N.E.R., regardless, apparently, of the feelings now mounting against it, and the reliance Brampton had to place on Messrs. Thompsons for their railway service. This was to continue and agitation was constant that the N.E.R. should come to the aid of Brampton.

Great political capital was made by blaming those responsible for the original routing of the N. & C.R. to miss Brampton, when the truth was that the N. & C.R. had no real desire to serve Brampton at all, while their 1825 branch proposal through Brampton Ridge, with its inclined plane and gradient of 1 in 36, would hardly have been a suitable solution either.

During the 1870s much was said and published in similar vein by opposing political factions, and by people complaining about the coal monopoly held at Brampton by Thompsons, which they believed was supported by the Earl of Carlisle's Trustees. Complaints were levelled at the N.E.R., too, for not building their own branch to Brampton, all of which serves to prove that at all times the majority of the local people wanted a railway and were not opposed to it.

By the third week of March 1872 the N.E.R. was surveying for a possible route into Brampton, their engineers considering three routes. Two of these would use the Dandy line, both leaving this at different points to terminate near The Sands. The third was by Rowbank, Beckside and Hamblesgate to a similar terminus. The last route was most favoured but costly, and the N.E.R. said that if their study to provide a loop line to Brampton was proven feasible, a clause covering it would be put into one of their applications to Parliament as soon as possible. On 6 September 1872 the N.E.R. said that they could not make a branch to Brampton at present. At this point Mr. Waugh again tried to promote his 3ft.-gauge light railway but still failed to raise the necessary funds.

This double blow to the locality is typified by this extract from a letter published in the *Carlisle Patriot* on 13 September 1872:

> ... I am sorry, because by the refusal we are condemned to almost starvation, by being compelled to burn the stuff sent to the coal hole, and it is my opinion as a working man that the Lord Carlisle should not act the part he does in winking at the monopoly of those representing him in these parts by practically insisting that we shall either burn anything that is sent to us, or starve without grumble.

(In local dialect the word "starve" means to go cold.)

The actual attitude of Lord Carlisle's Trustees was not known to such complainers, but it is plain from surviving papers that the Trustees were all for freedom of coal sales in Brampton, but how to get Thompsons to give up their sole right to the Brampton branch and the coal staith when they were integral with their lease was an acute problem.

During 1874-5 further applications to the N.E.R. to take over the branch again failed, for Thompsons would not give up the coal staith, even if the N.E.R. took over and ran the passenger services.

In March 1876 Thompsons proposed that the Trustees should purchase the necessary land to enable the existing line to be extended nearer the town and construct a station and coal depot there. Thompsons offered to pay the 3% interest on the outlay involved, provide all the plant, equipment, rails, rolling stock and locomotives. The cost of this scheme to the Trustees was estimated at £3,000 and Thompsons £4,000.

After careful consideration, the Trustees' adviser, Mr. R. Du Cane, said that the plan was feasible but that the Trustees had little power to undertake such a scheme, which he said in any case was only likely to facilitate the sales of Thompsons' coal at the proposed new depot at Pickerings Hill. This was duly conveyed by Du Cane to Thomas Thompson who was told that the line and its improved operation would benefit the town, but could not be supported financially by the Trustees. He went on to say that the people of Brampton must take up the problem themselves and that if they did, no doubt the N.E.R. could be persuaded to assist.

Discontent among the Brampton people continued, to culminate in a public meeting held in the Howard Arms Hotel in Brampton on Tuesday, 20 April 1880. The meeting was large and substantially supported by influential people ready to discuss the problem.

Again, blame was aimed at the original routing of the N. & C.R., which was, one speaker said, ". . . diverted to suit powerful private interests." Alternative routes for new branch lines were put forward, while the N.E.R., too, did not go unscathed. One speaker described the N.E.R. station at Brampton (or rather, Milton) as being ". . . like no station I have ever seen . . .", having low platforms, without any warning to that effect; there was no shelter on the eastbound platform, while the station name of Brampton was misleading. The traveller needing to get to Brampton must then travel, the speaker said, "... in a remarkable vehicle with two compartments in which both luggage and passengers must travel". The journey was described as, at least, alarming to the stranger, especially on its horseless run to the staith, together with the question of what would happen if the brake failed. For this, and the long trudge into the town, the fare of 3d. was charged.

The vehicle was said to have no cushions; travellers who were lucky enough to get inside being crushed together—ladies, gentlemen and workmen in working dress—and that although smoking was not allowed it was said to be frequently carried on. Even on normal days, one speaker related, the vehicle was usually full, with others hanging precariously on the outside, while on special occasions, such as electioneering and agricultural show times when extra accommodation was required, an open truck was put on and passengers expected to sit in that. There was no doubt at all that the effect on the commercial life of Brampton would be greatly disadvantageous until the town obtained more suitable railway facilities.

Another speaker pointed out the extra charge paid on goods for using the branch, while the coal sold at the staith was said to be the worst in the area. After many more points had been made, the meeting resolved to send a deputation of Brampton people to meet the N.E.R. Directors, but did not intend it to be a reflection on either the N.E.R. or Lord Carlisle's Trustees, for they needed new or improved railway facilities, no matter who provided them.

The proposer of the last motion was told that Major Thompson had offered to put a locomotive on the passenger service and improve the station at the staith, but that he (Major Thompson) doubted this would meet the requirements of the town. This scheme was not seen as the answer since it still failed to permit competitive coal traffic to use the staith.

One of Lord Carlisle's Trustee representatives reminded the gathering that the fault of a lack of competitive coal supply lay now within the province of the Brampton people themselves, for the restrictions prohibiting the laying down of coal and lime within the Barony of Gilsland by the N.E.R. had been abandoned in February 1875, thus leaving the way clear for the provision of such facilities anywhere in the barony. This, however, excluded the line leased to Thompsons, and as the only staith in the district was on this line, the monopoly effectively still existed.

The following extract from a letter dated 28 April 1880 throws some light on the problem:

> The N. & C.R. Acts prohibited the company from constructing wharfs and staiths for the deposit or sale of coal or lime on land acquired for other purposes in the Barony of Gilsland without the consent of the Earl of Carlisle.
> ... the clauses which prohibited the company from appropriating land for the erection of coal staiths sold to them for making a railway did not apply to

other persons wishing to erect coal staiths, and that so far as the Earl of Carlisle is concerned, any number of coal staiths could have been established in the Barony notwithstanding these clauses since 1829.

The letter from Mr. C. Stephenson, Secretary to Lord Carlisle's Trustees, ably states the case and removes the blame entirely from Naworth and back on to the people of Brampton.

During May 1880 Du Cane told the Trustees that the N.E.R. should take over the branch but that again the Thompsons were not in agreement. Complaints about the N.E.R. station at Brampton (Milton) were voiced throughout 1880 until, finally, the railway company agreed to improve it, but would not construct a new branch to Brampton. The work had commenced by November 1880, including raising the platforms by 10in., widening the eastbound platform to 20ft. and providing new waiting rooms.

The coal monopoly was again raised in the Carlisle press during early 1881. Lord Carlisle's representative, Mr. C. Stephenson, speaking for the Trustees, said that the N.E.R. had never been prohibited from selling or delivering coal on their own railway within the barony, only from setting up coal staiths in the barony, while private interests had always been free to do so since 1829. This statement appeared to have cleared up the problem of the coal monopoly once and for all, leaving the largely politically-motivated opponents without ammunition.

On Monday, 4 July 1881 the hopes of the Brampton people were evidenced in a tangible form when the old one-horse Dandy, after forty-five years of service, was replaced on the Brampton branch by what was described as "a powerful tank locomotive", bought from Neilson & Co. Ltd. of Glasgow, and a set of three comfortable ex-L.N.W.R. passenger carriages. With First and Third Class accommodation totalling fifty seats, there was little doubt now that this was a very welcome improvement. The local press said, "Messrs. Thompson, without solicitation, undertook to provide a steam engine and suitable carriages for use on Lord Carlisle's line of which they are lessees".

Improvements undertaken at the coal staith, Fig. 33, included a proper platform, a waiting room and a new approach road, while the branch itself was relaid with steel rails on wooden sleepers, indicating that the fish-belly rails on stone block sleepers dating from July 1836 had remained in use until 1881. When asked about the possibility of extending the branch nearer to the town, Thompsons did not rule this out, when funds became available.

The old horse-drawn Dandy made its last trip at 10.30 a.m. and soon afterwards the new locomotive, named *Dandie Dinmont*, drawing its train bedecked with flowers and evergreens, drew up at Brampton (Milton) station after travelling from Kirkhouse, being then boarded by the official party.

The party included Major Thompson, his wife and daughter, Mr. C. Lacy Thompson, Mr. James Thompson of Milton, and various other local people who had campaigned for the improvements. The train then set off "at a fair pace to Brampton coal staith", where a small crowd of spectators welcomed it. After its return to Brampton (Milton) Station, the station improvements were inspected before the party had lunch at Milton Hall. The new train ran at regular intervals during the day, operating a free service to allow people to sample the new service, which did the journey in three minutes compared with twenty minutes by the horse Dandy.

Mr. R. Du Cane, writing to the Trustees of Lord Carlisle, said that "The carriages which Mr. Thompson has put on are excellent in every respect—the 3rd Class so good that the 1st Class might be dispensed with". Fig. 35. He then added "If the Brampton people are not satisfied with the accommodation given and intended, they may make their own railway".

During the late summer of 1881 Messrs. Thompsons asked the Trustees if they would build a new road to the staith, from the Newcastle road, to improve access, while Thompsons proposed generally to clean up the site, construct a station house for £100, and a shed for the locomotive and carriages. The road did not materialise but a carriage shed was built.

The passenger service continued, but in the autumn of 1889 when the Thompson lease was due for renewal, Mr. Hugh Jackson, Chairman of the Brampton Railway Committee, suggested that the renewal might be used as a lever to obtain an even better railway service and an improvement in the quality of coal sold at the staith. Jackson said that the coal suffered from inefficient screening, which resulted in much dust and dirt being sold mixed with the round coals.

By this time the eighth Earl's Trustees had handed over the estate to George Howard, ninth Earl of Carlisle, who in turn let his successful business-woman wife, Lady Rosalind Carlisle, manage his affairs while he concentrated on his great interest in art and crafts, being a close friend of William Morris and his associates. Lady Carlisle told Hugh Jackson on 7 November 1889 that a strong expression of local opinion was needed from influential people, to the effect that the branch railway from the staith to Brampton Junction (renamed from Brampton in January 1885) would be better in the hands of the N.E.R. She continued by saying:

> This railroad question is a very delicate matter with the Thompsons . . . I think that a forcible expression of responsible opinion from businessmen in Brampton would show the Thompsons that there is a real and reasonable desire resting on solid grounds, to have free railroad communication to Brampton.

The Thompsons were approached but made it clear that they would not allow the branch line to be taken from their lease and that the passenger service was being run at a very low profit and that if it was not for the coal traffic and sales from the staith, it would be unwise to operate it. The following report was furnished to Lady Carlisle on 25 March 1890:

	1883-4	1884-5	1885-6	1886-7	1887-8	1888-9
Receipts	587	609	566	570	569	557
Expenses	545	555	594	581	541	587
Gain	42	44	—	—	28	—
Loss	—	—	28	11	—	30

No doubt thinking of Hugh Jackson's suggestion of using a lever to persuade Thompsons to relinquish their lease on the branch before their lease was renewed, Lady Carlisle arranged for the branch line to be inspected by the Board of Trade Inspector of Railways, Major-General Hutchinson, who duly visited the line on 22 March 1890. However, this reason is only one suggestion, others just as applicable being that once the line was found unfit for passengers Thompsons would be free of their obligation to provide the service and able to continue with the profitable coal traffic alone over the line. At the same time, it was hoped, the cost of putting the branch into suitable condition to meet the requirements of the B.o.T. Inspector would be sufficient to dissuade the N.E.R. from their intention to take over the line.

From this we gather that it was the idea of Lady Carlisle to have the inspection, but as may be seen, the hoped-for results appear to have been more in favour of the lessees, Messrs. Thompsons, than the people of Brampton.

The ruling of the B.o.T. Inspector was set out in the new lease to Thompsons. The Inspector, as was expected, said the line was unfit for passenger operation and required the following changes:

1. At Brampton terminus . . . all sidings to be provided with throw-off points connected with facing points by rod and key attached to a staff carried by the engineman. Coke stage to be removed from the main line, sharp curve near platform to have check rail, platform to end in ramps not steps, clock to be visible from platform.

2. Loop siding to be removed or provided with throw-off and facing points as above.

3. Loop siding at Brampton Junction to be similarly treated.

4. All points to have double connecting rods.

5. Fencing to be repaired and renewed when necessary.

6. Mile posts and gradient boards to be erected.

7. Rolling stock: engine to have six wheels and both it and the carriages to be fitted with continuous and automatic brakes. Carriages to be fitted also with continuous foot boards.

On 25 March Messrs. Thompsons wrote to Hugh Jackson:

> In the event of the N.E.R. deciding not to take possession of the railway, we are not in the position to fulfil all the requirements of the Board of Trade in connection with passenger traffic, and, therefore, we shall not be able to continue to carry passengers between Brampton Junction and Brampton coal staith.

The urgency of the question now became very apparent and feverish discussions were going on in Brampton, and their petition to the N.E.R. had been supplemented by a letter from the Brampton Railway Committee asking for temporary relief to meet the emergency which would arise by the end of April when the train service had to stop. The B.o.T. requirements were a great problem to Thompsons, but not, it was felt, to the N.E.R. The impression that the gradient on the branch was the problem is, in fact, erroneous, as the B.o.T. made the point that this was no obstacle to rolling stock and a locomotive of suitable type with continuous brakes. An efficient signalling and block working system was required but these were obviously no problem to the N.E.R., likewise the provision of suitable locomotives and rolling stock which they had already.

Although block working of the branch is mentioned it appears that the line was worked on the one engine in steam method.

An interesting fact now emerges in that Thompsons were amenable to the N.E.R. taking over the branch, provided they still had running powers over it for their coal traffic—this was to be the principal problem in the N.E.R.'s takeover of the line.

Other demands made by Thompsons in late March 1890 were:

> That we be paid the value of the rails and sleepers thereon, and also the value of the station, platform and carriage shed, but not necessarily the value of the locomotive and carriages.

In order to alleviate the position, suggestions as to the forms of alternative transport were considered, such as locally-run omnibuses or coaches to connect the town with How Mill station, while the newspapers even dared to suggest that the old Dandy might be reinstated!

On the fateful day, Wednesday, 30 April 1890, in accordance with their published notices, Thompsons withdrew the passenger train, although some hope was still held locally since the N.E.R. had not yet answered the Railway Committee's petition, and the proposal put to them by Thompsons that they should hire to them a properly equipped train for use on the branch.

Suggestions that a local company be formed to take over the branch came to nothing, and in the meantime omnibuses were being run between Brampton and Brampton Junction to connect with trains. The advantage of this was that they ran from the centre of Brampton, eliminating the long walk to and from the coal staith required in order to use the train service.

By the end of 1890 nothing had transpired with the N.E.R. and Thompsons were quite happily operating the branch for their coal traffic as usual. Although agitation continued, no one would apparently take the necessary practical steps, which position was to continue for over twenty years.

CHAPTER 9

Reopening Schemes

A number of schemes were talked about in trying to resolve the railway problem of Brampton, but only one of these was really worked out. This one, in 1903, was for a private railway to replace the "Dandy" line, which was also to serve the town of Brampton by providing a transport system actually in the town itself.

The scheme was investigated and reported on by Mr. S. T. Harrison of George Harrison & Co., engineers, electricians and millwrights, of Ure Bank Engine Works, Ripon, who presented his report dated 2 July 1903 to Mr. Lief Jones the following day, for consideration by Lady Carlisle and the Railway Committee.

The report, entitled "The Brampton Light Railway Scheme", was as follows. Mr. Harrison had met Hugh Jackson, and the difficulties of such a small scheme had been discussed, Harrison considering that Jackson was capable of piloting the scheme to its conclusion if accepted.

Both visited the site on 26-27 June 1903, going over each route, considering operational information on the old "Dandy line" and the number of passengers using Brampton Junction Station. Four routes were considered. One was to use the Dandy line to reach the staith, then pass behind Wesley House on to the Newcastle to Carlisle road (A69), across the Sands, over Pickering's Hill, down Moat Side and Main Street to opposite the Magistrates' Office, returning up Front Street via St. Martin's Church to the Market Place. The circuit was completed by returning along High Cross Street to rejoin its line in Main Street. The second proposal again went to the staith, behind Wesley House and on to the main road, across the Sands, down Lovers Lane to Craw Hall and into the Market Place.

The third route made use of the Dandy line in part, breaking away across Hamblesgate fields, over Tree Road, through Mansion House Park to High Cross Street. The fourth route was not specified, but was to follow the route used by the bus.

The first three would have required the payment of Thompsons for the value of the rails and sleepers, although many sleepers were by this time rotten. A grooved tram rail would be used and continue right through the town, being laid on a concrete bed with the rails level with the road surface; a depot would be made in Moat Side.

Some street widening would be necessary in the first scheme and speed limits imposed, while the second required some widening, and straightening in Lovers Lane and an entrance from Craw Hall; an expensive scheme. The third route would need an embankment over Hamblesgate fields, Tree House fields and Mansion House Park, a bridge over Tree Road and the purchasing of property in High Cross Street for a terminus; again an expensive scheme. Scheme four was possible but the cost of a tramway all the way would be prohibitive.

The first scheme seemed the best and Mr. Harrison considered it could be built over a 7-10 year period to spread costs, completing initially the section to the depot.

Thompsons had supplied the branch passenger figures for 1886/7/9:

1886	August	947	passengers per week
	September	903	,, ,, ,,
1887	January	698	,, ,, ,,
	February	549	,, ,, ,,
1889	June	1,314	,, ,, ,,
	July	987	,, ,, ,,

This gave an average of 900 passengers weekly, not including season tickets, parcels and mail traffics. On 25 March 1890 the Dandy line had an average income of £576. The fare was 3d. single so that the average income was equal to 46,000 single fares annually.

The figures for people alighting at Brampton Junction from N.E.R. trains in 1902 were:

Excursionists	2,850
Ordinary tickets	28,800
Contract tickets	2,300
Weekend, holiday tourist and special tickets	8,500
	42,450

After taking into account that 15% of passengers did not go to Brampton, and if another 25% did not use the railway, a figure of about 27,000 passenger journeys, 54,000 if doubled as return journeys, would give a fair estimate of, say, 1,000 single fares each week.

The current bus fare was quoted as 6d. The light railway might charge 4d., giving an income of £855 per annum on 52,000 single fares.

Of the type of traction, Harrison said an overhead electric trolley was too expensive, as were steam railcars—mainly due to high standby costs. He suggested a petrol motor-tramcar of 10 h.p. with a capacity of 16 passengers. Two cars would be required, the second being used as a standby and in busy periods. Two trailer cars of 16 passengers' capacity were also required. His estimates were as follows:

	£	s.	d.
Dandy line—purchase of old rails, sleepers and putting in good order	1000	0	0
5,000ft. of new single track for Scheme No. 1	2900	0	0
Land from coal staith to road	25	0	0
2×10 h.p. Motor-tramcars	1500	0	0
Cost of light railway order, fees, drawings and attendance at enquiry	200	0	0
	6075	0	0

WORKING EXPENSES

	£	s.	d.
Wages: 1 Mechanic driver and 1 Assistant driver ..	132	0	0
2 Conductors (1 Part-time)	52	0	0
Running expenses—petrol, oil, repairs	200	0	0
Repairs to permanent way and buildings	100	0	0
Rates, taxes, water, printing	30	0	0
Secretary's salary	20	0	0
5% of £6,100	305	0	0
	839	0	0

Mr. Harrison said such a line could not afford a full-time manager, and surplus income must be saved for replacements, etc., while if the local authority insisted on granite sets or wooden blocks for setting of the rails, the scheme would not be feasible.

The scheme was presented to the Parish Council and to Lord and Lady Carlisle, prior to seeking views and objections to its route and effects on property, with the idea of putting the No. 1 scheme into action by the autumn of 1903. This was not to be, as the objections proved too strong, and in the view of some the costs of re-routing and the acquisition of property for demolition in any case doomed the idea to failure.

On 27 January 1904, a public meeting took place to discuss the desirability of improving the travelling facilities by means of a light railway or other mode of transport.

The meeting, chaired by Hugh Jackson, received from Mr. C. Lacy Thompson some figures relating to the steam passenger service of 1881 to 1890:

YEAR	NUMBER OF FIRST CLASS	NUMBER OF SECOND CLASS	TOTALS
1885	440	43,169½	43,609
1889	316	43,272	43,588

The earnings of these figures were:

		£	s.	d.
1885	First Class	11	0	0
	Third Class	539	10	0
	Parcels (excluding N.E.R. parcels delivered by road)	24	0	0
	Mail	26	0	0
	Passes	7	0	0
	Total	£607	10	0
1889	Total	£605	10	0

Figures for the number of passengers travelling by the old Dandy on Brampton Agricultural Show days, using carriages lent by the N.E.R. to supplement the Dandy train were:

Year			Year		
1885	1,619½	passengers	1888	1,765½	passengers
1886	1,411½	,,	1889	2,164¼	,,
1887	1,590½	,,			

The discussion which followed said, among other things, that Mr. Harrison's passenger figures were underestimated, but that this was all to the good. The meeting agreed unanimously to carry out the scheme and passed the motion that it was ". . . highly desirable that travelling facilities between Brampton Junction and the town of Brampton should be improved by means of a light railway or otherwise".

Accordingly, a new committee of 28 members was set up, including Lady Carlisle, Hugh Jackson, Mr. Cook of the Carlisle Tramways Co., Lief Jones and C. Lacey Thompson. Their first meeting on 29 February 1904 resolved to remind the N.E.R. of the petition of fourteen years previously, when Lord Carlisle had agreed to sell them the line, and to see if Lord Carlisle was still agreeable to the sale. This proved to be the case and on 8 July 1904 the N.E.R. were offered the line provided they also paid Thompsons for the plant, etc.

The N.E.R. replied in October 1904, suggesting that Lord Carlisle make the line suitable for passenger traffic so that, with an appropriate arrangement with

Thompsons, the N.E.R. would then be pleased to operate the line. The N.E.R., in this hardly extravagant offer, no doubt remembered that in 1890 the line had been offered to them as a gift and had no intention of paying large sums for refitting the branch line or for a lease.

Negotiations dragged on, culminating by December 1905 with the lessees, Thompsons, insisting that the N.E.R. work all the traffic on the line, including their coal traffic, as they did not think the B.o.T. would permit Thompsons' trains to operate on a line carrying a public passenger service, and without adequate signalling, which only could be installed at a high cost.

The same month, Sir George Gibb, the N.E.R. General Manager, wrote to say that the line would be a great public convenience, but feared it would not yield a profit. However, provided a long lease at a nominal figure of £5 per year could be agreed, they might consider putting the line in order and operating it. A draft lease was prepared dated 18 December 1905, the main points being:

1. The N.E.R. to have a long lease of the line at a nominal rent, so long as Messrs. Thompson pay interest in full on the £10,000 plant.

2. In the event of Messrs. Thompsons' payment of interest being reduced on account of the railway plant being given up, the N.E.R. should make good the deficiency and pay rent accordingly. If the line should cease to be used for colliery purposes, the N.E.R. should pay interest at 3% on the capital value of the Brampton line which they give up, seeing that their coal will continue to be carried over the line on terms (to be arranged) not less favourable to them than that of the present arrangement. It must be understood that if the N.E.R. take over sole control of the line, an arrangement must be made for the carriage of Thompsons' coal as shall in no way place them in a worse position than they are at present, as far as the carriage of their coal is concerned.

3. Messrs. Thompson are bound upon termination of their tenancy to hand over to Lord Carlisle colliery plant to the value of £10,000. It is agreed that in the event of the N.E.R. taking over the line, the £10,000 be reduced by the capital value of the plant of the line (valued as a colliery line). The N.E.R. would, therefore, in turn upon a termination of their tenancy hand over the line in as good a condition as that in which they receive it, being of no less capital value than at present.

4. The N.E.R. should agree to extend to further lessees of the Naworth collieries the same facilities agreed at present with Messrs. Thompson.

5. If the agreement is carried through with the N.E.R. a suitable clause must be added to the colliery lease.

6. No legal expenses should be put upon Lord Carlisle in connection with the transfer of the line from Messrs. Thompsons to the N.E.R.

With various safeguards Lord Carlisle was, by late December 1905, ready to lease the line to the N.E.R. However, nothing materialised and on 19 April 1907 Hugh Jackson urged Lord Carlisle to find out the position, since it was sixteen months since the N.E.R. had agreed to work the branch.

In April two letters arrived from the N.E.R. to say that the matter was in hand and that the N.E.R. General Manager, A. Kaye Butterworth, had made some progress with Thompsons on the matter which would, it was hoped, form the basis of an agreement.

The position was still the same in October 1907 but on 2 December Mr. Philip Burtt, the N.E.R. Traffic Manager, wrote from York to say that they had practically come to terms with Messrs. Thompsons and, subject to the settlement between Thompsons and Lord Carlisle, they hoped to put on an "auto-car" service with a fare of 6d. First Class and 3d. Third Class early the following summer.

On 12 December 1907 some N.E.R. officials met Messrs. Thompsons at Brampton to make the final arrangements, pointing out that for the present they did not intend to extend the line nearer to Brampton. The legal proceedings were long and it was not until the end of March 1908 that the draft lease reached Mr. Burtt at York. Sadly, the whole project was upset by the Roachburn colliery disaster in January 1908 and the subsequent announcement by Thompsons of their decision to terminate their lease of the Naworth coalfield and railways.

In spite of the demise of Messrs. Thompsons at Naworth, the N.E.R. proceeded with their deliberations and on 25 May 1908 were negotiating directly with Lord Carlisle, with a view to obtaining a fifty-year lease on the Brampton branch, who, in turn, was thinking more in terms of a twenty-year lease. The shorter lease was prompted by a number of offers to lease the coal staith, which Lord and Lady Carlisle hoped would become a public siding, so ending the erstwhile coal monopoly.

Mr. Burtt of the N.E.R. met Hugh Jackson on 26 June 1908 and inspected the branch, the outcome being that it must be relaid and the route levelled before passenger services began, as the line was quite unfit for N.E.R. locomotives and rolling stock. The work considered necessary would disrupt coal supplied to the staith for several weeks, but it would be stocked to overcome this and the work carried out as quickly as possible so that services might commence on 1 January 1909.

As to the coal staith, the N.E.R. wanted it on a long lease, appointing their stationmaster as the agent to sell coal on a 5% commission—while lowering his salary appropriately! This commission would be added to the coal he sold as the N.E.R. profit came from carrying the coal. Private coal traffic would be delivered by the waggon load to the staith and no commission charged.

It was to be the coal staith which would hold up proceedings next—owing to the lack of agreement on a suitable rent, and the tonnages likely to be handled there. A figure of 9,000 to 10,000 tons had been stated by the Parish Council and the N.E.R. as likely, and a rent of £100 per year quoted. Lack of space for a free

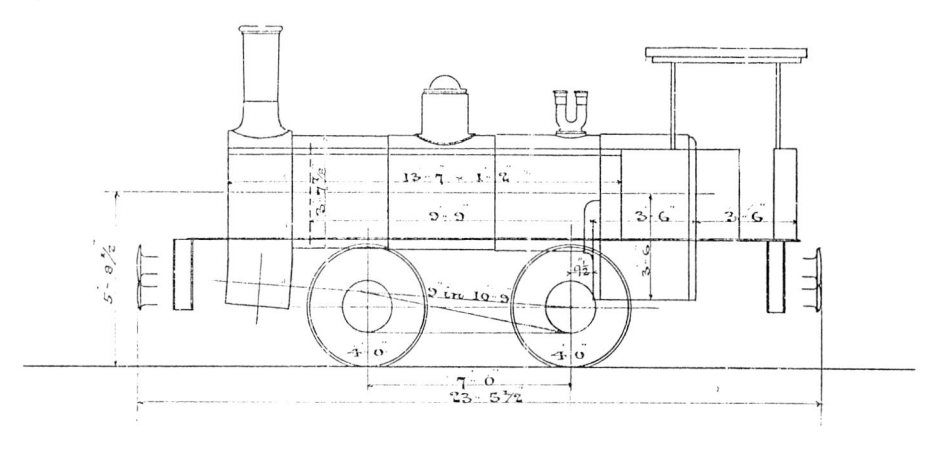

Fig. 60 Outline diagram of *Dandie Dinmont* 0-4-0Toc (N 2738/81).
(*Mitchell Library, Glasgow*)

Fig. 61 *Dandie Dinmont* at the end of its career dumped in a siding, probably in the late 1920s, and at Hallbankgate.
(*Collection of B. Webb*)

Fig. 62 *Dandie Dinmont* after rebuilding by Barclay in 1903 and in use as a mineral locomotive. *(Collection of B. Webb)*

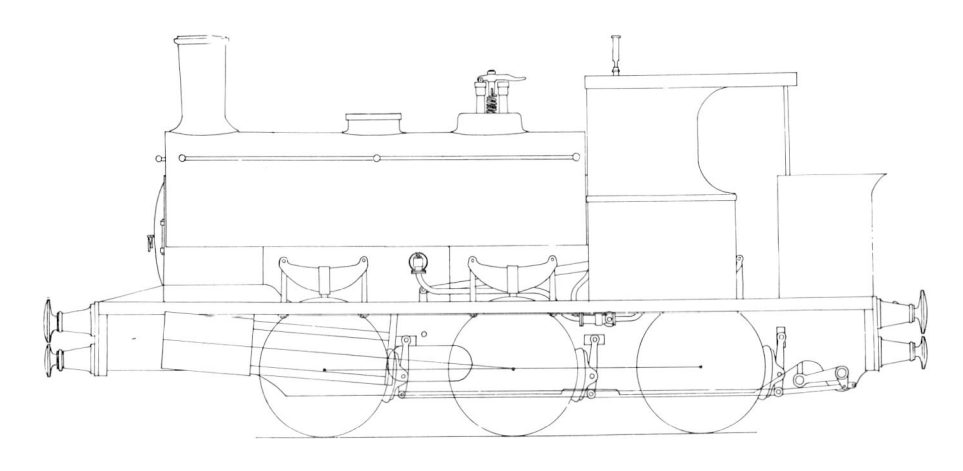

Fig. 63 Side elevation of *Sheriff* 0-6-0SToc (AB 903/00), the last locomotive purchased by Messrs. Thompsons. *(Andrew Barclay, Sons & Co. Ltd.)*

Fig. 64   *Sheriff* at work near Midgeholme about 1907.   (*Collection of F. Jones*)

Fig. 65   *Belted Will* shunting, probably around 1920.   (*Locomotive Club of Great Britain*)

Fig. 66 Official photograph of *Naworth No. 6* 0-4-0SToc (AB 1365/14) purchased by the Naworth Coal Co. Ltd. after Thompsons demise. (*Andrew Barclay, Sons & Co. Ltd.*)

Fig. 67 *Naworth No. 6* standing in Kirkhouse sidings opposite the Gasworks buildings during the 1930s. Loco now fitted with small coal bunker. (*L. G. Charlton*)

Fig. 68 Official photograph of *Tindale* 0-6-0SToc (AE 1954/25) as built prior to naming and sale to the Naworth Collieries Co. Ltd. in 1926. *(Collection of B. Webb)*

Fig. 69 *Tindale* shunting Kirkhouse sidings in May 1946. *(Harold D. Bowtell)*

Fig. 70   *Tindale* climbing from Kirkhouse up the incline plane to Hallbankgate amid the snows of winter. *(Fleetwood Shawe)*

Fig. 71   Frames of *Tindale* on the Co-op siding at Hallbankgate in 1952. *(J. W. Armstrong)*

Fig. 72 Official photograph of *Stephenson* 0-6-0SToc (AB 1879/26) purchased by Naworth Collieries Co. Ltd., and the largest locomotive to work on the railway.
(*Collection of Fleetwood Shawe*)

Fig. 73 *Stephenson* at work near Whites Cut in May 1946. (*Harold D. Bowtell*)

Fig. 74 *Stephenson* standing at Hallbankgate in 1951. (*J. Hayes*)

Fig. 75 The last two operative locomotives under the N.C.B. were *Alice* 0-6-0SToc (AE 1460/03) purchased secondhand by Naworth Collieries Co. Ltd., and *Stephenson*. Here they are seen at Planehead Hallbankgate in the early 1950's. (*Collection of B. Webb*)

public siding was noted, as was the disinclination of the N.E.R. to accommodate private depots due to their traffic interfering with that of their own.

Figures of coal, lime and stone sold at the staith were obtained from Thompsons for the year ending May 1908:

Coal ordinary	5,760 tons
Small coal	1,037 ,,
	6,797 ,,
Coke	88 tons 5 cwt.
Coal and coke total	6,885 tons 5 cwt.
Lime	404 tons 4 cwt.
Stone	1,020 tons 4 cwt.
Total tonnage	8,309 tons 13 cwt.

During July 1908 the N.E.R. decided on a lower offer for the railway plant on the branch, which was valued, in their opinion, at £650 and not £1,000 as previously, the change being due to its poor condition and its use only as a mineral railway. The permanent way was put at 12s. per yard and the stone platform at £132. This revision was, the N.E.R. said, due to the termination of Thompsons' lease and the fact that they could no longer fulfil their obligations, and to Lord Carlisle's obligation to purchase the railway as a mineral railway from Thompsons.

The N.E.R. said they had offered Thompsons a carriage rate for their coal of 6d. per ton, but were now free to negotiate their own terms with colliery companies, and wanted only to take over Lord Carlisle's obligation at £650. Moreover, they said that if this was not agreed to, they would discontinue negotiations.

The matter was now rather delicate and the advice of Sir Hugh Bell, Lord Carlisle's friend and adviser, having been sought, the matter was allowed to drift since there was obviously little financial attraction for the N.E.R. from the branch.

After discussions and then a meeting between Lord Carlisle, Sir Hugh Bell, Mr. Burtt, Mr. Forster (Lord Carlisle's mines agent and viewer), Mr. Du Cane and Lief Jones in London, Sir Hugh Bell said, "The N.E.R. are anxious to meet the convenience of Brampton but foresee a loss on the operation. Lord Carlisle is willing to meet the wishes of the people of Brampton without getting any personal advantage from the scheme".

The main problem now was that when negotiations had been almost completed between the N.E.R. and Messrs. Thompsons, they had given up their lease, altering the position entirely. The N.E.R. had dealt for years with Thompsons, but felt they could not offer the same terms to a new lessee with whom they had no experience, nor contemplate the coal staith being in a third party's hands, though they had no objection to Thompsons or Lord Carlisle having the coal depot.

The N.E.R. said that they needed the coal depot to give them their profit on the branch, saying that if the depot handled 7,500 tons annually the scheme would work out as follows:

Rent asked	£100
Wages of men	£200
Repairs, etc.	£50
	£350

5% commission on 7,500 put at £1 is £375

Lord Carlisle said he would take £75 rent and Mr. Burtt said the N.E.R. would give £25.

From this the way seemed clear to return to the agreement being finalised with Thompsons and continue from there. However, the question of haulage from Brampton Junction was to provide another period of delay. If the coal depot belonged to Lord Carlisle and he worked it, the N.E.R. would have to deal only with his Lordship and charge 6d. per ton haulage, but if the N.E.R. themselves had the depot and operated it they would have to charge 1s. per ton haulage. The next step was the price of the line, the figure of £1,429 16s. 0d. being agreed with Thompsons, which was allowed to stand as satisfactory.

From these points the matter progressed and it was during November and December 1908 that the lease was being worked out. On 29 December 1908 Lord and Lady Carlisle and Mr. Forster set out the following:

1. The railway would be leased for fifty years at £5 per year.

2. The Naworth colliery must reserve the right to cross the North Eastern Railway at Brampton Junction.

3. The Naworth Coal Co. should have a siding at Brampton Junction.

4. Should a number of coal cells be reserved for the exclusive use of Naworth Coal Co. at the coal staith?

5. Is the Naworth Coal Co. right in thinking that its waggons would only be taken to the staith once or twice a week, and should the right to take them more frequently be safeguarded?

6. Lord Carlisle would not manage the coal depot and either the N.E.R. or Naworth Coal Co. must do it.

7. If the N.E.R. had the depot, Mr. Forster agreed to try to arrange access to it for the colliery company, coal traffic to be hauled when ready or daily, and also a lower rate of haulage than 1s. if possible.

It was agreed that if these last three points were accepted, the N.E.R. could have the depot.

By February 1909 Hugh Jackson, who had heard nothing of these transactions since June 1908, due to their confidential nature, wrote to Lady Carlisle to enquire if any further progress had been made; in due course his questions were answered.

In March 1909 the N.E.R. reduced their offer of October 1908 of £100 rent for the coal staith to £50, proposing also to carry the Naworth coal over the branch for 9d. per ton instead of 1s. The reduction in the coal haulage rate was still considered prohibitive by the Naworth Coal Co., who pointed out that the N.E.R. proposed to carry other collieries' coal for 3d. per ton. Such were the problems which continually dogged the negotiations over the branch line. Lord and Lady Carlisle continued to try to aid the situation by offering improved rentals for the coal staith but problems still persisted.

Mr. George Clark of the Naworth Coal Co. stated that the N.E.R. were certain to want to alter the present colliery line which crossed their Newcastle to Carlisle main line at Brampton Junction on the level, a legacy of Lord Carlisle's demands of 1829 and, that the level crossing was considered dangerous and very difficult to keep in good condition, not to mention the expense. By this Mr. Clark was inferring a possible loss of access to the Brampton branch from the colliery railway, a suggestion Lord and Lady Carlisle could not contemplate, but they had no objection to the installation by the N.E.R. of a different type of crossing, provided Lord Carlisle's interests were safeguarded.

On 6 August 1909 a plan of Brampton Junction showing the proposed diversion of Lord Carlisle's railway which the N.E.R. desired to make at the point where it crossed the main line was studied by Lord and Lady Carlisle with the railway company's representative, and it was said that no objection would be made to the proposed zigzag crossing to replace the diamond crossing, even if the N.E.R. decided not to lease the line. Fig. 34.

Throughout the summer of 1909 the Naworth Coal Co. was arguing about the charges the N.E.R. proposed to make for the use of sidings at Brampton Junction, and bearing in mind the possible loss of the coal staith, this was hardly surprising. In August 1909 the Naworth Coal Co. informed Lady Carlisle that they needed the coal staith for selling Roachburn coal, which was not liked in Carlisle, and would not be able to continue to operate the stricken colliery at all if this outlet was removed—even with this only 110 tons had been sold during July.

By the end of 1909 it was decided to continue the lease of the staith to the Naworth Coal Co. on a yearly basis, and separately from the colliery lease, to prevent any continuation of monopolistic coal sales. At the same time, the N.E.R. were to have a private siding at the staith.

The rent for the staith was to be £60 per year provided the Naworth Coal Co. maintained it, and they were reminded that their £60 rent was identical to that to be charged to the N.E.R. for their lease, who were to spend £300 in improvements to the staith.

On 2 August 1910 the N.E.R. General Manager, A. Kaye Butterworth, wrote Lord Carlisle that the matter was still under consideration, but that the N.E.R. must have sidings for the retailing of coal at the staith in addition to the Naworth Coal Co. Butterworth continued at length, stating that the sum of £1,429 16s. 0d. had been offered for the material on the branch because Messrs. Thompsons had agreed to consign all their traffic via the branch railway, so securing a sure income to the N.E.R. He said ". . . our engineer has never appraised the permanent way material at more than £500 to £650 and that was five years ago".

Butterworth said the railway had depreciated since 1905 and thus it was necessary to incur expenditure in the region of £3,500, in addition to the £1,429 16s. 0d. to be paid to Lord Carlisle, before passenger services could operate. Also, there was the cost of a locomotive and rolling stock which would be exclusively used on the branch. As to traffic potential, Butterworth said the passenger service probably would give only a slender gain, while there was no agreement with Naworth Coal Co. about their coal traffic using the branch, and that in 1890 when Thompsons withdrew their passenger traffic, the line had been offered to the N.E.R. free of charge. He then suggested that the 1890 offer should be remade to enable the modifications to be done for about £2,000.

Eventually, the N.E.R. put its proposals again to Lord Carlisle when, on 1 November 1910, A. Kaye Butterworth said he recommended his directors to take over the line under the arrangement previously discussed with Mr. T. E. Forster, as follows:

1. The company to pay Lord Carlisle the sum of £500 for the rails, sleepers and platforms at Brampton staith.

OR

2. The company to take over the existing railway and equip it for passenger working, without payment to Lord Carlisle. After the line has been brought into use and working expenses have been deducted from the gross receipts, the balance to be divided as follows:

Lord Carlisle	..	One-third
N.E.R.	..	Two-thirds

This would be their final offer.

Lord Carlisle was, however, obviously losing out here because of the £1,429 16s. 0d. he had paid to Thompsons for the branch in 1908, and thought £500 too low. He said he would accept £1,025 for the line, which was still double what the N.E.R. was prepared to pay.

Later, in December 1910, Butterworth said they would not pay £1,025, saying that the N.E.R. ought to have the line free, but said they could split the difference between £1,025 and £500 and arrive at £762, offering, in fact, £750.

Sir Hugh Bell, bearing in mind that the line was likely to be a burden on the N.E.R. and that really they probably did not want it at all now, recommended Lord Carlisle to sacrifice £250-£300 to secure the service Brampton required. The branch would be offered to Lord Carlisle upon the lease being given up by the N.E.R., but not at the same price at which it had been taken over in view of the modifications made to it.

Troubles again arose with the Naworth Coal Co., who were operating the staith, and this gave Lord and Lady Carlisle an opportunity to decide to let the staith be included in the N.E.R. lease of the branch.

In order to appease the Naworth Coal Co. Lord Carlisle instructed his agent, Mr. Forster, to tell them that this was one of the requirements of the N.E.R. in taking on the branch.

A draft agreement for the branch was prepared by Forster on 12 January 1911. This ran as follows:

1. The railway between Brampton Junction and Brampton Staith to be leased to the N.E.R. for a term of fifty years, the N.E.R. being at liberty to determine such lease at the end of any year of the term on giving Lord Carlisle twelve months' notice of their intention to do so.

2. The N.E.R. to pay the yearly rent of £5 in respect of the railway.

3. The N.E.R. to pay Lord Carlisle £900 for permanent-way materials and platform at Brampton Staith.

4. The N.E.R. to provide a passenger service between Brampton Junction and the staith and also to work the mineral traffic to Brampton Staith.

5. The N.E.R. to take the coal depots at Brampton Staith at a rental of £60 per year, the company making all necessary alterations and repairs at their own cost and undertaking to provide seven coal cells and allow Lord Carlisle's lessees to have exclusive use of not less than four such cells paying a rent to the company not exceeding £10 a year for each cell. If the cells are given up, or any of them at any time, by the lessees, they are to have the right to retake them.

6. The rate on coal handed to the N.E.R. at Brampton Junction by the lessees of Lord Carlisle's Naworth collieries for conveyance between Brampton Junction and Brampton Staith to be 9d. per ton in owners' waggons.

7. The N.E.R. to be at liberty to charge their ordinary scale of rates from other collieries on the N.E.R. system to Brampton Staith.

8. The railway to be maintained during the lease in good workable condition by the N.E.R. and on determination of the lease, Lord Carlisle to be entitled to purchase the permanent way materials, station buildings and railway plant, or such parts thereof as he may desire, at a price to be settled in default of agreement by arbitration but if Lord Carlisle shall not desire to purchase, the N.E.R. to be at liberty to take up and remove the said materials, buildings and plant.

9. Lord Carlisle's right of crossing the N.E.R. at Brampton Junction and all rights which he may have with regard to using N.E.R. sidings at Brampton Junction and other powers and easements not to be prejudiced, but the N.E.R. to have power to vary the position of the crossing at Brampton Junction in accordance with the plan already prepared by them and to provide a proper and convenient crossing at the determination of the lease.

The N.E.R. said that apart from clause 5 it was all right, but that they would like the Naworth Coal Co. to consign all their coal over the branch. This proved impossible to obtain in the form of a written agreement, but as it seemed the most economic transportation for Naworth Coal, it would, no doubt, continue.

In April the N.E.R. added clause 10—"Lease or agreement to be prepared in a form satisfactory to the N.E.R. solicitor". This was approved by Lady Carlisle in April 1911.

Further small points, such as the use of farm crossings on the branch, rentals for water supplies laid along its route, the future of the coal office owned by Lady Carlisle as successor to her late husband, and the weighing machine owned by the Naworth Coal Co.

All was signed up and on 1 November 1912 the copy of the lease was put in Naworth Estate Office—it ran from 29 October 1912.

CHAPTER 10

The Resumption of Passenger Services

Before the Brampton branch could be reopened for passenger trains the N.E.R. had to re-lay its one mile, eight chains route from the coal staith to Brampton Junction, and the 1836 stone arch over the Brampton to Alston road (A689) had to be replaced since the County Council wanted to widen the road through its narrow arch.

Through the intervention of Lady Carlisle, the County Council paid £250 towards the cost of the scheme, which was to be carried out by a new steel girder bridge, Fig. 37, which at 28ft. was 8ft. longer in span than the old one and was to be supplied by Finlays of Motherwell, with locally-built stonework. The track bed had to be raised in a narrow part of the cutting by placing 6,500 cubic yards of earth.

The new station, to be called Brampton Town, was to have one platform 160ft. long by 15ft. wide built of solid masonry with concrete copings. The buildings, of wooden construction, included a centrally-placed booking office, parcels office, waiting rooms, etc.; these were all gas lit. The entry to the station was past the weighbridge and along the access road which was to be resurfaced.

Alterations to the coal staith, Fig. 38, included pulling down the old lime depot, while a run-round loop was to be installed at the platform. Preparations for reopening in late July 1913 continued and it was announced that thirty-eight trains per day would operate to meet all main-line trains for a fare of 4d. single and 6d. return.

What a truly remarkable day for Brampton was Thursday, 31 July 1913. The elaborate reopening ceremony was performed by Lady Cecilia Roberts in the presence of crowds of people at the Town station at 12.15 p.m., Sir Walter Plummer, representing the N.E.R. Directors, presiding.

Lady Roberts unlocked the station gate with a silver key, Fig. 39, presented to her by the N.E.R., and made a short speech, before boarding the inaugural train which set off for Brampton Junction amidst exploding fog signals. Both stations were decorated with flags and bunting, with Venetian masts lining the entrance road to the Town station and a large banner over the entrance gate proclaiming "Success to the Brampton Branch Railway". Fig. 40.

At Brampton Junction the party was photographed, amidst crowds, and the special train joined the N.E.R. Directors' saloon and its locomotive in the platform, Fig. 42. Fig. 43, In addition to Lady Roberts, the party included Wilfred Roberts, the Misses Winifred and Christina Roberts, Lady Aurea Howard, Lief Jones, M.P.,

C. Lacy Thompson, plus N.E.R. officers and directors and, of course, Mr. and Mrs. Hugh Jackson of the Brampton Railway Committee.

The party reboarded the train and returned to the Town station whence, led by Brampton Town Band, they walked to lunch at the Howard Arms Hotel.

The branch passenger service was always operated by a class BTP 0-4-4T locomotive based at Carlisle London Road shed, and the N.E.R. auto-car push and pull train set—usually one coach, but on the first day, and on special days, two or more carriages were used, often in sandwich formation. The locomotives travelled to and from Carlisle daily, two or three locomotives being available for the duty, No. 1089, working the service on that first day.

The service proved excellent, but was to be relatively short-lived after World War I started in 1914 and the resultant need for economies in public transportation, for which the Brampton branch was an obvious candidate. However, the service continued, the goods traffic being worked mainly by such classes of 0-6-0 tender engine as classes 398, C, E and P-1 which were based at Carlisle.

The expected blow was not to fall until 1917, when the N.E.R. informed Lady Carlisle on 12 February that the line would close on 1 March, since locomotive shortages caused by the need to supply locomotives for use in Europe had to be met by the various British main-line companies.

Both passenger and goods services ceased, and this had to be accepted by the local people, who hoped that upon the end of hostilities the branch would quickly be reopened; this was not, however, to be the case.

A local meeting of the Railway Committee decided to ask the N.E.R. about the branch, and Hugh Jackson wrote to them on 20 January 1920. Their reply of the 23rd said that the N.E.R. was not yet in a position to reopen the branch but would bear it in mind.

Lady Carlisle was called upon to urge the N.E.R. to restart the service and also to support a scheme being proposed to the Ministry of Agriculture that a light railway be built on the north and south sides of Brampton. The urging soon bore fruit and the N.E.R. resumed services on 1 March 1920. Fig. 44.

No doubt the reluctance of the N.E.R. to resume services was prompted by its doubts about profitability, and, therefore, the fares were increased. Complaints brought substantiating figures from the N.E.R. in March 1921 after one year's operation.

Services	Operating Cost	Receipts	Loss on operation
Passenger ..	£3,500	£700	£2,800
Goods ..	£500	£300	£200
Totals ..	£4,000	£1,000	£3,000

From this it was obvious that no railway could afford to continue to operate a branch line with an annual deficit of £3,000.

The Brampton Railway Committee, therefore, decided to call a special meeting, inviting Mr. E. F. Wilkinson, District Passenger Manager, and Mr. Lambert, Divisional Goods Manager, of the N.E.R. to come to Brampton to discuss the situation. The meeting took place on 29 August 1922, chaired by Hugh Jackson who, after speaking about the work of the Committee, came to the problem which was to be the main item, the future of the branch line. Jackson said the Committee were of the opinion that the loss was caused by the fares of 6d. Third Class Single, 7d. Third Return, which had risen from 4d. and 6d. each respectively. The fares were considered quite ridiculous for so short a line, when the N.E.R. only charged 1¾d. per mile on the main line, and a plea for the return to the 4d. single fare was made.

The loss of traffic, due to the increased fares and growth of motor bus services, was to be the death knell of the Brampton branch, and both Wilkinson and Lambert said closure was inevitable, although they appreciated the assistance of the Railway Committee and were sorry that the result was to be the closure of the line.

On 26 October 1922 the N.E.R. gave notice of their intention to terminate their lease of the branch on 29 October 1923. Suggestions that the N.E.R. should put on a motor bus service to replace the train came to nought.

In order to gain some time, the Railway Committee asked the N.E.R. to continue goods services after the cessation of passenger services, this being agreed twice by extensions to the end of November and, finally, the end of December 1923.

By now, of course, the L.N.E.R. were in control, following the grouping of the railways in January 1923. In the meantime the line was being valued for the executors of the late Lady Carlisle, who were carrying this out in pursuance of the right they had held since 1913 when the lease was finalised.

The L.N.E.R. inspection saloon visited the line on 6 November 1923 when officials of the railway, the estate executors and the Naworth Coal Co. toured the branch. It was observed that the line was in very good condition, much too good for a purely mineral line future, while the station buildings had no future as dwellings. The executors of the estate would have liked the N.E.R. to lease the line to the Naworth Coal Co. at £100 per year, or that the Naworth Coal Co. should purchase the line, rather than that they themselves should buy it.

The valuation notice for the branch was delayed, arriving on 11 January 1924 after total closure had taken place. It ran as follows:

VALUATION OF BRAMPTON BRANCH RAILWAY PERMANENT WAY MATERIALS

	£
2,006 yards second-hand plain line, ballast, etc., at 30s. per yard	3,009
40 yards second-hand points and crossings at 32s. per yard	64
1 rail buffer	25
1 4-ton weighing machine *in situ*	15
	3,113
2,825 yards of fencing at 3s. 6d. per yard	494
	3,607
Waiting rooms and booking office *in situ*	140
Sleeper coal house	10
	150

The high valuation put off the executors from its purchase and resulted in overtures to the Naworth Coal Co., which was in poor financial condition due to difficulties with Gairs Colliery. The coal company had doubts whether or not the L.N.E.R. would allow their colliery locomotives and trains to cross its main line at Brampton Junction, although if this could be resolved, perhaps the L.N.E.R. might allow them to rent the branch.

By now coal for Brampton was going by road, so whether it was let to the coal company or the estate, its viability would be doubtful.

On 30 January 1924 the L.N.E.R. sent the following lease clauses to Mr. Lief Jones for the executors to consider:

1. Lease the railway for £150 per year—the lessee to pay the tax.
2. Railway to be maintained and upon end of lease returned to the L.N.E.R. in the same condition as when leased.
3. Lessee or his agents (Naworth Coal Co. Ltd.?) to work the railway, accepting traffic from the L.N.E.R. at Brampton Junction.

These points were duly put to the Naworth Coal Co., who replied during February 1924 to say that as they would not control the coal staith they were not interested in the branch line because it would not benefit their coal sales. They would also require another locomotive and the granting of free access over the L.N.E.R. main line.

Discussions continued, but the L.N.E.R. were becoming impatient and were informed by Lief Jones that they could start to lift the rails, leaving the bridge and fences as agreed in the 1913 lease; lifting and dismantling commenced in September 1924. The bridge remained, in fact, until December 1941, when it was dismantled to aid the war-time scrap drive; the coal staith was sold in 1925.

From 1924 until May 1939 the track bed of the Brampton branch was leased to the L.N.E.R. as a footpath to Brampton Junction station, and it still serves this purpose today.

CHAPTER 11

The Locomotives 1836-1953

The locomotive history of Lord Carlisle's railway is obscure in its early years because of the apparent lack of surviving records. Practically all coverage on the subject is restricted to previously published work and the notes of railway historians, at the best incomplete, and often conflicting—all published in the last seventy to eighty years.

James Thompson expressed an early interest in locomotives, maintained throughout the 1820s despite the views of a majority of his contemporaries; here one thinks of the lack of vision of the N. & C.R. concerning locomotives. Thompson's tenacity saved the day, for by the correct routing of the N. & C.R., free of inclined planes, it was built on a level route enabling the N. & C.R. directors to introduce locomotives once they realised their mistake.

The first locomotive to operate on Lord Carlisle's railway, according to contemporary reports, was *Gilsland*, a small Stephenson 0-4-0 tender engine, said to have been brought to Carlisle by Edward Sheldon, an engineer of Stephensons in 1835. The locomotive may have been Sheldon's property and it may have been plying between Kirkhouse and the N. & C.R. at Milton during the summer of 1836, although we have no proof of this. On the other hand it could have been owned by Stephensons with Mr. Sheldon simply in charge of it.

Gilsland's purpose at Carlisle is a mystery unless it found employment on the actual construction of the western section of the N. & C.R. However, *Gilsland* was apparently lent to Lord Carlisle by Mr. Sheldon, for it was used on 15 July 1836, together with another locomotive, *Atlas*, at the official opening of Lord Carlisle's railway, when they operated on the same train between Kirkhouse and Brampton coal staith. The fact that neither locomotive was owned by Lord Carlisle has been overlooked, for *Atlas* was actually the property of its makers, Stephensons, and, according to contemporary reports, only on loan to the N. & C.R. until their own locomotive of the same name was completed, being evidently intended for export.

A few days later, on 19 July, both *Gilsland* and *Atlas*, together with two N. & C.R. locomotives, *Samson* and *Hercules*, worked the inaugural trains at the opening of the western portion of the N. & C.R. between Carlisle and Greenhead, a day so full of mishaps—locomotive failures, broken couplings, etc.—that it will never be forgotten, although to recount these again here would be out of place. The main culprit was *Gilsland*, whose fate was, no doubt, influenced by its performance that day, for it was recorded as shipped by Mr. Sheldon via the Solway Canal to Ireland later in 1836. Attempts to discover its fate in Ireland have so far failed. Mr. Sheldon himself was later one of the partners in the world-famous Carlisle company of engineers and crane makers, Cowans Sheldon & Co. Ltd.

From this it will be seen that *Atlas* and *Gilsland* were, indeed, employed on Lord Carlisle's railway, but were never his property, thus ruling out the theory that both were later rebuilt at Kirkhouse.

With the disposal of *Gilsland*, the coal and lime traffic on the colliery railway reverted to horse traction, continuing as such until the first locomotive was put to work in April 1837.

The first locomotive purchased by Lord Carlisle was *Rocket* and followed James Thompson's recommendation on 2 October 1836 that a locomotive was needed to operate the Midgeholme Railway to bring the traffic to Hallbankgate. Even though James Loch doubted the economy of the suggestion, Thompson's calculations were referred to Nicholas Wood, who confirmed the idea. The outcome was that John Ramshay was sent off within a week or so in search of a suitable light, second-hand locomotive. Ramshay carried letters of authority to the managers of the Bolton & Leigh and the Liverpool & Manchester Railways from Loch, the result being the purchase of the *Rocket* in October 1836, according to Liverpool & Manchester Railway records. James Thompson and his brother, Mark, are recorded in surviving colliery records as having journeyed to Liverpool to see the locomotive and to buy it for the colliery railway.

The redoubtable *Rocket*, Robert Stephenson No. 19 of 1829, built for the Rainhill Trials, was by 1836 considered far too light and of low power for the traffic, and its sale was, no doubt, a welcome release. It was, of course, a very much different *Rocket* which was to be moved by sea back to Carlisle—*back* to Carlisle because the fact was that it had been shipped from Carlisle to Liverpool in 1829 after being conveyed by road from Newcastle in dismantled form. *Rocket* now sported a smokebox, its cylinders having been lowered to near horizontal from their previously steeply-inclined position, while its original tender had been replaced by one of much more substantial design.

The putting into traffic of *Rocket* was delayed, according to statements made by Thompsons, until April 1837. The reasons for this could have been either to allow for its re-erection in the then meagre facilities at Kirkhouse or perhaps for an overhaul. In the latter case it has been suggested that the overhaul, if it did take place, was undertaken at Stephenson's works at Newcastle.

The £300 locomotive was put to work on the Midgeholme Railway until 1840, by which time it had been found far too light for the growing tonnages on the line, and in any case two of Thompson's locomotives were by then available. Its career was short and its only mention so far discovered in surviving records is in the lease document of May 1838, when it was valued at £150, a reduction of 50% since Lord Carlisle purchased it.

The fact that Lord Carlisle purchased the *Rocket*, and not James Thompson, is quite contrary to what has been stated previously in both the Thompson family records and in published works on the locomotive. The fact that it was recorded in Thompson's lease of 1838 proves, beyond doubt, that it did not belong to Thompson until after that date, for it would seem unlikely that Thompson would lease his own locomotive!

The well-known exploit of *Rocket* on 10 August 1837 is worthy of mention when, on the occasion of the East Cumberland election, it was supposed to have covered the four miles from Halton Lea Gate to Hallbankgate in four-and-a-half minutes carrying the Alston returns. It is said to have travelled tender first, driven by James Thompson's brother, Mark, on its 60 m.p.h. dash—a very dubious claim in the writer's opinion, although, no doubt, a fast run did take place.

During its working life on Lord Carlisle's railway, *Rocket* was based near Tindale Village at Mack Doles Hole, but was laid aside at Kirkhouse from 1840, remaining there in semi-dereliction until towards the end of 1850, when enquiries were instigated with a view to the machine being exhibited at the great exhibition in 1851. Accordingly, *Rocket* was sent in February 1851 to Stephenson's works at Newcastle for attention to make it suitable for exhibition. For some reason it got no attention, nor did it go to the exhibition. Whether this was due to the reluctance to spend the necessary money, or to the problem of deciding who should pay for it, is not clear.

Opinions as to what happened to *Rocket* from 1851 until 1862 are that it either returned to Kirkhouse or remained at Stephenson's works, gaining further dereliction in the process; the latter suggestion is, in the writer's opinion, the most likely. Indeed, when during the late 1850s Mr. J. D. Wardale, Stephenson's chief draughtsman, was trying to establish the locomotive's original lineaments, it was reported in Warren's book, "A Century of Locomotive Building", that he obtained some of his dimensions ". . . from the engine as standing in the works yard".

The locomotive remained the property of Thompsons until its presentation to the Patent Museum in London during September 1862. Some hurried and erroneous "restoration" work was carried out by Stephensons which failed to take into account the fact that the 1862 remains were vastly different from the 1829 locomotive. Fortunately, its sadly-deficient remains were restored, or rather "de-restored" some sixty years later, and it is as such that we can see it today in the Science Museum at South Kensington, a poor tribute to its glory of 1829 and its £500 prize.

By mid-1838 the small locomotive shed at Kirkhouse adjacent to the bottom of the inclined plane was built. Fig. 44. This shed, with its tall Gothic arch doorway and double doors, was still standing roofless in 1952, but was demolished soon afterwards.

The second locomotive to operate under Thompsons was also the first to be built at Kirkhouse workshops, which was starting to expand its facilities under the

Thompsons' lease. This machine, *Belted Will*, Figs. 48 and 49, was completed either in late 1838 or early 1839 to the designs of James Thompson and named after the nickname given to Lord William Howard. This locomotive was an 0-4-0 tender engine with vertical 11in. × 16in. cylinders set inside the boiler, a somewhat outmoded type for contemporary work.

A number of components including the boiler, cylinders, and 3ft. 6in. wheels were supplied by Robert Stephenson & Co. Ltd.

Warren depicts "Thompson's engine" in his "Century of Locomotive Building", stating "As rebuilt by Robert Stephenson & Co. Ltd. in 1839, and fitted with gab valve gear".

This locomotive has provoked much speculation, being variously attributed to locomotives built by Thompsons, two brothers who were engineers at Marley Hill, or by Thompsons of Wylam. Another suggestion is that Warren's illustration is one of the mysterious Springwell locomotives, built or rebuilt in some form or another.

Yet another claim is justified by the writer, based on a somewhat debased engraving depicting *Belted Will* used in the 1889 Kirkhouse fete invitation card, Fig. 50, but showing undoubtedly the same locomotive as that in Warren's book. Is the mysterious "Thompson's engine" really the *Belted Will* of James Thompson design and of Kirkhouse build? The writer suggests that it is.

The second Kirkhouse product appeared probably in either 1839 or 1840 and may have been similar to *Belted Will*, but named *Mosstrooper* after the Border brigands once notorious in the locality. Statements that this locomotive suffered difficulties occasioned by its inside cylinders fouling the rollers on the inclined plane seem strange, for one doubts that James Thompson would construct such a problem locomotive. Have the previous writers assumed that the locomotive had inside horizontal cylinders, whereas it might have had a similar arrangement to its predecessor, vertical cylinders inside the boiler? A number of spares were supplied by Stephensons during the 1839-1846 period.

It was not until the third locomotive product of Kirkhouse that we have more definite information. This machine was another tender engine, named *Loch* after James Loch, and was the last locomotive to be produced under James Thompson, being completed, probably, during 1848. The drawings, Figs. 51 to 53, of this locomotive are annotated "James Thompson, Kirkhouse, No. 3 Patent, February 1st, 1845".

The mechanical design of *Loch* was based on Stephenson's No. 3 patent locomotive type, having typical open light plate frames, the long boiler layout—that is, with the firebox outside the wheelbase, itself an 1841 Stephenson patent. The firebox was of the Haycock type, having a domeless boiler and steeply-inclined outside cylinders. *Loch* was cabless and had its centre coupled wheels without flanges to allow sharp curves to be negotiated. The boiler was constructed from five plates lap-jointed, longitudinally along the whole length of the boiler barrel.

It seems that *Loch* was the first long-boiler type British industrial locomotive. The main details of *Loch* were:

Cylinders	13in. diam. × 22in. stroke
Wheel diameter	3ft. 9in.
Wheelbase	9ft. 11in.
Length over buffers	20ft. 7½in.
Length over buffer beams	20ft. 2½in.
Height over chimney	11ft. 6in.
Boiler pressure	90lbs.
Boiler diameter	3ft.
Number of tubes	78
Diameter of tubes	1⅝in.
Boiler barrel length	11ft. 10in.
Thickness of boiler plates	⅜in.

Loch operated mainly on the Midgeholme line, working from the Hallbankgate locomotive shed, built during the 1840s. It was withdrawn during 1885, when it was taken to the Howard Colliery and jacked up to allow its wheels to revolve freely and operate as a stationary engine, assisting that colliery's winding and pumping engines. To enable the wire ropes to pass over *Loch*'s wheels, grooves were cut in its tyres. It continued on this duty until the colliery closed in 1896 and was scrapped soon afterwards.

The final production of Kirkhouse appeared sixteen years after James Thompson's death, that is, in 1866, although it seems it was based on his designs, at least in some degree. This machine was yet another outside cylinder tender engine of 0-6-0 layout, again of long-boiler type, and named *Garibaldi* after the red-shirted Italian patriot, for some obscure reason.

Of similar size to *Loch*, it was more powerful with 14in. × 22in. cylinders and 100lbs. boiler pressure. Running on 3ft. 9in. wheels, it had a domed boiler with the dome towards the front of the boiler barrel, a brief weatherboard cab, later extended by fitting a short roof and windowless cabside sheets.

One interesting point common to all the tender engines on the railway was the four-wheel tender. This was not, as has often been claimed, to allow turning on the Kirkhouse turntable, because these turntables (there was more than one) were actually waggon turntables used to permit waggons to gain access to right-angled sidings serving various buildings at Kirkhouse. The suggestion that access to the fitting shop was via one of these turntables is not borne out by surviving plans of Kirkhouse, so locomotives did not use them.

Garibaldi worked on the Midgeholme line between Hallbankgate and Lambley, but was traditionally employed, according to local opinion, once each year on passenger duty on the Brampton branch, when it operated a shuttle service between Milton Station and the coal staith, with borrowed N.E.R. carriages, on the occasion of the Brampton Show. This would appear to have ceased in 1890, following the discontinuation of passenger services on the Brampton branch.

Garibaldi was probably withdrawn around 1901 when the new Barclay locomotive, *Sheriff*, was delivered.

At this point one wonders just how many parts of these four locomotives were actually made at Kirkhouse with its foundry and machine shop? As in other cases it seems likely that Thompsons link with the Stephensons may have resulted in sets of components being sent from Newcastle for erection at the Kirkhouse shops.

By the early 1870s it was necessary to increase the locomotive stock, for coal production carried by the railway was averaging 145,000 tons per year at this time, and, fittingly, the order, the colliery railway's first new order to an outside contractor, went to Robert Stephenson & Co. Ltd. of Newcastle.

The locomotive was to be a typical long-boiler 0-6-0ST with outside cylinders and a square box-saddle tank, stovepipe chimney, domed boiler and a meagre front weatherboard cab with a completely open back. The coal was carried in bunkers situated in the cabside lower panels. Figs. 54 and 55.

The locomotive was given the name *Tichborne*, after the fraudulent claimant to the Roger Tichborne baronetcy, who was a butcher from Wapping, London—a strange choice, it would seem, for a locomotive working in the wilds of Cumbria.

For some reason—excessive weight or, perhaps, restricted operation due to limited fuel capacity—*Tichborne* did not prove popular, and so it was that the railway's first tank engine came to be converted during 1879 at Kirkhouse into an 0-6-0 tender engine with, of course, yet another four-wheel tender. Figs. 56 and 57. So Robert Stephenson No. 2011 of 1872 began a new life as No. 4 with its name painted on its tender side panels, working mostly from Hallbankgate to Lambley, but later, after the opening of Roachburn Colliery, the traffic from that colliery to Midgeholme washery and Hallbankgate.

At the end of the Thompson era *Tichborne* was to be rebuilt yet again, as an 0-6-0T, a side tank. The reasons for this could have been the reduced size of the railway and the lessening need for tender engines.

About 1901-2 *Tichborne* had received attention from Barclays, who overhauled it and fitted an improved cab, new boiler and firebox, but of its 1907-9 conversion to a side tank some confusion arises. This rebuild was, according to some opinions, instigated by Thompsons and carried out at Kirkhouse by the staff there, but suggestions that Barclays undertook the work at either Kirkhouse or at Kilmarnock seem more likely in view of the somewhat impoverished nature of the collieries at this period. Other suggestions are that the rebuild was carried out by the Naworth Coal Co. Ltd., who had taken on the lease in 1908 following Thompsons' demise. In this case the new lessee had little use for Kirkhouse, so once again the likelihood of Barclays doing the rebuild arises; unfortunately, Barclays have been unable to shed any light on the question.

Fig. 76 *Alice* in a sorry state during the last few days of operation of the railway in March 1953.
(*Collection of B. Webb*)

Fig. 77 View of the "shared centre-rail" section of the incline plane looking towards Planehead in October 1952.
(*L. G. Charlton*)

Fig. 78 The "meetings" or passing loop midway up the incline plane looking towards Hallbankgate Planehead in 1952. (*J. W. Armstrong*)

Fig. 79 Planehead in 1952. Incline control cabin on right. (*J. W. Armstrong*)

Fig. 80   Planehead coal depot and top of incline plane looking towards Kirkhouse.
(*Fleetwood Shawe*)

Fig. 81   Howard Screens on the Midgeholme railway in N.C.B. days.   (*Fleetwood Shawe*)

Fig. 82 View of the Midgeholme line between Tindale and Whites Cut showing the siding put in to serve the small Prior drift. *(Fleetwood Shawe)*

Fig. 83 N.C.B. and B.R. wagons standing in Whites Cut loading bay to carry coal brought by road from the nearby Low Midgeholme drifts. *(Fleetwood Shawe)*

Fig. 84 Foresthead lime kilns about 1920, situated along the old Blacksike branch.
(*Collection of B. Webb*)

Fig. 85 A culvert on the Gairs railway built in 1908/9. (*Fleetwood Shawe*)

Fig. 86 Part of a 15ft. long Fish-Belly type wrought iron rail found near Blacksike in 1972.
(Brian Webb)

Fig. 87 Coal wagon built by Gloucester Railway Carriage & Wagon Co. Ltd. for Maria Thompson & Sons Ltd.
(Historical Model Railway Society)

Fig. 88 Side elevation of a typical chaldron waggon in use during the period of James Thompson. The letters TK mean Thompson Kirkhouse. *(Brian Webb)*

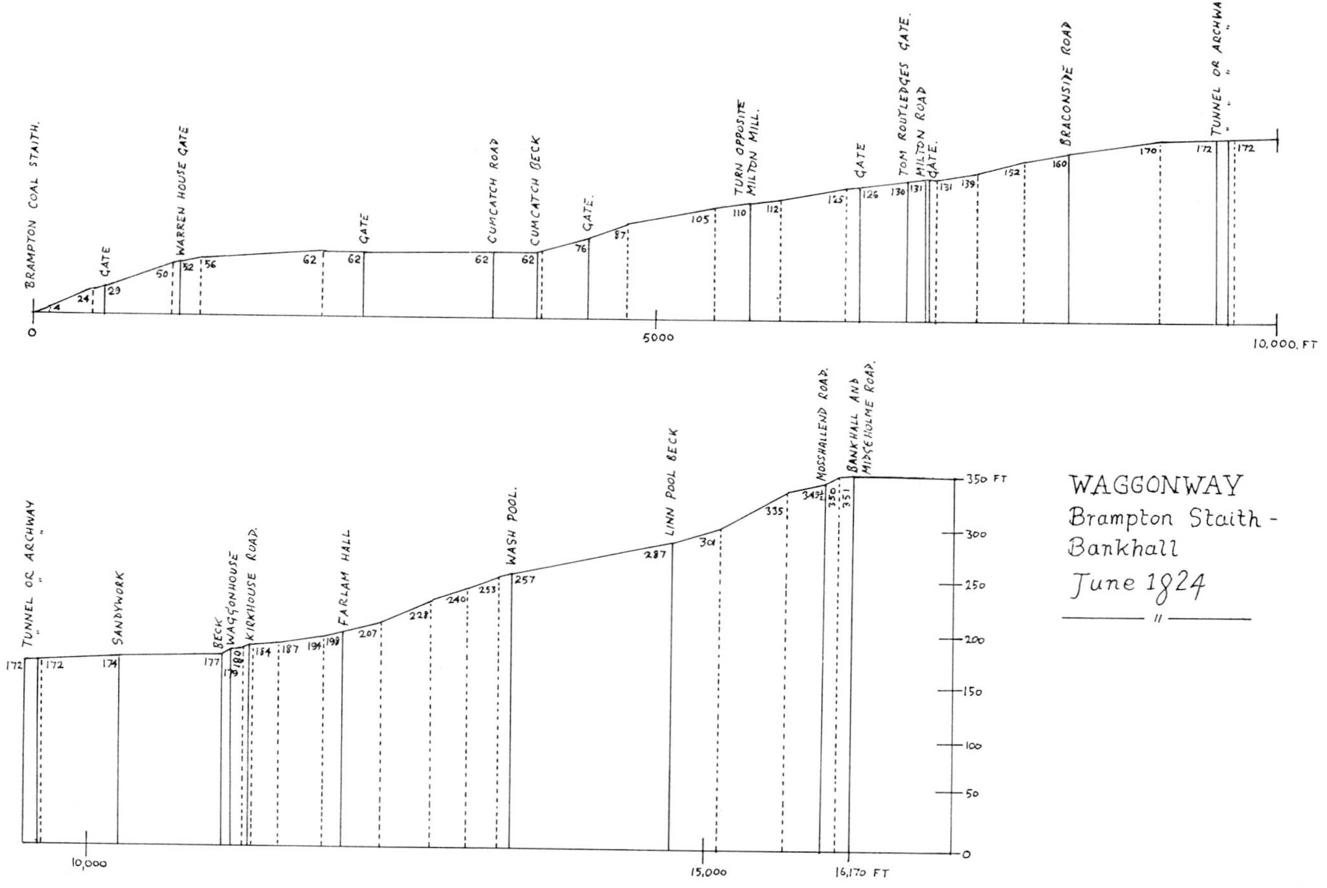

Fig. 89 Gradient profile of 1799 waggonway illustrating its obvious unsuitability for improvement, June 1824.
(David A. Gordon)

The rebuild in a fully-lined livery was photographed in 1908, it is said, at Brampton staith, Fig. 58, still as No. 4, but renamed *Belted Will*, reviving the name of the controversial 1838-9 locomotive. Its sphere of operations in its new form was mostly the Kirkhouse to Brampton staith line and the Gairs Railway, but it enjoyed only a dozen or so years' work, being little used after 1920, and was scrapped some five or six years later.

The original dimensions of *Tichborne* in 1872 were:

Cylinders	14in. diam. × 22in. stroke
Wheel diameter	3ft. 9in.
Wheelbase	9ft. 11in.
Length over buffers	20ft. 2½in.
Length over buffer beams ..	20ft. 7½in.
Height over chimney	12ft.
Height over weatherboard ..	11ft.
Boiler pressure	130 lbs./sq. in.

Prior to the conversion of *Tichborne* to a tender engine, Stephensons delivered another new locomotive in the form of another 0-6-0 tender engine with outside cylinders. This unit became No. 5 and was Stephenson No. 2351 of 1878, being the only locomotive not to carry a name on the colliery railway. No. 5 was quite typical of Stephenson practice, again with long-boiler layout and coupled to a four-wheel tender. Fig. 59.

Little is known of this locomotive, apart from the fact that it operated mainly from Hallbankgate locomotive shed, being overhauled by Barclays in around 1903 and tendered for again in November 1913, continuing to operate until the mid-1920s, when it was apparently scrapped during 1924-5. Its main dimensions were given as:

Cylinders	14in. diam. × 22in. stroke
Wheel diameter	3ft. 9in.
Wheelbase	9ft. 11in.
Length over buffers	22ft. 3in.
Length over buffer beams ..	21ft. 3in.
Height over chimney	11ft. 5in.
Height over cab	10ft. 3in.

Possibly the most well-known locomotive of the fleet, apart from *Rocket*, was the outside cylinder 0-4-0T built during 1881 by Neilson & Co. of Glasgow—Works No. 2738 of 1881, Figs. 60 to 62—for use on the passenger service operated between Brampton Junction station and the coal staith. It was to supersede the horse-drawn "Dandy" service which was still in use from its introduction in July 1836—by this time somewhat outmoded, to say the least.

The new locomotive was, at first glance, appropriately named.

However, its name, *Dandie Dinmont*, was not after the horse-drawn carriage, but the literary character in Sir Walter Scott's writings.

Finished in green with two concave corner-lined panels on its tank sides, it had its name painted on its leading panel. Of somewhat austere appearance with its typical Neilson stovepipe chimney, full-length tanks carried to the front of the smokebox, a very brief weatherboard and roof cab with completely open back (the coal being carried in cabside bunkers), it was married to a rake of three carriages. The carriages were ex-L.N.W.R. four-wheel vehicles with three compartments suitably refurbished and, although "vintage", quite superior to the mode of conveyance they replaced.

The service commenced on Monday, 4 July 1881, being operated with two or three carriages, as required, the locomotive always remaining at the outer end of the train facing Brampton Junction, pulling its train to that station and propelling it on the return trip.

By 1885 *Dandie Dinmont* had been modified, in that its cab was fitted with a full-width front weatherboard and side panels, and although the rear was still open, it presented no real problem due to the cab's close proximity to the train. Some difficulties in surmounting the initial gradient from the staith had prompted the provision of larger sandboxes, which were sited above the front buffer beam and operated by rodding carried over the tanks from the cab.

The passenger service operated until Wednesday, 30 April 1890, when Board of Trade requirements, which Thompsons felt unable to meet, were enforced.

Dandie Dinmont was stabled in the small engine shed at Kirkhouse, leaving its rolling stock at the staith. Upon the cessation of passenger services, it found employment on general work such as shunting and the lighter mineral work, although not proving totally satisfactory for this task.

Barclays rebuilt this locomotive in mid-1906, when it was given a new cab and chimney, and was probably reboilered also. Its new livery was Caledonian Railway blue, lined out with only one convex-cornered panel on the tanks, the name being painted in the centre.

The work was carried out under Order No. 6807 of 1906. Barclays also tendered for overhauling it in November 1913. The locomotive was ordered on 21 January 1881 under order No. N/E 529. (By coincidence, N/E 528 was for an identical locomotive for the Maryport & Carlisle Railway, carrying Works Number 2737 of 1881.) Together with an earlier example, Neilson 2649 of 1880 for the M. & C. Railway, these three Cumbrian tank locomotives were the only ones built to this design. The Neilson order book states:

> The chimney and cab are to be of the ordinary company construction: the injectors to be placed so as not to be affected by a gradient of 1 in 18: the two rods between the brake blocks will require to be carried a little higher than in the Maryport & Carlisle engine, as some of the girders [*sic*] stand 12in. above the top of the rail.

The reference to "girders" alluded to the fact that the locomotive had to be able to clear the rollers on the Kirkhouse inclined plane.

The M. & C. Railway examples were built to a low profile with considerably reduced chimney and cab height.

The main dimensions of *Dandie Dinmont* were:

Cylinders	14in. diam. × 20in. stroke
Wheel diameter	4ft.
Wheelbase	7ft.
Length over buffers	23ft. 5½in.
Length over buffer beams	21ft.
Height over chimney	11ft. 6in.
Height over cab	10ft. 9in.
Boiler pressure	130lbs.
Number of tubes	140
Boiler barrel length	10ft. 0½in.
Heating surface (tubes)	644 sq. ft.
" " (firebox)	52 sq. ft.
Bunker space	30 cu. ft.
Water capacity	600 galls.
Weight in working order	22 tons
Grate area	9.5 sq. ft.

Under the ownership of the Naworth Coal Co. and Naworth Collieries Co. this machine operated mostly from Hallbankgate, taking its share in the work of the railway, even including the steeply-graded Gairs Railway. From 1926 it was usually the spare engine spending periods dumped outside at Hallbankgate, being finally cut up, it is said, around 1929-30.

Locomotive accommodation by the 1880s included the sheds at Kirkhouse and Hallbankgate, but after 1870 a larger building with repair facilities was in use on a site opposite the coke ovens at Kirkhouse. This building was incorporated into the Kirkhouse Brickworks during 1926-7. Statements that this building dated from the very early days, and was where the locomotives of the 1838-66 period were constructed are quite erroneous.

The final locomotive to be purchased by Thompsons was ordered in July 1900 in the form of a large 0-6-0ST from Andrew Barclay, Sons & Co. Ltd., Kilmarnock. This outside-cylinder machine carried Works Number 903 of 1901 and was named *Sheriff* in honour of Mr. Lacy Thompson, who was, at the time, Sheriff of Cumberland. It was despatched from Barclays' works on 16 May 1901 carrying a brass nameplate with "Sheriff" in 4in. letters. It was painted dark blue, lined with concave-cornered lined panels in black, edged both sides with white. Figs. 63 and 64.

Sheriff was a typical Barclay product of the period with stovepipe chimney, open-backed cab and large rear coal bunker, replacing *Garibaldi* on the railway.

Thompsons stipulated some modifications in their order, requiring four sprung buffers at each end to permit both normal coal waggons and chaldron waggons to be handled, increased width between the frames, special cab windows, footplate and cab, asking that the right-hand coal box be omitted and the left one fitted out as a tool box and provided with a lid. In order that *Sheriff* would be able to negotiate the inclined plane without fouling the rollers and pulleys, the motion and brake gear were to be not less than 12½in. clear of the top of the rails, which was achieved by fitting wheels 5in. larger than standard.

The main dimensions were:

Cylinders	14in. diam. × 22in. stroke
Wheel diameter	3ft. 10½in.
Wheelbase	11ft.
Length over buffers	24ft. 2in.
Length over buffer beams	23ft. 2in.
Height over chimney	11ft. 2in.
Height over cab	10ft. 4in.
Width over buffer beams	8ft. 2in.
Boiler pressure	140 lbs.
Boiler diameter	3ft. 7in.
Length of boiler	14ft. 9¼in.
Bunker space	60 cu. ft.

At the end of the Thompsons period, Naworth Coal Co. no longer required *Sheriff*, so it was sold in 1908 to J. & F. Wake Ltd. of Darlington, the plant and machinery dealers, who resold it to the Waterloo Main Colliery at Leeds during 1909. Afterwards *Sheriff* went on to work for Trafford Park Estates Ltd. and later for Nicholls Nagle & Co. Ltd. (Brown & Polson Ltd.) at Trafford Park, and was scrapped, named *Colonel Moseley*, in 1929, it is thought.

So it was that *Tichborne*, No. 5 and *Dandie Dinmont* were taken over by Thompsons' successors, the Naworth Coal Co. Ltd.

The formation of the Naworth Coal Co. Ltd. in 1908 and their takeover of the railway, together with diminished colliery system, combined to reduce the locomotive requirements. Thus, they managed to operate the railway east of Hallbankgate to serve Roachburn Colliery, to Tindale where the Bishop Hill branch served Henry Pit and Tindale Quarry and the line to the washery at Midgeholme, with one locomotive, and the Gairs Railway to serve the new Gairs Colliery, also with one locomotive, leaving one locomotive as standby. The section to Kirkhouse Brampton Junction and the Brampton coal staith was operated by either locomotive after descending the inclined plane.

The railway from Halton Lea Gate to Lambley was taken up in 1909-10, thus severing forever the eastern outlet and access to the Alston branch, at least so far as Naworth coal was concerned.

The conversion of *Tichborne* into the 0-6-0T *Belted Will* resulted in the loss of its lower buffers, indicating that between 1901 and 1908 chaldron waggons had ceased to be in general use on the railway. Fig. 65.

Roachburn Colliery closed in 1912, so the railway east of Tindale was rarely used for a short period, since the washery at Midgeholme was now no longer required. At the same time, the N.E.R. takeover of the Brampton branch meant that Naworth locomotives would no longer cross the N.E.R. at Brampton Junction, a further reduction in locomotive requirements.

However, trials for coal at Whites Cut enabled the opening of a colliery there during 1913 and brought the railway back to use east of Tindale. New motive power was also needed to assist the aged trio in handling traffic.

Duly, a new locomotive was obtained (the only one to be purchased by Naworth Coal Co.) from Barclays in June 1914. Bearing Works Number 1365 of 1914 and named *Naworth No. 6*, Fig. 66, it was a standard machine, an 0-4-0ST with outside cylinders, and soon proved its usefulness on the Gairs Railway, which was difficult to operate with the older locomotives.

Apart from the required extra clearance, obtained by fitting two extra leafs in its bearing spring, *Naworth No. 6* was quite standard with the following main dimensions:

Cylinders	14in. diam. × 22in. stroke
Wheel diameter	3ft. 5in.
Wheelbase	5ft. 6in.
Length over dumb buffers	20ft. 8in.
Length over buffer beams	19ft. 9in.
Height over chimney	11ft. 2in.
Height over cab	10ft. 4in.
Width over buffer beams	8ft. 2in.
Boiler pressure	140lbs.
Boiler diameter	3ft. 9in.
Length of boiler	14ft. 8in.

For some reason *Naworth No. 6* had large flat dumb buffers and very small coal space, although a small bunker was fitted by the coal company later. Fig. 67.

At the end of the lease of the Naworth Coal Co. the traffic was being worked from Gairs and Venture Collieries, both served by the Gairs Railway, with Whites Cut and Prior Pits served by the Midgeholme line, which in 1924 terminated at Whites Cut. The locomotive stock stood at four: *Belted Will, No. 5, Dandie Dinmont* and *Naworth No. 6*.

The Colliery Railway ceased to operate until a new lessee was found, who took over in 1926, this new concern trading as the Naworth Collieries Co. Ltd. Upon their reopening, they promptly disposed of *Belted Will* and *No. 5*, feeling that the restricted system remaining was quite capable of operation by *Naworth No. 6* and *Dandie Dinmont*.

The opening of the Midgeholme quarry and its crushing and handling plant at Midgeholme on the site of the washery and coke ovens prompted the need for new motive power, and two locomotives were ordered. Since quick delivery was essential, the orders went for one locomotive each to Barclays and the Avonside Engine Co. Ltd., Bristol, both possibly supplying from stock.

The Avonside example was Works Number 1954 and dated 1924 on its works plate, but delivered in 1926 named *Tindale*, its main dimensions being:

Avonside type B3 0-6-0ST outside cylinders.

Cylinders ..	14in. diam. × 20in. stroke
Wheel diameter ..	3ft. 3in.
Wheelbase	9ft. 8½in.
Length over buffer beams	19ft. 11½in.
Width over buffer beams	8ft.
Height over chimney	11ft. 4½in.
Boiler pressure ..	160lbs.
Heating surface (tubes) ..	446 sq. ft.
Heating surface (firebox)	52 sq. ft.
Bunker capacity ..	1 ton
Water capacity ..	750 galls.
Weight in working order	29¾ tons
Grate area	8 sq. ft.

The clearance for the incline fixtures was achieved by not fitting brake crossbeams, etc., but otherwise *Tindale* was a standard product. Figs. 68 to 71.

The Barclay locomotive was one of its makers' characteristically chunky and very robust 0-6-0ST's of standard outside-cylinder type, carrying Works Number 1879 of 1926 and named *Stephenson*, Fig. 72, in painted letters on its saddle-tank sides, being delivered from stock in December 1926. As with *Naworth No. 6*, two extra leafs in the bearing springs gave the incline clearance required. Principal dimensions were:

Cylinders ..	14in. diam. × 22in. stroke
Wheel diameter ..	3ft. 5in.
Wheelbase	10ft. 3in.
Length over buffers	26ft.
Length over buffer beams	23ft. 1in.
Height over chimney	11ft. 0½in.
Height over cab ..	10ft. 3¾in.
Width over buffer beams	8ft. 2in.

Boiler pressure	160lbs.
Boiler diameter	3ft. 7in.
Length of boiler	15ft. 0¼in.
Bunker capacity	1 ton 15 cwt.
Water capacity	700 galls.
Tractive effort	14,198lbs.
Weight in working order . .	30½ tons

Both these 1926 acquisitions were kept busy on the Gairs and Midgeholme lines handling coal from Gairs and Venture, Mint Hill drift (loaded at Prior Dyke) and the stone traffic from the Tindale Granite Co.'s Midgeholme quarry, the Naworth Lime Co.'s Bishop Hill quarry at Tindale and shale traffic from Foresthead to Kirkhouse Brickworks.

The next move was the decision to scrap *Dandie Dinmont*, surplus since 1926, which was carried out in 1930, so disposing of the last Thompson locomotive.

The next disposal took place in 1935 when *Naworth No. 6*, which of late had been the spare locomotive, was sold to Brereton Collieries Ltd. in Staffordshire, passing to the N.C.B. in 1947, who moved it to Rawnsley Shed in 1961. It was finally cut up in 1962 at Cannock Wood Colliery by Cashmores.

The imminent closure of Gairs Colliery, whose falling traffic was mostly in the hands of *Tindale*, meant the railway was again to be reduced, so for some twelve months during 1935-6 only two locomotives were to be found on the railway, *Tindale* and *Stephenson*. These were quite adequate for the Whites Cut coal traffic and the mineral traffic to Kirkhouse and Brampton Junction.

The hope of a revival of the fortunes of the railway by expanding coal production from the Low Midgeholme drifts (which was loaded at Whites Cut for transit to Howard Screens), the small though steady output of Venture Drift from 1933 to 1939, plus the possibility of traffic from a firm interested in zinc residue extraction from the Tindale Spelter works waste tips, made the company seek another locomotive.

During 1936 this arrived in the shape of a second-hand Avonside 0-6-0ST with outside cylinders. This, the final locomotive acquisition, carried Works Number 1460 of 1903, being built for South Leicestershire Collieries, Snibston Colliery, moving to the Ford Motor Co. Ltd. at Dagenham and then to George Cohen & Co. Ltd., from whom it was purchased. It was named *Alice* and was less powerful than *Tindale*, its main dimensions being:

Avonside type B2.

Cylinders	14in. diam. × 20in. stroke
Wheel diameter	3ft. 3in.
Wheelbase	9ft. 8½in.
Length over buffer beams . .	19ft. 8½in.

Height over chimney	11ft. 2½in.
Width over buffer beam	8ft.
Boiler pressure	140lbs.
Heating surface (tubes)	414 sq. ft.
,, ,, (firebox)	52 sq. ft.
Bunker capacity	1 ton
Water capacity	620 galls.
Weight in working order	28 tons
Grate area	8.25 sq. ft.

Although less powerful than *Tindale*, the only external differences between this locomotive and *Alice* were that *Alice*'s boiler was lower pitched, while her wheels had thick cast iron centres with six thick spokes, and *Tindale* had ten spokes of normal proportion.

After the closure of Gairs Colliery in 1936 the two Avonsides and *Stephenson* were quite adequate for the output of Venture and Low Midgeholme Drifts, two locomotives being steamed daily to operate this traffic, the Foresthead shale traffic and the falling stone traffic. During World War II the traffic remained much the same except that the stone traffic ceased.

After nationalisation the N.C.B. took over the three locomotives, and although allocated numbers 26 (*Alice*), 27 (*Tindale*) and 28 (*Stephenson*), they never carried them. Figs. 73 to 76.

Plans to expand coal production through a new drift at Whites Cut proved abortive, nor was the reopening of Midgeholme King Pit in 1951 of any help to the railway, since its output was taken by road.

The railway continued to collect coal from Whites Cut—the production of the Midgeholme drifts, together with some of Lambley West's coal—in fact quite high tonnages.

The stone and shale traffic had ceased due to the change to road transport, so that when the last drift closed in March 1953 the railway was doomed.

By this time *Tindale* was out of action with a condemned boiler and, although considered for repairs, was scrapped at Hallbankgate in 1954.

After track lifting (*Alice* working the demolition trains) both *Alice* and *Stephenson* were taken to West Wylam Colliery during May 1954. *Alice* was in poor condition with wooden plugs in the corrosion holes of the saddle tank and was sent on to North Walbottle Colliery and scrapped there in January 1956.

Stephenson was stored after having its tyres turned up at West Wylam, and upon the closure of the colliery was sent to Burradon Colliery, being noted there in March 1962, where it was cut up in September of the same year.

Thus ended 126 years of locomotive history, starting from the *Rocket* in 1837 and ending with, appropriately, *Stephenson* in 1962.

CHAPTER 12

The Scene Today

For the industrial archaeologist and railway historian much of interest remains to be seen today of the collieries and their railways.

At Brampton one may inspect the remains of the coal staith where the site of the coal and lime cells, the passenger platform and bridge of 1913 vintage over the A689 road, albeit reduced to its abutments, can be easily seen. After crossing the road it is possible to walk along the 1836 "Dandy line" to Brampton Junction station, the route being easily followed.

Of the 1799 waggonway route, few earthworks remain until the point where its route intersects that of the British Railways Newcastle & Carlisle line. Here some few hundred yards east of the level crossing, where there is a public footpath across the railway, one will find on the up side a short length of waggonway embankment. Following the route via the A689 road, the site of the 1799 "Sandy Arch", in reality a tunnel under this road, may be traced leading into a shallow cutting on the south side of this road, now sporting some very sturdy trees. Once across the rough track to Kirkhouse Brickworks a shallow embankment is to be seen heading towards Beck Cottages and Farlam Hall grounds.

Between Beck Cottages and Hallbankgate little can be seen but the route is traceable from a point almost opposite the derelict 1836 inclined plane control cabin to pass east across the road towards Clowsgill, traversing the fields where some earthworks remain.

From Clowsgill it is easy to follow the line on its southerly course from near Cleskets where the 1799 route, first in a shallow cutting and then on an embankment, heads towards Howgill, this course being retained by the railway for most of its existence.

To the west from a point where the route crosses the road is the line of 1822-3 to Foresthead quarry and Blacksike. Returning now to Brampton Junction station (itself worthy of some attention) one notes the northern bay platform, once the habitation of the "Brampton Dandy" service, and the discernible raising of the platforms still evident in the platform faces.

Moving now to the eastern end of the station we can see the "Y" junction, the left-hand B.R. line heading to Newcastle and the overgrown right-hand cutting to Kirkhouse. This latter route is the 1836 line which replaced the 1799 waggonway.

One may follow this through to Kirkhouse, noting immediately the obstruction caused by filling in the Birky Brow arch. Just before Kirkhouse to the left is the

113

sand pit. Here the site widens to form the site of the Kirkhouse sidings, now heavily overgrown and despoiled by tipping.

To the left can be seen the remnants of some of the old gas-works buildings, followed immediately by the area occupied by the old coke ovens and, latterly, the site of a concrete plant. The old Bog Cottages are now an office.

On the right are the Kirkhouse Brickworks followed almost immediately by the remainder of the stone buildings of the Kirkhouse workshops and farm. Of railway interest are the waggon repair shop and the office where James Thompson worked from 1808 to 1851.

Retracing our steps we start to climb the inclined plane to the left of Kirkhouse and continue in cutting and on embankment to reach Planehead, the journey being blocked twice en route due to the filling-in of the arch carrying the road to Kirkhouse and by the demolished stone arch which once spanned the A689 road—the "Priests' Arch". Figs. 77 to 80.

At Planehead there are still the coal depot and offices, the Planehead incline control cabin and the stone-built engine shed.

Once across the road the route forks away westward, skirting Clowsgill to its west (the 1799 route ran through the centre of the quarry) to continue to Howgill. At this point we can trace two lines veering eastward, one to climb across the face of Tindale Fell, reaching an altitude of over 1,000ft. and used from about 1802 to 1838; the other eastward curve is the 1835 branch to Howgill Colliery which crossed Howgill Beck via a bridge—the stone abutments of which can still be seen.

Yet another route, more easily discerned, heads away in a westerly direction passing the drift-scarred fellside on its climb to Gairs Colliery. This line was put in about 1908/9 and was lifted soon after closure of Gairs Colliery in 1936, but the lower sections were not lifted until 1941.

Back at Hallbankgate the easterly route of the railway attracts the attention. Within a short distance ample evidence exists of the hectic mining activities of the Howard, Templegarth and Greenside Collieries, not to mention the Howard Screens which were only demolished after the N.C.B. tenure ended.

At a point near Blue Gate Farm we note the war-time attempt to open a small drift, before passing into the deep cutting which provided the site of the loading facilities for the Roachburn Pit of the early 1860s and the ill-fated Roachburn Colliery, 1893-1912. The remains of Roachburn Screens, together with the nearby colliery site, repay a brief study.

Only a few hundred yards further on we come to the small hamlet of Tindale and the vast desolation of the waste banks of the old Spelter works. This valley, divided by the massive Tindale railway embankment, was once the home of a thriving industrial community complete with its own school and shops. It was at a place called Doles Hole that Stephenson's "Rocket" was stabled between 1837 and 1840.

At the eastern end of the embankment a spur line led off westwards to serve the Spelter works, local quarries and some drifts and lime kilns. High on the Fell above Bishop Hill can be seen the site of the Henry Pit and its rope-worked tubway scarring the heather-bracken hillside.

Continuing east, the route is both in cutting and on embankment and passes the site of Prior pits with their siding accommodation, soon to emerge alongside the A689 road and Whites Cut. At Whites Cut the loading bay for Low Midgeholme coal is seen, together with some partly-demolished modern brick buildings—the remnants of the N.C.B. attempt to extract coal from this ancient mine. Figs. 82 and 83.

We now cross Midgeholme embankment with the River Blackburn and its culvert at its eastern end and arrive at High Midgeholme. If one looks left down the Blackburn, one notes the scarred Low Midgeholme valley stretching away north-easterly beyond the A689 road—the site of active drift mining for hundreds of years, the final drifts closing only in 1953.

High Midgeholme itself is a scene of desolation with the wind whining through the rusting metalwork of the stone plant built on the sites of the coke ovens and coal washing plant. There, too, is a narrow-gauge trackbed to serve Midgeholme quarry, but only sheep now follow its route. Fig. 90.

A little further, and again some ruinous red-brick buildings are to be seen—this was the proud King Pit. Operated from 1828-9 until 1893 by Thompsons, it was disturbed from its slumbers in 1951 by the N.C.B. in an effort to reopen its coal reserves, an attempt which ended in 1955.

After King Pit the route becomes more overgrown due to the lack of track for a longer period, but it is uneventful until Halton Lea Gate is reached. Here is the depot built to serve the railway by James Thompson, and the level crossing where the line crossed the A689 road. As one looks eastward the line may be seen passing the spoil heaps of Lambley West Colliery and a little further on that of the Old Lambley Colliery. Of the once-extensive Hartleyburn Star Pit, only a small mound of waste remains to mark the formerly prosperous mine. This is further north on the common, but of the other contemporary mine further east no trace can be seen. Once past Lambley Colliery the line changed ownership, for it joined end-on to the N. & C.R. Lambley Fell branch, passing under a footbridge and thence to connect with the Alston branch of B.R. Figs. 91 and 92.

The journey over, one's thought, too, travels back over the history of this once thriving coalfield and its railways and marvels how an industrial development of such magnitude could have been operated for so long, given the sparse population and village lifestyle common to the district.

To convert an essentially rural area from the farming life to industrial work for almost two centuries, and then to revert to it, has not proven an easy task. The effort and enterprise of the coalmasters and their workers may never again be witnessed, so their tribulations and hardships, happily almost unknown today, must not be forgotten.

APPENDIX 1

Copy of a letter from George Stephenson to John Ramshay and James Thompson.

Liverpool.
August 23rd 1824.

Messrs. Ramsay [sic] and Thompson,
Gentlemen,

Agreeable to your request, I have examined the country in the vicinity of Brampton, Carlisle, and Gillsland [sic] on the probality [sic] of forming a Railroad through the Lord of Carlisle's coalfield, and also to form a junction, with the one proposed from Newcastle Upon Tyne; the vale of Gillsland appears the most favorable [sic] ground for the junction; in this vale is the summit level between the two Seas, and considerably lower than any part of the neighbouring Country; taking this line a suitable level could be obtained for the Locomotive Engines to travel thereon between the two extreme points, and taking after them 50 tons of goods; and travelling at the rate of 4 to 5 miles pr [sic] hour; such a project if carried into effect would be of great advantage to the public; and incalculable benefit to many of the Land owners through which it would pass; but in all probability almost ruinous to the Lord of Carlisle's coal works; as many coal fields would be opened out on the East, and North, of his Lordship's, which would compete with his interests, as coals would be sent to Carlisle from those new Collieries at a very trifling expence [sic] more than his Lordship could send them; this would not be all. The public line would very likely be projected from Carlisle to the neighbourhood of Whitehaven, where a communication would be formed with Ships of large burden; so that the hazardous passage to the mouth of the Carlisle Canal would in a great manner be done away; this projection would also pass through more Coal fields, and at such a distance as would enable them to reach Carlisle Market, and sell at very low prices, on this account the market would be constantly glutted; on these grounds I think sufficient reasoning has been shewn for the Lord of Carlisle to oppose the public Line, at least in passing through his Estates, his Lordship forming a private Railway from his own coal works to Carlisle would have a very different effect, and supposing the Newcastle projection to join his, and also Collieries to be opened out upon that line, – His Lordship would be empowered to lay on such a tonnage rate on coals passing through his private property, as would ensure him as much profit as though he worked the Collieries himself, and also obliged them to sell at high prices; all tonnage except coals and Lime might be charged the same as on the public Line:

Satisfying myself that these conclusions I have drawn are correct, and also coroborated [sic] by Mr. Thompson – In conjunction with this gentleman I then set forward to examine the country for a line the most direct from the

Collieries to Carlisle, and succeeded in finding a very favorable one, commencing in the extensive coalfield East of the Tern [sic] Lake vale, and falling into another which runs parallel to the Lake, and continues forward on favorable ground to the South side of Kirkhouse, where the ground gets undulating but nothing serious, as its Banks are principally sand and gravel, which is easy to excavate, and also is an excellent material for finishing the road, if worked by Locomotive or permanent Engines. (Horses require a more expensive material.)

The line from the latter place would then stretch forward almost in a direct line to Carlisle.

The limited time I had to spend in your neighbourhood prevented me examining the intervening ground, from where we should cross the river to Carlisle; but from the ocular view I got of the Country, I think it is favorable – I cannot make out any accurate estimate what such a line would cost without making a close survey, and taking the levels of the Country, but judging of the levels that have been taken for a Canal, enables me to know that a very desirable level may be got for a Road; the descent from the Collieries to Carlisle, is such that a loaded waggon would run by itself the whole distance, and a Locomotive Engine would return with from 20 to 30 empty waggons – a Branch might be taken from this Line to the south side of Brampton; and a Depot ought to be made about half way between the latter place and Carlisle, to suite [sic] the Penrith trade; this would shorten the cartage in that district very much – The main Line would commence on a suitable level for projecting it towards Alston, where a ready communication might be formed with the Stockton and Darlington Railway.

Supposing these projects to be carried into effect, and the coal field opened out in the way Mr. Thompson proposes, and the increased sale which must evidently take place, there is little doubt of his Lordships profits on these works being from 20 to 30,000 £ pr annum as he must have the market entirely to himself; in case this Line should not be extended to Carlisle, it is evident a new line must be made to Brampton, from the coal field Mr. Thompson proposes to open a favorable one might be formed from that field to Brampton; so that one Locomotive Engine, and one self acting plane will do all the work that is done at present, except one horse kept at the pit drawing the waggons to and from the train of carriages which ought to be ready on the arrival of the Engine – An estimate was shewn to me by Mr. Thompson for extending the Line to Carlisle, which I think very properly drawn up, and I have no doubt of its accuracy – and I think it is only fare [sic] to state, in justice to Mr. Thompson that I have never seen any coal works apparently better conducted than those under his care.

    I am Gentlemen
     Your Obedient Sert.
      George Stephenson.

APPENDIX 2

Copy of a letter to James Loch and James Thompson from George Stephenson.

Newcastle on Tyne
November 18th 1825.

Sir,

    I have, agreeably to your request, accompanied Mr. James Thompson, and have examined that part of the intended line of Railway from Newcastle to Carlisle, which passes through the Lord of Carlisle's Estate, with a view to ascertain, whether the Branch proposed by the directors of the above undertaking, from his Lordship's private Railway near Brampton, is laid out in the best line for his interest.

    After examining that neighbourhood in every direction, I find it is impossible to form a junction with public line as it is laid out, so as to enable his Lordship to convey his coals as cheap as they may be led from other Coal-fields; and it is my opinion, that the proposed Branch might be laid out in a more favourable route for the Lord of Carlisle: but supposing it be done in the best manner possible, he cannot convey coals from his Coal-fields, so cheap as they can be done from Col. Coulsons Estate. My reason for such a statement is this: that the Lord of Carlisle's Coal-field lies from 2 to 300 feet higher than the Colonel's, and at almost as great distance from the market. A horse will draw from 10 to 12 Tons, exclusive of waggons, on the main line; that is, from the Colonel's coal pits to Carlisle; while the same horse could not do more than half that weight on his Lordship's private road, except on that part which is making from Midgeholme, where a horse will travel with quite as much as on the main line.

    Mr. Thompson has suggested to me some improvements in the old line, after passing the Midgeholme junction, which might be done to great advantage. One inclined plane will be required near Kirkhouse; and I think it is practicable, after passing that plane, to form such a junction with the main or public line, that a horse would travel with double the load he does now; but not by the line which is pointed out by the Directors: that must be done either by a permanent engine or self-acting plane, which, cannot convey goods so cheap as horses on a good line.

    It appears to me that Lord Carlisle's family has, from time to time, expended large sums of money in forming Railways from his Coal-field to Brampton, which must have been a great benefit to the public. By such expenditure he has been enabled to supply the public with coals cheaper than the neighbouring coal-owners: now supposing the public line to be formed in the way it is laid out, he will then be in a worse situation than he was before he had any Railway, though it is true the public will be benefitted by such a measure.

I beg to be understood, that it is not my wish to advise you to attempt preventing the public's obtaining such a benefit; for the same benefit could be given to them if the line was laid out to his Lordship's best interest. If Lord Carlisle has considered to give up such a privilege to the other Coal-owners, nothing more need be done on His part, even if such a clause be in the Bill preparing for Parliament, that the proposed Branch be made, and that no more than $\frac{1}{2}$d. per Ton per Mile be charged on this part of the line: this will not bring his Lordship on a par with Colonel Coulson at the junction.

A considerable allowance ought to be estimated on the leading charge for the breakage of waggons on the inclined plane, which will not come into such charge on the main line.

If the intended Bill can be deferred until another year, I think, by a plan which Mr. Thompson has suggested to me, his Lordship's interest might be protected. I mean by extending a line into Scotland as far as Annan, (by way of Longtown,) at which place I understand there is a good harbour; and a branch could be taken off this line to Carlisle. The projection from Brampton to Carlisle and Annan, ought I think to be formed by a separate Company, so that his Lordship could have the line laid out the best for his interest, and at the same time yield as much benefit to the public.

I have examined with Mr. Thompson a part of the country towards Longtown which is extremely favourable for a railway; and I have no doubt the Scotch gentlemen will take it very eagerly, on account of the great scarcity of lime in that neighbourhood; and no doubt the sale of your coals would be extended into Scotland. It is probable that a good deal of back carriage might also be got from Annan to Allendale, and also to Newcastle it being a good shipping port. It certainly would be a great advantage to Lord Carlisle, if the Newcastle Railway should not extend to Brampton, as it would then leave the whole of the market to himself; and if he wishes to favour the public with low-priced coals, he could do it with more honour this way than to be compelled by competitors.

      I am Gentlemen
        Your Obedient Sert.
         George Stephenson.

Fig. 90 View looking West along the course of the Midgeholme railway at High Midgeholme in September 1972. The ruinous buildings of the Tindale Granite Co. occupy to the left the site of Midgeholme washery and to the right the coke ovens. (*Brian Webb*)

Fig. 91 View eastwards along the Hartleyburn/Lambley line showing the old Lambley colliery waste tips to the right and the cattle overbridge. September 1974. (*Brian Webb*)

Fig. 92 Close-up of the cattle bridge over the N. & C. Lambley Fell branch which formed a head-on junction with the colliery line at the point marked by the gateway. (*Brian Webb*)

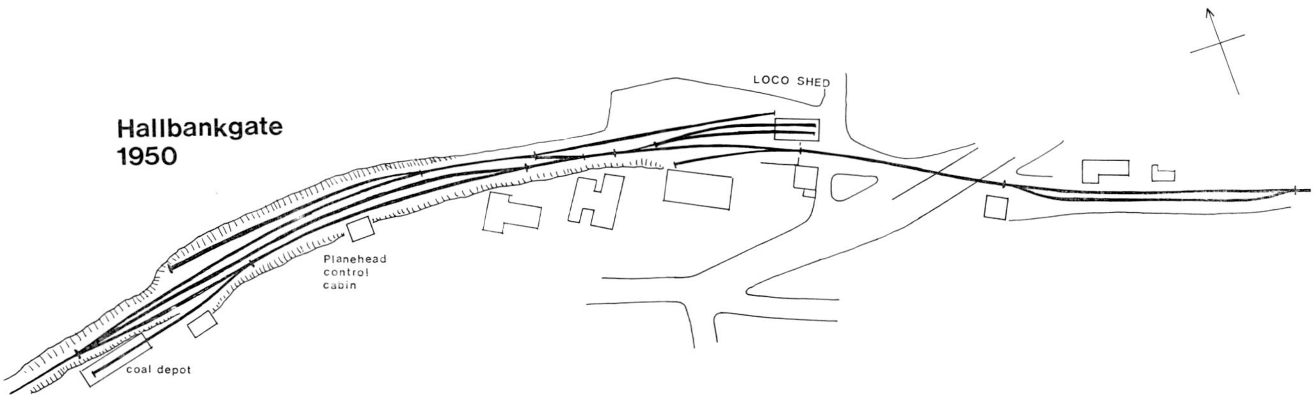

Fig. 93 Plan of the layout at Hallbankgate Planehead about 1950.

(Collection of B. Webb)

APPENDIX 3

Copy of a letter to James Thompson from Robert Stephenson.

Newcastle on Tyne
March 17th 1828.

Dear Sir,

Your letter of the 15th inst. to my Father duly received this Morning, in answer to which, I beg to lay before you the following remarks, on the two lines of Road represented by the sections contained in Your Letter.

On the Comparative value of the two lines of Section for the conveyance of Goods in a descending direction, very few observations are required, the superiority of the one over the other being so decided – in the first place, on the Corby line of Road, one Species of Power without interruption may be employed, and so far it is preferable, as all delay in transferring Goods from Horses to inclined Planes, and again from the latter to the former, is avoided, which process in every situation is attended with a loss of time, however simple and efficient the means employed may be. Add to this advantage a still more important one, viz the saving in Wear and Tear of Ropes and Rollers on the inclined Planes, and the obviating the risk which is inseparable, not only for this machine but all others of a like nature.

The ascent of the Corby line is so nearly uniform that it may be regarded as such. A Horse will pass with any weight downwards, as at this rate of descent the friction of the Waggons and their gravity are nearly equal: consequently the power of a Horse on such a Line is only limited by the empty carriages he can return with.

In the present case one Horse will return with 5 empty waggons weighing $5\frac{1}{2}$ or 6 Tons capable of containing 10 or 12 Tons of Goods; this therefore is the weight a Horse may be estimated to travel with, on the Corby line of Section, being on the whole more favourable than the level line of Road, where the Horse's power would be limited by the weight of loaded Waggons, whereas on such a descending line as Corby the weight of empty carriages is the only limit. On the Newby Line, we find 4 Miles of ascending Road, with the empty Waggons at the same rate of ascent as the Corby Line: which as a matter of course fixes the same limitation on the Horse's Power, viz 5 empty Waggons; so far therefore, the two lines of road are on an equal footing – I have already alluded to the disadvantage of a self acting plane, if it can be avoided both on account of the Wear and tear and risk.

Under such circumstances as these the trifling advantages which may be supposed on a partial examination of the two Sections, that arise in behalf of the Newby line, having 3¾ Miles at a moderate Ascent and one Mile level quite disappears. These gentle ascents might have been in certain Situations favourable, but in the present instance the Power of a Horse is restricted by an Ascent of 4 miles ascending 29 feet per mile in one direction with empty Waggons, and by a level in the other direction with the loaded Waggons, which completely counterbalances any increase of Power which might be gained by a reduction of the ascents on the other parts of the Line.

      I remain, Dear Sir,
        Yours very Truly,
          Robert Stephenson.

P.S. My Father has just read the above and his views perfectly coincide with those expressed. R.S.

RAIL GAUGES

APPENDIX 4

Part of a letter from James Loch to James Thompson dated 23 October 1825.

Dear Mr. Thompson,

 I have received your letter detailing your Success with your mission to Newcastle, with Mr. Thompsons proposal to make a tunnel near the Staith at Brampton so as to have an inclined plane to join the publick [*sic*] line opposite Walton house. I am inclined to think that this is a very favourable arrangement for Lord Carlisle, provided they agree to limit their tolls to 1d. a ton per Mile and 1½d. a ton per Mile on the Railway and inclined plane respectively as you mention. The Clause making such a limitation must be a general Clause and not a particular one, which Parliament wont admit. – it must however be distinctly understood that they agree also to form their railway of the same width of Lord Carlisles and the sooner you communicate this to be his Lordships determination the better. I am sure that Mr. Thompson is far too reasonable, not to see the propriety of this; indeed upon publick [*sic*] grounds.

APPENDIX 5

Copy of a letter from James Loch to Nathaniel Clayton of the Newcastle & Carlisle Railway dated 3 November 1825.

Dear Sir,

I wrote to Mr. James Thompson on the 23rd stating that if the Railway Company agreed to make the side Branch up to Brampton and would agree not to charge more upon coals than 1d. per ton per mile on the railway and $1\frac{1}{2}$d. per ton per mile on the inclined plane and that they agreed to make their Railway the same width as the Midgeholme branch, belonging to Lord Carlisle, which is the same width as the Darlington Railway, his Lordship would oppose no obstacle to the passing of the Bill – of course his Lordship will expect that the act shall contain some distinct pledge, that the branch Railway shall be completed, but this I doubt not will readily be granted as the Toll on the Carriage of his Lordships Coal and Lime, will form a material part of the tonnage on the Western end of the Railway. The width of the Railway will I conceive be easily accommodated also, as it must be a material object to have all the leading ones of the North of England of the same width.

Yours etc.,
James Loch.

APPENDIX 6

Copy of letter from James Loch to Messrs. Clayton dated 13 November 1825.

Dear Sir,

I have been favoured [sic] with your Letter of the 9th and one from Mr. James Thompson of the same date. Lord Carlisle cannot expect to pay a less tonnage on the General Line, than the rest of the public, and relying on your assurance that no higher rate than $1\frac{1}{2}$d. per ton per mile is at present conceived necessary upon the inclined plane to Warren House, his Lordship expects that every consideration will be given to the matter; that this may speedily be settled. Mr. James Thompson writes to me that it was left to his determination, and Mr. Thompson one of the Directors of the proposed Railway – You have omitted to mention anything respecting the width of the Railway, but Mr. James Thompson says that he was assured that the wedth [sic] of the Railway should not be less than 4 feet 8 inches nor wider than 5 feet, and that if the latter width was determined on, the Company would alter the width of Lord Carlisle's Midgeholme branch and Waggons.

Yours etc.,
James Loch.

NEWCASTLE & CARLISLE RAILWAY ROUTES

APPENDIX 7

Extracts from Benjamin Thompson's report to the Directors of the Newcastle & Carlisle Railway 14 June 1825.

. . . to the point above Haltwhistle, where it becomes necessary to strike into the Vale of the Tipple, and pursue the line advised by Mr. Chapman to the Summit level. From this elevation, in place of that Gentleman's level course south of Naworth Castle Demesne and a Descent of 370 feet afterwards by a succession of inclined planes, I conceive it to be practicable to go down the Irthing upon a declivity suitable for a horse way, and by doing so, reach Carlisle without subjecting the road to the serious obstruction, and danger of any such expedients.

. . . It would afford a free, easy and uninterrupted passage between end & end would be dependent on no adventitious aid, and leave passengers and goods secure from all danger. Its locality would always, and every where yield the greatest possible portion of public accommodation from the circumstance of its passing through the best and most popular part of the district, as well as the lowest in regard to level, and yet upon investigation it will be found that Gentleman's [sic] Houses and Grounds will be far less exposed to annoyance by this, than by the other line, and if I am not very much mistaken, the cost of establishing a road upon it would be a great deal lower also. Impressed with the high importance of supplying to the public a rail road that shall be entirely exempt from interruption and impediment of every kind, I am anxious to recommend to your Serious consideration, not only the abandonment of inclined planes, but also the use of any other than Horses as the motive power. There is, I believe, a strong feeling of dislike in country Gentlemen generally, through the Kingdom against Locomotive Engines, and we were given to understand, that this is especially the case between Newcastle and Carlisle . . .

. . . It is in my opinion, most important to secure the same free and independant [sic] progress over a rail road which is so esential to the well being of a common Highway; but inclined planes and locomotive engines are, both of them, incompatible with such object; long detentions and perpetual danger attend the first, and horses will not mix with, or face the latter individuals excepting they were on a large scale business, could not be their own carriers, and the end of it must be that the company would necessarily have to take the whole conveyance into their own hands.

. . . It is to appropriate the two roads to distinct purposes. One, for the carriage of raw and heavy materials. the other for the exclusive use of passengers and the lighter and more valuable species of merchandise. The first might be worked by heavy horses at the ordinary rate of slow travelling – the second with lighter Horses and at a speed of 8 miles an hour. The first road would require sidings, for the convenience of passing each other; but the second might avail itself of the first for that purpose.

Extracts from Benjamin Thompson's report to the Directors of the Newcastle & Carlisle Railway 19 February 1828.

Gentlemen,

In compliance with the desire you this day expressed of receiving my opinion on the comparative Merits of the two recently projected lines of Road diverging from each other at Brampton Beck at or near the point where it is understood Lord Carlisle's Colliery Railway is meant to fall into the proposed public Road – such two lines meeting again at the Penrith Road a little south of the Turnpike Gate leading out of Carlisle . . .

The two points just alluded to, of Separation and re-union, are 10 miles apart by the line going South of Unity, crossing the Gelt on the left of the Southernmost Quarry some quarter of a Mile below Middle Gelt Bridge, and passing the Stone House Estate into the Vale of How Beck near the Spinning Mill, and afterwards by Corby &c &c to Carlisle, which from the high demand of Sir Hew Ross to a passage over his lands, seems to be the only practicable line left for your choice, exempt from an inclined plane. By the other line, which necessarily requires the adoption of an inclined plane to descend from the high Grounds above Brampton to the low Haughs near the Gelt – pursuing its course to and crossing the Irthing considerably above the junction of those Rivers, beyond the latter of which it unites with your originally surveyed line – the distance between the two before referred to points is only $9\frac{1}{2}$ Mls.

The first of these lines would, according to an estimate I laid before you some time ago, cost about £18000. in formation, *only*, of the 3 Miles from Brampton Beck to the Irthing – while the $3\frac{3}{4}$ Miles by the other line from Brampton Beck to the Irthing, would cost no more than about £5,500 including the inclined plane, engine and Machinery. – the ground being in one case particularly favorable, and in the other as much the contrary, for the purpose required.

From the circumstance of obtaining a fall of about 170 feet in the space of three quarters of a Mile by means of the inclined plane, the road is rendered considerably easier to animal draught, both upwards and downwards; . . .

As connected with the arrangements of Lord Carlisle's Colliery, I consider this line as one calculated to yield him nothing but accommodation. I understand an Inclined plane is either in progress or contemplated upon his Lordships private Railway at Kirkhouse; from which place to the city of Carlisle I suppose the distance by the proposed line may be between 10 and 11 Miles. This might be considered an easy days Work, out and home again, in consequence of the inclined

Plane near Capon Tree; for the Horse and Driver upon their arrival there would detach themselves from the load, and, walking down the plane, re-possess themselves of it at the bottom where it would be found awaiting their arrival. And so upon their return with the empty Waggons from Carlisle, they would quit them at the bottom and walking to the top resume the same again there. No time, assuredly, being lost, on either passage, in waiting for the Mechanical operations of the Inclined Plane. this would be an undoubted relief to the Horse, and, certainly not retard, but expedite his Work, and shorten his Days Labour. It may be observed as a further conductive to Lord Carlisle's Interest and convenience, that a short inclined Plane from the top of the proposed one near Capon Tree, and to be operated upon by the same Engine, would deliver his Lordship's Coal and Lime at the West End of Brampton at the Turnpike Road Side very advantageously for the Road leading to Longtown &c, thereby dispensing with his Lordships present very defective and almost impassable railway . . .

APPENDIX 8

Extracts from a letter from James Thompson to James Loch 26 February 1828.

. . . This report is quite different from the opinion I had formed and which I have stated to you. My statements were not made on precise data but from what I learned verbally as to the levels from Mr. Studholme, the surveyor of this end of the line, and from my own local knowledge of the country, and I still think yet, on close examination (unless I am quite mistaken as to what the real descent of each line is to be) that the preponderance will be found in favour of the Hayton line for a descending Trade . . .

As to the Inclined plane I certainly think it will be a great inconvenience, supposing the Horses do walk down the plane (which is no where the practice that I know of) if a number of Horses are going together there must be a great deal of time lost before the last Horse gets his Carriages up or down putting out of the question all accidents which Inclined planes are liable to, When on this subject I beg to insert an extract from a Report of the directors Dec 3d 1825 James Losh Chairman it will shew their aversion to Inclined planes at that time. – "The Directors deem it an advantage of *great importance* that an open line of way has been obtained, exempt from *inclined planes* and easy of preformance [sic] by animal power, whereby the Carrier relying on his own resources is independent of auxiliary power and its *delays* and *risks* and the property under his charge is always secure from *danger* and the conveyance of it certain as to time."

As to the plane down to the Turnpike West of Brampton I consider it quite unnecessary and would be laying expence upon coals for no advantage. as the

Town of Brampton would be supplied as well from the Top of the plane or by a short level branch to the South side of the Town, also it would be good for the Longtown Trade . . .

Should the line go by Hayton, Brampton &c would be supplied from the road leading to Talkin at very little further distance than at present, or a branch may be made very near the Town without any Inclined plane, and of course entirely abandon the present old Railway . . .

P.S. I confidently look forward to some great improvement in locomotive Engines before many years pass by, and to their general adoption on Railways, in that case this Inclined Plane would be an awkward thing between Kirkhouse and Carlisle. J.T.

REFERENCES

The work undertaken by David A. Gordon in cataloguing the vast amount of material contained in the files of the Howard of Naworth Muniments cannot be allowed to pass unacknowledged. Upon the transfer of these from Boothby, Brampton, to Durham University, a mine of information hitherto not available for public research was opened out, and David Gordon took full advantage of this.

From 1966 his effort saw the majority of the data relating to the collieries and railways copiously noted, typed and filed. The documentation by an identical process of some of the estate records still held privately at Brampton enabled the research to become some three-quarters completed by his death.

The present writer was able to use the above references to complete the collation of material, and then by a process of integration to build up a very full picture of the Naworth coalfield and its railways. Without the preparatory work set out above, the preparation of the manuscripts upon which this study is based would have been almost impossible.

Due to the complexity of the material used here, it has not been possible to use a detailed bibliographical reference system within the text; indeed, space alone prevents this.

It is hoped, however, that the following lists of files and bundles will be sufficient for anyone who wants to see at first hand the wealth of data available.

University of Durham. Department of Paleography and Diplomatic. Howard of Naworth Muniments—59A; C170; 203; 204; C565; 590 No. 1; 590 No. 2; C591; C592; C593; C596; C607; 612; 630; C645; C646; C665; C672; C687; C693; C695; 713; 714.

Privately held at Brampton. Estate Records which will in due time be transferred to Durham—R2; 10; 15; 24; 49; 54; 58; 65; 111; 112; 112A; 113.

GENERAL INDEX AND NOTES FOR THE GUIDANCE OF READERS

NOTES

The proliferation and extent of the work of James Thompson for Lord Carlisle is very apparent throughout the book and for this reason to mention individual page numbers in this index is pointless.

Figure numbers for illustrations are in bold type.

All maps and plans are from local or preserved records. Many original sketch maps have been redrawn to preserve their original character, others have been completely redrawn where this was not possible.

The scenario for this work is a small portion of Cumbria and Northumbria and the reader is advised to study the general maps (Figs. 1–3) for the full picture of the Naworth Coalfield and its railways. Comparison with 1 inch or 1:250000 O.S. maps enables easy identification for those who wish to inspect at first hand the area concerned.

INDEX

Allgood, Mr. 9, 39, 44
Alston 9, 10, 19, 22, 39, 42, 45–6
Alston Branch 57–9, 69, 108, 115
Avonside Engine Co. Ltd. 110–11

Backstand.. .. .. 61–2, 67
Barclay, Sons & Co. Ltd., Andrew 104–7, 109–10
Baron House 36, 44, 47, 56, 60
Bedlington Ironworks 7, 8, 14
Bishop Hill 35, 43, 47, 56–7, 59, 67, 108
Blacksike Colliery 7, 35, 9, 47, 53, 56–7
Blenkinsopp Colliery 2, 7, 9, 21–2, 32, 36–7, 39, 43, 47, 49, 50–1, 59, 72
Blue Gate Drift 68, 114
Bolton & Leigh Railway.. .. ..50, 100
Brampton Branch Railway 19, 20, 22, 25–7, 30, 40, 43, 60–1, 73–6, 78, 80–1, 109, 119–20, 127
Brampton Branch Receipts 79, 80, 84, 86
Brampton Branch Board of Trade Inspection 80–1, 87
Brampton Junction Station (alias Brampton or Milton) .. .. 69, 73–4, 76, 78–9, 83, 91, 99, 105, 109, 113; Figs. **34, 42–3**
Brampton Light Railway Scheme 83–6
Brampton Coal Staith .. 10, 20, 46, 73, 79, 80–1, 88–9, 90, 95, 113; Figs. **32–3**
Brampton Town Station .. .. .. 95, 113; Figs. **38, 40, 44, 46, 41, 45**
Brampton, N.E.R. Lease of Branch 87–94
Burradon Colliery 112
Byron Drift 59–63

Caledonian Railway 74
Carlisle, Brampton & Glenwhelt Railway .. .. 9–13, 15, 27, 31, 117; Fig. **9**
Carlisle, Brampton & Milton Railway 74
Carlisle, Lord .. .. numerous
Carlisle, Lady Rosalind 2, 63, 79, 83, 85, 90–1, 95–7
Carlisle-Newcastle Canal Proposal 3, 8, 17
Catch Pit 9, 36
Chapelburn Drift 68–9
Chapman, William 12, 17–18, 26

Chaldron Wagons	6, 109; Fig. **88**
Clesketts	5, 7, 43, 113
Clowsgill Quarry	2, 3, 5, 59, 113–14
Coal depots	48, 50, 77–8
Coanwood	59
Coanwood Coal Co. Ltd.	62, 65
Cohen & Sons, Geo.	71
Cost of lines	3–4, 10–11, 14–15, 18, 35, 40–5
Coulson, Col. J. B.	7, 50
Cowran hills/cutting	31
Cumrew Limeworks	7, 50
Dandy carriage/wagon	46, 48, 50, 73–5, 77–8; Fig. **28–9**
Denton Colliery	67
Duke Coal Co.	71
Fairlie, Robert	75
Farlam Hall	5, 6, 39, 47
Featherstone	59–60, 65
Featherstone Colliery	60
Featherstone Coal Co. Ltd.	65
Featherstone Colliery Co. Ltd.	65–6
Foresthead	60
Foresthead Quarry	67–9, 111, 113; Fig. **84**
Foresthead & Blacksike Rly.	7, 46, 63, 70, 113
Gairs Colliery & Rly.	62–3, 66, 98, 105, 107–9, 111–12, 114; Fig. **85**
Gapshields Colliery	32, 36, 39, 47, 56–7, 65–6, 68–9
Geltsdale Colliery/George Pit	7, 35, 39, 47, 56, 58
Glasgow, Dumfries & Carlisle Rly.	74
Glasgow & South Western Rly.	74
Graham, Sir James	31–2
Greenside Drift	59, 114
Guide Pit, Croglin	8, 36, 39, 47, 56
Hallbankgate	5, 26, 35, 38–9, 41, 44, 47, 58, 60, 70, 100–1, 114; Fig. **93**
Halton Lea Gate	36, 57, 64, 101, 108, 115
Hartleyburn	2, 36, 39, 45, 50
Hartleyburn Coal Co. Ltd.	69
Hartleyburn Colliery/Rly.	9, 36, 39, 44, 46–7, 54, 58, 115

Havannah Drift	7, 56, 71
Hawthorn Ltd., R. & W.	49
Henry Pit	35, 39, 47, 56, 59, 60–2, 64, 108, 115
High Fell Colliery	65
Howard of Corby, Henry	31
Howard Pit/Screens	59, 60–1, 64, 67–71, 103, 114; Fig. **81**
Howgill	2, 5, 36, 43–4, 46, 56, 59, 60, 63, 71, 113–4; Fig. **8**
Howgill Drift	36, 39, 43, 47, 53, 56, 58, 114
Inclined Planes	12, 18, 22–3, 26–30, 39, 43–4, 47, 50, 56, 58–9, 107, 114, 119; Figs. **77–80**
Jackson, Hugh	79, 80, 83, 85, 88, 91, 96–7
Jessop, Josias	17
Kerr, Stuart & Co. Ltd.	67
King Pit, Midgeholme	36, 47, 54, 56–7, 59, 60, 69, 70–1, 112–15; Fig. **21**
Kirkhouse	13, 22, 28–9, 30, 39, 43–4, 46–9, 53–5, 57, 60, 62, 65, 69–70, 73, 100–1, 103–5, 114; Figs. **16, 17, 19, 20, 23–6**
Kirkhouse Brick & Tile Co. Ltd.	67–8, 107, 111, 114
Lambley	2, 9, 39, 58, 103, 108
Lambley Colliery	57–60, 64, 115; Fig. **91–2**
Lambley Extension	58
Lambley Fell Branch	59, 69, 71, 115; Fig. **92**
Lambley West Colliery	69, 71, 112, 115
Lawson, Thomas	6
Leasing of collieries & railways	53–6, 60–3, 65–6, 68–9
Liddel, Matthew	53, 56–7
Liverpool & Manchester Railway	50, 100
Loch, James	3, 9, 10, 12, 19, 20–1, 25, 27–30, 32, 41, 46, 49, 50, 53, 56, 100
Locomotives: *Alice*	111, 112; Fig. **75–6**
Atlas	49, 74, 99, 100
Belted Will	Frontispiece, 102; Figs. **48, 49**
Dandie Dinmont	78, 106–11; Figs. **35, 36, 60–2**
Garibaldi	103–4
Gilsland	49, 74, 99, 100
Goliath	49
Hercules	49, 99
Kerr Stuart "Wren" type	67

Loch	102–3; Fig. **51–3**
Mosstrooper	102
Naworth No. 6	109, 111; Fig. **66–7**
Rocket	Frontispiece, 100–1, 105
Samson	49, 99
Sheriff	104, 107–8; Fig. **63–4**
"Simplex" petrol loco	67
Stephenson	110–2; Fig. **72–5**
Tichborne/Belted Will	104–5, 108–9; Figs. **31, 54–8, 65**
Tindale	110–12; Fig. **68–71**
No. 5	105, 108–9; Fig. **59**
Maryport & Carlisle 0-4-0T	106
N.E.R. No. 60	Fig. **44**
N.E.R. No. 1089	96
N.E.R. Loco classes BTP, C, E, P-1, 398	96

Loco sheds	58, 69, 101, 103, 105–7, 114; Figs. **27, 47**
Longridge, R. B.	8, 14
Losh, James	27, 29, 32
Low Midgeholme Drifts	68–71, 115
Low Pit	59
Lyneholme Burn Colliery	65
L.N.E.R.	97–8

Macadams (Contractors)	23
Maryport & Carlisle Rly.	106
McKay (Contractor), John	43
Mickley Coal Co. Ltd.	65–6
Midgeholme	2, 9, 27, 45, 60, 68–9, 70; Figs. **21, 90**
Midgeholme Rly.	10, 12, 14, 18–19, 21–3, 26–7, 35–6, 38, 43, 46, 50, 100, 103, 109–10
Miners (Industries) Trust Fund Ltd.	66
Mint Hill Drift	66, 111
M.R.H. Minerals Ltd.	65, 69–70

N.C.B.	69, 112
Naworth Coal Co. Ltd.	63–5, 90–4, 97–8, 104, 107–9
Naworth Collieries Co. Ltd.	65, 107, 109
Naworth Limeworks Ltd.	67–8, 111
Neilson & Co. Ltd.	78, 105–6
Newcastle & Carlisle Rly.	9, 12, 13, 17–33, 37–8, 40, 43–5, 47–9, 51, 58, 74–7, 99, 121, 124–7

Newcastle & Carlisle Rly.—Brampton Branch	19–22, 25, 27, 29, 30
Compromise North & South Route	26–30
North Route	18, 19, 21, 25–6, 28–30, 121–2, 124; Fig. **9**
South Route	17, 18, 21, 26–32, 121–2, 125–7
North Eastern Rly.	59, 75–7, 80–2, 84, 86–7, 89, 90–2, 94–5, 97
North Walbottle Colliery	112
Opencast mining	72
Passenger Fares/Receipts	46
Peps Pit	66
Planehead	47, 70, 114; Figs. **79, 80, 93**
Plenmeller Colliery Co. Ltd.	65–6
Prior Dyke Drifts	27, 56, 64, 66–7, 115; Fig. **82**
Rails	54–5
Rail Gauges	20–2, 35, 38, 57, 73, 122–3
Rail types—Cast iron	5, 7, 15, 55
Patent iron	54–5
Wrought iron/malleable iron	5–7, 10, 11, 14, 15, 55, 72; Fig. **86**
Wood	3, 5
Ramshay, John	14, 27, 46, 50, 53, 56, 58, 100
Reagarth	68
Recovery Pit	55, 71
Rennie, John	20
Riggfoot	35, 43–4, 55, 67
Roachburn Colliery	59–63, 67, 70, 88, 104, 108–9, 114; Fig. **22**
Roberts, Charles	66
Roberts, Lady Cecilia	95; Fig. **39**
Ross, Sir Hew Dalrymple	26–7, 29, 30–1
Sheldon, Edward	99, 100
Shop Pit	5, 59
Spelter Works	56, 65, 67, 70, 111, 114
Star Pit, Hartleyburn	36, 47, 57, 115
Stephenson, George	3, 12–14, 20–2, 25, 29, 30, 57, 70, 117–20
Stephenson, Robert	30, 121–2
Stephenson & Co. Ltd., Robert	99, 100–2, 104–5
Stockton & Darlington Rly.	21, 123
Studholme, John	27, 29–30

Talkin Colliery	2, 3, 5, 7, 9, 35, 39, 47, 56, 59
Tarnfoot Quarry	35, 59
Tarnhouse Colliery	2, 3, 5, 7, 9, 35, 39, 47, 56
Taylor & Worsley (Contractors)	46
Telford, Thomas	18, 20
Thompson, Benjamin	18, 20, 23, 25–6, 29
Thompson, Charles Lacy	60, 62, 78, 85, 96
Thompson, James	numerous
Thompson, Major	77–8
Thompson, Maria	8, 57, 60
Thompson & Sons	55, 57, 59, 60, 74, 76, 78, 88
Thirlwall Colliery	60, 62, 65
Tindale	26, 27, 35, 56, 70, 101, 108, 114
Tindale Fell	2, 5, 6, 35–6, 46–7, 55, 59, 114; Fig. 8
Tindale Granite Co.	66, 111
Tramway	66
Tramcars, Petrol	84–5
Turntables	103
Valuation of collieries/railways	53–4
Venture Drift/New Venture Drift	59, 64, 66, 109–11
Waggonway, Earl of Carlisle's	1, 3–5, 10, 21, 38–41, 44, 46, 73, 113; Figs. **4–8, 89**
Wake Ltd., J. & F.	108
Warren "A Century of Loco Building"	101, 102
Wear Valley Rly.	58
West Wylam Colliery	112
Whites Cut/Whites Cut Colliery	27, 56, 64, 68–71, 109, 111, 115; Fig. **83**
Wood, Nicholas	38, 41, 50, 53, 100